Leo Potishman Fund Series
in the Social Sciences
Robert H. Talbert, Managing Editor

VIOLENCE IN THE CITY

**Leo Potishman Fund Series
in the Social Sciences**

VIOLENCE
IN THE CITY

BLAIR JUSTICE

Leo Potishman Fund
Texas Christian University Press
1969

Library of Congress Catalog Card Number: 73-86501

CONTENTS

DEDICATION

*To those who are convinced that the
conditions that breed violence
can be overcome without violence.*

FOREWORD

I consider *Violence in the City* by Blair Justice a powerful
book. This is true in spite of, and in part because of, the
fact that it bristles at points with statistics based on significant data that substantiate insightful hypotheses relating
to the causes of violence so widespread today.

The author has made the people he studied more than
ciphers or mere statistical units. He actually "sat where they
sat," moved among them, talked with them in "natural dialogue," and interacted with them in tense situations. He has
painted them as he sees them. He knows the backgrounds out
of which they have come and the situations from which they
are trying to emerge. He tries to "tell it like it is" where
their behavior is concerned. He sees their strength and their
weaknesses, and he makes clear distinctions between their
creative acts and their follies.

As I read *Violence in the City* I was often disturbed
and/or deeply moved. For example, when I read the chapter
on the "Rebel without a Cause," I found a clear distinction
between those who participate in collective violence, directed
toward the attainment of some social objective, and individual, or lonewolf, violence as a response to a sense of frustration. The author's stories of Phil Fitch and James Norris
are very moving stories.

Both Fitch and Norris grew up in impossible situations—at least in situations that made any career except a
criminal one an unexpected outcome. Fitch responded by the
iron rule of *lex talionis* to the very end, except in fuller
measure—two eyes or two teeth for one and for the violence
and the hate heaped upon himself by others. He never became his "own man," but remained as reflexive as a "knee-
jerk" to any stimulus applied to him. On the other hand,
James Norris began to think, while he was in solitary, "about
the bitterness inside him . . . the bum rap he got" from wife,
home, the father he never had, people who pretended to be
his friends, the world, the system, the cops, the judges, and
"every goddamn son-of-a-bitch" he considered responsible
for his "rap" as a habitual criminal. But this attitude was
no good. He finally decided that "there was one thing I could
call my own, and that was me—myself. . . . I had been worse

than nothing. I had been a thing belonging to other people. I was just like somebody's knee when the doctor hits it with a hammer. I just reacted to what goaded me, and as long as I did that, I didn't have any control over my life. . . . I didn't even have me. I was nothing, just a knee jerking this way and that. . . ."

Then he said when he got out of solitary: "I didn't do any reforming. I just became me. Somebody who was going to have his own thrust."

But Phil Fitch never got a thrust of his own. He grew up in the "Bottom," the most underprivileged ghetto in a city which is one of only two metropolitan centers in the United States without a housing code, and one in which live more than 300,000 Negroes, many of whom have come from many points of the compass to find lodging and some means of subsistence. His story, as well as that of James Norris, is reminiscent of, but worse than, what is implicated in Stephen Leacock's parody on "I remember, I remember;" and both men had plenty to remember. Leacock was writing in Harper's Magazine for July 1927, lines that ran straight "Out of the Lion's Mouth," containing some provocative words. These lines ran:

> I wish I could remember
> The house where I was born
> And the little window where perhaps
> The sun peeped in at morn.
> But father can't remember
> And mother can't recall
> Where they lived in that December—
> If it was a house at all.
> It may have been a boarding house,
> Or a family hotel,
> A flat or a tenement;
> It's very hard to tell.
> There's only one thing certain
>   from my questioning as yet,
> Wherever I was born it was
>   a matter of regret.

What Phil Fitch remembered was that he had a very tired mother, two brothers in prison, and a sister who was a prostitute. His only way to respond to frustration was the "knee-jerk" way. He would adjust by making others fear him as the violent "big-shot;" and, to evoke fear, he killed the white driver of a Cadillac, a perfect stranger to him. Thus he belonged to that large group of lonewolves who respond as such and never as a member of an activist group seeking to redress a social injustice. He was a "rebel without a cause."

Although James Norris was a lonewolf, in his case I think the author has presented the clearest case of a man who was trying to become "his own man" that I have ever known. He died determined not to be controlled by frustrating circumstances. After reading Adler, James, and Sartre, he decided they were saying to him: "Do your own choosing. Be your own man;" and he accepted the manner of his death, facing a taunter's knife, as proof of his own integrity.

Those who are given to collective action may engage in rioting that seems senseless. If they have a cause, it is not clear to them. They are "knee-jerk" crowds, responding to rumor with random destructiveness. The Black Power Revolutionary has a cause in which he tries to gain superiority on what Adler would call the "useless side," gaining "power over" instead of "power with" the majority. He is for "Black power" and "whitey" weakness.

The main thrust, however, of the Civil Rights movement is to gain a "piece of the power" through contact and communication with the power structure. Justice describes the process at length.

The author advances a number of significant hypotheses relating to the causes of collective action, including rioting, in his study of *Violence in the City*. The following propositions represent these hypotheses only in part, but they will serve to indicate the direction of his interviewing research:

1. The greater the focus of the spotlight on a city as an area in which rioting is expected, the greater the likelihood that a riot will occur—the principle of a self-fulfilling prophecy.

2. The more aware the underprivileged become of the way of life of the more privileged, the less satisfied the former are with the *status quo;* at the same time, they come to expect more for themselves and to take measures, even violent measures, to improve their status.

3. Attitudes of violence leading to riots will grow with an increasing knowledge of such events and with the advent of rumors that allege that brutality is being practiced by police, for example, during their occurrence.

4. The more mobile an underprivileged population and the denser it is—i.e., the less widely dispersed it is in a city— the more susceptible that population is to rioting.

Although his data are based mainly on Houston and on "natural dialogue" interviews conducted in the main by Negro interviewers, he has made it clear that his data have a real bearing on the problems of violence everywhere.

The author presents a program which he thinks industry could follow to bring the city out of its shambles, but I will let him tell that story himself. He argues: "I do 'know that it is time to end the destruction and violence, not only in the streets of the ghetto, but in the lives of people'." He sees doors opening upon a vista of the future city in which none of its people will have to say of it what James Thomson's derelict philosopher said of his experience in London:

> As I went through the desert thus it was,
> As I went through the desert.

The city will never be Utopia; but it will be easier for all its people to sing in the United States:

> To see . . . thine alabaster cities gleam
> Undimmed . . .
> America, America . . .

Austin L. Porterfield

ACKNOWLEDGEMENTS

A number of people have helped make this book a reality. Initial support came from the Texas Department of Mental Health and Mental Retardation, through the assistance of Dr. George Constant, long-time board member, and Dr. Shervert Frazier, then mental health commissioner. Dr. Constant was particularly interested in the effects of slum conditions, and the chapter I turned over to him in July 1968 on "Rebel Without A Cause" was one answer to what happens to too many people who are subjected to slums.

The U.S. Department of Justice, Law Enforcement Assistance Administration, gave early and generous support to my studies. This agency was concerned with the whole question of detection of potential community violence, and what could be done to correct conditions that seem related to both the underlying and precipitating causes of civil disorders.

Funds also came from the Advanced Research Projects Agency, as administered by the Center for Research in Social Change and Economic Development at Rice University. It was at Rice and the Center that much of the work on this book was carried on. I am indebted to a number of persons connected with the center who gave support, including Edward Norbeck, chairman of the department of sociology/anthropology at Rice.

I am equally grateful for the opportunity I have had to observe community problems from first-hand experience by working on the staff of Mayor Louie Welch of Houston. He has been consistently receptive to programs designed to help correct some of the problems pointed up by studies we did in Houston and elsewhere. Through Mayor Welch, it was also possible to gain cooperation of authorities in Los Angeles and Oakland to learn about conditions there contributing to community violence in those cities.

Douglass Price-Williams, chairman of the department of psychology at Rice, was one of the original investigators in the early studies of the Center for Research in Social Change and is due credit for analyzing data on opinions of Negroes in Watts and Oakland, compared to attitudes of black people in Houston. As noted in the chapter on "Degrees of Unrest and Effects of Action," he also designed a chart showing how levels of unrest in Houston varied by geographical area. In addition, I am grateful to Dr. Price-Williams for his initial review of my chapters on "Rebel Without A Cause" and "The Black Revolutionary," as they were first drafted in the spring and summer of 1967.

Helpful suggestions on several parts of the manuscript came from Robert H. Talbert, chairman of the department of sociology and anthropology at Texas Christian University, and his predecessor, Austin L. Porterfield, both of whom encouraged its publication, as did James W. Newcomer, Vice-Chancellor for Academic Affairs and Director of the TCU Press. Judy Oelfke and Harrell Moten of the TCU Publications Office assisted in helping prepare the manuscript for publication. Professor Talbert as managing editor of the Leo Potishman Fund had the responsibility for guiding the manuscript through publication.

I am particularly indebted to many persons who typed various drafts and who aided in the illustrations and art work. Among the typists and manuscript assistants were Susan Andries, Julie Louis, Elizabeth and Joyce Weedman, Delores Porter, Hifa Rezak, Marilou Gamst and Jo Giese. Deni Seinfeld, secretary at the Center for Research, also was a source of assistance. As for the illustrations, I am grateful for the help of the planning department of the City of Houston and Dick Bigler.

George Beto, director of the Texas Department of Corrections, and Howard Sublett, warden of Wynn unit, were extremely cooperative in the research I did within the prison system and the many interviews conducted with inmates in 1966.

Most of all, though, the people who helped make this book possible were the field interviewers, the people who went out in the community and asked the questions that needed answering. Dr. and Mrs. Melvin Sikes and Mary Ellen Goodman were initially responsible for helping me organize an interview team. Later, with grant support, other teams were trained and furnished invaluable help. Members included Durward Collins, K. S. Falls, Brenda Barnes Green, R. L. Gray, A. M. Alton, R. L. Ross, Mary K. Dunham, Jacquelyn Bernard, W. C. Hunt, Betty Hunt, Beverly McWashington, E. L. Lott, Mary A. White, S. Y. Williams and a number of others.

The interviewers were aware of how close the city came

on a few occasions to community violence. As indicated in
the pages that follow, many people, both black and white,
helped to avert violence so that other means could be taken
to combat problems. Al Henry and Donald Crockett were of
special help. So were a number of police officers, who demonstrated restraint and good judgment. Also, Ernest Carswell,
Brenda Green, Doug Holford, Ronald Rea, Eddie Corral—
each has contributed through work in the community toward
helping neighborhood people find ways to improve their lives.
Jo Alys Long and Ofelia Jaime have furnished "backup
support."

Without the assistance of all these people, this book may
well have had a different ending.

Blair Justice

INTRODUCTION

In the summer of 1965, I began doing surveys of attitudes in the Negro community in Houston. I did this with the assistance of Negro interview teams that used a "natural dialogue" technique of finding out what black people felt about their problems. The "natural dialogue" was something devised from more than 15 years of experience in reporting. It is a conversational, no note-taking technique of interviewing people. And it seems to elicit feelings that otherwise go unexpressed.

Riots and racial strife were not on many people's minds in the nation's sixth largest city in 1965. There was not much interest in the surveys until the Watts riot occurred in Los Angeles in August of that summer. Then rumors began circulating that Houston was going to have a riot over the Labor Day weekend. Suddenly my field work became of interest. I was asked to present it to the mayor. He did not want to believe that Houston Negroes felt a Watts riot could occur in the city. A group of us, including members of the Negro interview team, worked up a list of recommendations for reducing tension. In a second meeting the mayor and police chief went down the list, and we discussed steps suggested. The Labor Day weekend came, and Houston got by without a riot.

By the fall of the next year, after I had joined Mayor Louie Welch to work in race relations, enough data had come in to suggest not only what the greatest tensions and most pressing problems seemed to be but also what might be done about them. As a first step, I worked up a series of recommendations that Mayor Welch announced in December 1966 as "Project Partner."

Even then it was clear that the biggest issue in the minds of people, both black and white, was violence. Problems in employment, housing, education, police relations—all were emotionally charged with the question: Would they bring violence? By October 1966, I had come face to face with people in Houston who felt that rioting was the only way to stimulate action on such problems. I disagreed then. I disagree even more today.

1

But riots were not the only form of violence in question. There was also the problem of crime in the ghetto. Negro crime was, and is, a pressing issue—and many of the ghetto people we interviewed expressed repeated concern about it. On delving deeper into the problem of riots, as they occurred across the nation, it became clear that many of the factors contributing to them were also playing a part in the breeding grounds of Negro crime.

In Houston, there still seemed to be time to mitigate some of the precipitating and underlying causes of violence. At least, this seemed true in the black community. However, on the campus of Texas Southern University, a predominantly Negro school in Houston, tension was mounting. It began spilling over in a series of incidents. There were many nights and a number of days spent working on problems at TSU—one of which was the city street running through the campus—but the lid finally blew off two weeks before the semester's end when a gunbattle took place between students and police.

After that, tension in the whole Negro community mounted precipitously. The community temperature showed an ominous rise. And consequently, during the summer of 1967—a summer the nation will never forget—we spent many additional nights on the streets, working with non-violent militants and enlisting their help in carrying the message to the community that there are better ways to attack problems than through violence.

Houston came close to riots on at least two occasions—just how close can be appreciated only by those who were on the streets in the midst of the potential explosions. I remember arriving at one turbulent scene in a pajama top and thinking, after seeing Molotov cocktails tossed in the street and hearing the bullhorn of the demonstrators, "This is it." But it wasn't. Police agreed to hold back to give us time to ask a small group of non-violent militants to go into the cluster of demonstrators and persuade them to disperse. The band did disperse—finally—but they already had knocked out six store windows, in addition to tossing Molotov cocktails into the street. There were some citizens the next morning who criticized us for the broken windows, arguing the police should have moved in and made mass arrests. That was just the kind of move the demonstrators had hoped for, because they knew that hostility toward the police was high enough to get the community to riot if police could be drawn into a confrontation. There was no confrontation—and no riot.

But the night from that summer that I will probably remember the longest came a month later when a white service station operator shot a Negro man. A rumor raced through the neighborhood that a policeman had shot to death a black man at the service station. My first act on reaching the scene and learning the facts was to call the mayor by mobile phone and ask him to request all radio stations, particularly those with listeners predominantly in the black community, to help dispel the rumor. The media promptly cooperated because the facts were that the only involvement by police was the taking of the wounded man—he was shot in the leg, not killed—to the hospital.

A potential riot, however, was already underway. The service station was burned to the ground, and a supermarket down the street, owned by a man of Chinese extraction, was also set ablaze. Two stores in the block were looted. In the middle of all this, I received a call on the mobile phone from the mayor giving me a number and saying the person trying to reach me had an urgent message for me. I phoned the number. It was a friend, a conscientious person concerned about "getting something done for black people." He had heard the news of the service station burning and the supermarket set on fire, and of the crowds in the street. He wanted to give me this message: "Let them do their burning. It will be a catharsis. They need this." I hung up.

One reason I hung up, and the reason I relate this story, is that I cannot ever accept the notion that violence brings good. I am talking about the initiating of violence. I already knew from the surveys we did in the wake of the TSU violence that tensions were high in the community and the fuel for an explosion was just waiting for ignition. And here was this man—this white man, far removed from the scene of battle—asking for the explosion.

We got through that summer without the massive violence he prescribed. Eight months later, we got through the assassination of Dr. Martin Luther King without a riot. And for all this, I will long be thankful to the many who helped. But from such experiences, I believe I have had enough brushes with violence to be convinced that "a Watts" or "a Detroit" solves nothing. I have heard enough loud and angry voices to conclude that emotional rhetoric is a poor substitute for just plain hard work on conditions that have existed much too long but are not going to vanish magically by being shouted away. I have listened to—and, when called upon, engaged in—heated discussion of the race issue from Houston to California to Washington, D. C. Two colleagues at Rice and I went to Los Angeles, Oakland and San Francisco to ghettos where riots had occurred to find out what the underlying and precipitating causes seemed to be there. In November 1967, along with a number of other people, I was called to Washington to testify at the hearings on riots conducted by Senator John L. McClellan's Subcommittee on Investigations, which was probing causes nationwide.

But despite all the probing, there is still the threat of violence in cities—and there is still violence itself. It is both collective and individual. In this book, I have tried to delve not only into some of the causes of it all but also the *effects*. I have tried to touch on some of the factors of unrest that I believe have been skimmed over too lightly. And, with considerable detail, I have tried to show what the effects of violence are on community people. The effects are far-reaching, indeed, and if my white friend had known them on the night he called, I do not believe he would have recommended what he did.

The violence discussed in this book is clearly not the only kind that occurs in urban America. The nation is permeated with violent acts, from slaughter on the highways to the much less public abuse of children at home. Violence cuts across all lines of color, income, religion and education, so in focusing on that which involves mostly black people, there should be no interpretation that acts of violence are peculiar to the Negro community. There is no doubt that black people are disproportionately the greatest victims of violence—both in terms of individual crime and the consequences of riots. But because there has been so little attention given to *effects* of violence in the Negro community and because confusion persists about why violence occurs among black people, this book is on the subject of race as it relates to unrest, tension—and violence.

There will be some material in the book that the average reader may consider too sociological, statistical or theoretical for his interests. This may be particularly true, for instance, of the chapter on "the Establishment," but I felt that people ought to know that there is much rich theory by outstanding

authorities, both living and dead, disputing the popular notion that there is some monolithic group in every city that
makes all the decisions and holds all the power. Parts of the
chapter on "Rebel Without A Cause" will also be hard reading, because of the statistical detail. But Phil Fitch and
James Norris are also in that chapter, and I hope no one will
pass up their stories.

To scholars, if they read this book, there will be even
greater portions of it that may seem "journalistic." This is
especially true of the way I have written the case studies
included in "Rebel Without A Cause," but I wanted to bring
home to the reader the stark feelings and naked emptiness
that mark the lives of human beings who have known little
else than violence in their day-to-day existence. This is individual violence—crime on the streets.

As to riots—the collective kind—I believe that the *before-and-after* studies on violence that are included in this
book may be the first of a systematic nature to be presented
on what happens in a community as a consequence of violence. Certainly the 7,156 interviews, of which these studies
are a part, constitute the largest survey done in any one city
on tensions in the black community.* I hope the findings may
be of preventive value to cities where eruptions have already
occurred and can be kept from recurring. The results also
may be of use to those relatively few cities that have escaped
community violence. It is in the opening chapter that findings are given on the effects that violence has, effects that
add to community tension and increase the potential for even
greater violence. I hope the tabulations and statistics that
must necessarily be presented to demonstrate the effects will
not keep the layman, who is usually repelled by arrays of
figures, from reading on and grasping the reasons behind
one simple message: There are better ways to change things
than through violence, for violence only begets violence.

Steps taken to head violence off or to keep it from
spreading—without use of police power—are of specific con-

---

*This total does not include 1,052 other interviews conducted in Houston
in collaboration with colleagues at Rice University, using a different
survey team than the one I directed in my independent study. It also
does not include 613 interviews that were completed in Watts, where the
"natural dialogue" technique was used and in Oakland, California. Chapter 5 presents findings from Watts and Oakland, in comparison with
Houston.

cern to this book. We all recognize that much attention must be given to the root causes of violence if we want to correct injustices and eliminate long-term factors of social unrest. But at the same time, there must be short-term positive approaches to keep bloodshed from occurring while the root causes and long-term factors are being worked on. Once the boiling point for a riot is reached, the most compelling question is: How can death and destruction be averted? In the chapter on "Degrees of Unrest and Effects of Action," I try to show the steps taken in one city to head off violence, together with the results obtained. Without measurement of the results, action can end up being taken for the sake of action, and the consequences can be the exact opposite to what is intended. Since Houston has faced incipient riots in the community—including firebombings and limited looting—there has not only been the need to take action, but there has also been the opportunity, through community interviews, to follow up immediately and measure the effect. Again, I hope the findings will be of benefit to others.

I have also included in this book a chapter on black campus unrest because I think there are lessons we can learn from student strife that apply equally to the community in terms of understanding the psychology involved. Although outbreaks of violence have now spread to predominantly white colleges and universities, it should be remembered that black schools were faced with rebellious students first. The problem of unrest on Negro campuses is still not solved, but one or two of the recommendations suggested for dealing with it should apply to black and white schools alike.

As for the community off campus, I have included, in another chapter, some proposals on opening up wider avenues of opportunity for people who want to become a bigger part of the mainstream of society. And finally, I have tried to tell what is being done *here and now* to help give the individual who is still caught in the ghetto a way out—a way without violence.

Although I firmly believe that the problem of violence in the city requires understanding before effective solutions can be offered, I hope this book does not stop with just an analysis of the problem. It frankly does in some chapters. In others, I have tried to include ideas on *what can be done* and *what is being done.* I have also gone one step further. In addition to the programs and proposals I mention, which are generally of a brick-and-mortar type, I have also offered at the end of all chapters a list of points that pertain to principles of *belief*. The degree to which we succeed in eliminating violence in the city is going to depend not only on what kind of programs are put into effect but also on how much agreement is reached as to what we believe is right, just and true in this society. In the midst of controversy and confusion, it is often hard to know what to believe. Although the end-of-chapter statements are presented under the heading of "What Should We Believe? Points to Consider," they clearly represent a summary of my own point of view, as one individual citizen. They are offered for others to consider in arriving at their own conclusion about what is right, just and true in regard to people of the ghetto.*

---

*See Appendix A for definitions that the author uses for various terms, such as "ghetto" and "black community."

CHAPTER 1

THE *SEAD* FACTORS OF UNREST

Community violence, like cancer, is foreshadowed by danger signals. Common signs of trouble include a high unemployment rate in the ghetto, police abuse and slum housing. But whether these danger signals spell a riot depends on the setting in which they are found—both the psychic setting and the ecological setting. The psychic setting refers to the expectations level that people have toward their lives and the attitudes they have toward the adverse facts of their existence. The ecological setting involves the way people are distributed in space, how they organize—or fail to—in their neighborhoods and the effects all this has on the unity or disunity of their interests and action.

To probe the potential for rioting, it is not enough to know the number of substandard houses in a certain section of the city. More essential is how the people there accept living in slums, whether they can envision a better life for themselves. It is not enough to know what the unemployment rate is. More crucial are the expectations of the idle people and the degree of frustration and anger they may have from finding no work, or work that has no future. It is also not enough to know whether people say police mistreat ghetto dwellers. More important is the way with which any abuse is accepted.

It is also not enough in any attempt to understand civil disorder in this country to say that riots are caused by "oppression." Oppression, in the form of racial discrimination and deprivation, existed from the time the first 20 blacks from Africa were sold by a Dutch shipmaster at Jamestown, Va., in 1619. Although there were slave rebellions during the years and outbreaks of race riots in the period of both world wars, massive community violence did not start occurring until the 1960's. Why? There are several reasons, and they apply to what will be discussed in this chapter as the "sead" factors of unrest. Briefly, the reasons include: (1) By the 1960's, many Negroes had heeded the admonition that "edu-

9

cation" is what they needed, and the gap between the average
number of years they had gone to school, as compared with
that for white people, narrowed to just two years. But, still,
the Negro found that he could not get the jobs he had been
promised if he would only go out and get some education.
The education he got was inferior and even if it had not been,
there was still discrimination in employment. So the doors
remained shut. His *expectations* for a better life had been
raised, but his *realization* of them was negligible. Result:
frustration and rage; (2) An outgrowth of the frustration
was a plunge into civil rights organizations, made up of both
black and white people who figured that if they got laws
changed, the plight of the Negro would be eliminated. They
organized, the laws did change, but life remained the same
for many black people. They still found doors shut, and there
was more frustration and rage; (3) While this frustration
and rage was mounting, mass migrations were occurring to
northern ghettos. There were *expectations* that life in the
North would be better for the black man. But realization of
the expectations fell far short. Result: more frustration and
rage; (4) Life in the northern ghetto was really harder in
many ways. Parents from less densely populated parts of the
country were ill-equipped to rear their children in a congested, complex urban environment. The price the children
paid for their parents' inadequacy was a high degree of tension and unrest from the first days they spent on the streets
of their new home: the city. They shared the disappoint-
ments of their families and were aware that high expectations had gone unfulfilled.

So, the question of riots is vastly more complicated than
reducing it all down to "oppression" and "racism." It is
deeply embedded in psychological, as well as sociological, factors. And a leading psychological factor is this matter of
expectations. Expectations, as we will see, are a product of
not only what people think exists elsewhere but also what
they have seen and experienced in their own lives.

After the Watts riot, various officials from the South
and the Southwest toured the Los Angeles area and remarked
on the number of "tidy houses and neat lawns" that they
found. They could not understand what the problem was in
Watts. To them, the living conditions seemed better than those
in the ghettos of Southern cities. They expected to find the
conditions worse, since Watts had rioted and many cities in

the South and Southwest, particularly Texas, had escaped violence. They could look at the conditions only through their own eyes, and not through those of the people of Watts, who expected something better. When a California sociologist toured the slums of Houston, not long after Watts, he was astonished that there had been no community riot. He said the abject conditions in some areas compared only with the squalor of slaves in the Old South. He viewed the conditions through one set of expectations—thinking that since there had been no riot, conditions could not be too bad—and the people who lived there viewed them through another. They had never seen Watts or how the people lived there. They remembered most their rural past and the shacks they tried to escape by moving to the city. It wasn't that they did not want anything better than what they found in the city; they simply had adapted and recognized no way out.

"The unaware, the contented—those who would be placated with little or nothing, they are the tragedies," as it was put in *From the Street,* a study made for the Department of Health, Education and Welfare. It asked: "Can we expect the ghetto dweller to be vocally disgusted with garbage-littered streets if he has never lived in any other condition?"[1]

What ghetto dwellers will or will not accept is a function not only of their own expectations but what they come to believe other people expect of them. If the spotlight of public attention casts them in the role of rioters, this is a factor that must be considered in how they will behave. If the spotlight carries the insistent suggestion that people should act out feelings of rage and hate, this too is a consideration. Although the public spotlight may not cause riots, it can be a catalyst in an explosive social mixture. The influence of the spotlight is great because it constitutes an all-pervasive carrier for arousing emotion and for suggesting to people what they *ought* to be or *ought* to do, not necessarily what they actually feel or wish to do. When the feeling and wish to do violence are actually present, as they may well be in people who have been held down, the suggestion that they should act out what they feel and wish is enough to trigger a release in many. The role of rhetoric and sensory stimulation has been largely neglected in so many of the sweeping statements made on the causes of civil disorder in the United States. James Q. Wilson of Harvard University has recognized it enough to insist that the impact of rhetoric must be added to material deprivation as a causal factor in riots. He says:

> Only a fear of being thought illiberal may prevent us from con-
> sidering that the probability of a riot is increased by demands
> for 'Black Power,' by a constant reiteration that white bigotry
> and racism are at the root of all the problems besetting the Negro,
> by the reaffirmation of the (untrue) assumption that most Ne-
> groes live wretched lives and that matters are going from bad to
> worse, by constantly predicting apocalyptic violence if 'something
> isn't done' and by 'discovering' the nontruth that all Negroes are
> alike in their hatred of 'whitey' and their tacit or open approval
> of extreme solutions for their plight.[2]

What I am calling the spotlight factor embodies the
powerful role that supercharged suggestion and multi-sensory
stimulation have in social unrest. The spotlight carries these
not only through daily newspapers and television and radio,
but also through paperback books and weekly news and picture magazines, which are more likely than all others to present the black-white picture in polarized terms.

The rhetoric and sensory stimulation given people are
not just sterile abstractions but are made up of all the visual,
auditory and kinetic cues and signals that tell them what it
is they ought to be doing and believing to be worth anything.
Right after the outbreak of civil disorder in Chicago following the assassination of Rev. Martin Luther King, I was in
that city and a newspaperman told me what he saw when
he first arrived in a neighborhood where only one store window had been broken. "A TV crew pulls up," he said, "and
this cameraman yells at a kid—'Come on, you people, you
can do better than that. Look mad! Shake your fist!' And
this kid does it—for the camera—then others start doing it.
Then they start yelling, 'hate Whitey,' and knocking out a
bunch of store windows and looting the stuff inside. The
cameraman gave them the spotlight and the cues and they
responded accordingly."

Whole cities have been given the spotlight. After the
Watts explosion, for instance, Oakland was put Number 1 on
the list of cities expected to riot next.[3] The Oakland ghetto
received national publicity. The spotlight cast the Oakland
ghetto dweller in the posture of angry rebel. Oakland had a
riot a few months later. Did the public attention influence
what happened there? If theories of self-fulfilling prophecies
have any validity, the spotlight factor cannot be ignored as
having some effect on people's behavior.

The *Report of the National Advisory Commission on Civil Disorders* stated that mass media cannot be said to cause riots. But it added: "No doubt, in some cases, the knowledge or the sight on television of what had gone on elsewhere lowered inhibitions, kindled outrage or awakened desires for excitement or loot—or simply passed the word. Many ghetto residents we interviewed thought so themselves."⁴ Surveys we conducted in the Negro community of Houston turned up the same finding. Alexander F. Miller, chairman of the Human Rights Commission of New Rochelle, N. Y., has cited "too faithful reporting of inflammatory statements" as one source of "the spark for igniting the explosion" in the urban ghetto. Certainly, any city that becomes the target of attention because of its racial conditions is going to have "inflammatory statements" said about it and the spotlight turned on it. But the degree to which the spotlight is turned on is not only a function of how bad ghetto conditions are but also how much self-restraint and responsibility the media—particularly national television networks—practice in playing up the violence and vocal outcries of those who do not truly represent the people living in those conditions. If a TV crew rushes in to find "angry youths rebelling against white racism and oppression," it will have no trouble getting youths to strike such a posture. In the process, it will also contribute to encouraging others elsewhere to strike the same "hate-whitey" pose, thus giving subtle sanction to violence as a means of change.

None of this should be interpreted to mean that there should be control over the mass media or how much attention television, radio or the press may give to community violence. Attention *ought* to be given to the need for change in a society that keeps a person from developing whatever potential he has. Attention *ought* to be given to conditions that are an insult to human dignity and decency. But giving attention to conditions that need to be changed is one thing; repeatedly suggesting to people that the acting out of hate and violence is an expected mode of behavior is another. It is naive to believe that the messages being disseminated through all the cues and signals bombarding people have no effect, and it is equally naive to say that what is being disseminated necessarily reflects reality. It may be quite true and "real" that a few highly-vocal black nationalists call for violence and that a bunch of kids start breaking store windows, but it is not necessarily "reality"—reality in the sense that this represents the sentiments of black people in general or is the behavior they sanction.

The spotlight, of course, varies in intensity. It varies according to the media from which it emanates, it varies according to the city that is touched by it, or bathed in it. To understand how both the psychic setting (the spotlight factor, the expectations and attitudes of people) and the ecological setting (the dispersion of the ghetto) all provide a framework for analyzing urban unrest, a single city will be examined here for purposes of illustration.

Houston will be the city, and the views of its racial unrest will be based on an acronym derived from the four "sead" factors: the *s*potlight that gives the city a certain public image and conveys a certain message to the people; the *e*xpectations and *a*ttitudes of the ghetto, and the *d*ispersion, which is the effect that space, distribution of people—and their social organization—have on their actions and concerns.

Spotlight

What kind of spotlight has Houston been in during its brief history? Until May 1967, it was not even in the public spotlight in terms of racial strife. The city had a race riot in August 1917, but it made few national headlines because the country was preoccupied with World War I. In May 1967 there was the violent upheaval at Texas Southern University. In July 1967, and again one month later, Houston came close to riot, but in both cases, the violence that the city experienced was not community-wide and hardly qualified it for a position on the same list with Newark or Detroit or even Cambridge, Md. However, any incident during that explosive summer captured headlines somewhere, and in Dallas, one newspaper played up six broken windows in Houston with the massive violence occurring elsewhere in the nation during that July.

The primary purpose of the present chapter is not to focus on the *causes* for the violence that did occur in Houston in 1967, but on its *effects* and on factors that influence unrest. This will be done by presenting a general profile of the city in a framework of the "sead" factors of unrest—both *before* any collective violence and *after*. What I hope we can learn from this is not only the influence of the psychic and ecologic settings but also the effects that even limited violence has on a city. The consequences of collective violence have not been studied nearly as completely as the causes. Because of the importance of these consequences, considerable detail will be provided on the before-and-after violence studies I made in Houston, and on the way violence influenced the attitudes of Negroes toward police, toward Black Power, toward the use of violence to gain a goal—and toward support of such figures as Stokely Carmichael and Cassius Clay.*

In 1956, even before the Manned Spacecraft Center came to the area, Lloyd's of London was being quoted by the *New York Times* as saying that within 100 years, Houston would be the largest city in the world.[5] Only three years earlier, *Holiday* magazine had decided Houston was one of 12 of the most "exciting cities in North America."[6]

Ebony magazine has from time to time joined in the chorus of attention given to Houston. In 1952, it said "Houston is sometimes called the 'Bagdad of Negro America'."[7] George Fuermann, in 1962, added that "it is also said that Houston Negroes have a higher per capita wealth than those of any other American city."†[8]

Just how many inhabitants of "the Bottom," until recently the most concentrated Negro slum in the city, have heard this is problematical. But it is a matter of record that as far as living expenses in the city, the U. S. Department of Labor has listed Houston as the largest city in the United States with the lowest cost of living for a family of four.[9]

---

*No definition will be attempted in this book for the term "Black Power." In October 1966, a two-day series of seminars on Black Power was held in Houston with the featured speaker being James Forman, Stokely Carmichael's right-hand man in the Student Nonviolent Coordinating Committee at the time. Interviews were conducted with those who attended the programs, and 54 different definitions were recorded from 123 young men and women, all Negroes. The definitions ranged from "mob violence" to "nonviolence," from "fighting, killing and burning" to "social, economic and political power." The most prevailing theme in the definitions was Black Power is meant to arouse emotions and promote separatism. This being the dominant finding, Black Power will be used in this book in that context, and the words will be capitalized to distinguish it from the "black power" that has now emerged as meaning a bigger voice and a greater stake in the mainstream of society.

†Fuermann, a well-known Houston columnist and author, does not cite the source for this optimistic report.

Houston has been picked for all sorts of honors, some of
them dubious. It has been called one of the noisiest cities
anywhere. It has led the nation in the number of murders, it
has been the only known city that has had oil wells drilled
on its city dump—and received royalties from them.

But Houston is not so materialistic that it has been regarded as having no heart. William S. White, writing in
Harper's, said Houston "was the first large community in the
United States to feed the depression hungry with no questions asked, no kind of means test, no social worker's cross
examination, no stigma and no nonsense."[10]

Houston, then, escaped being given a riot role to play
during most of its short history. But after the Watts outbreak in the summer of 1965, the city did seem to get the
jitters over the potential for violence during the Labor Day
weekend.

A survey conducted after the explosion in Los Angeles
showed that Houston Negroes—121 of them whose attitudes
were sampled at five "listening posts"—considered tension to
be higher in Houston as a result of the rioting in Watts. And
"natural dialogues" conducted among 110 low-income Negroes during the same period indicated that some 70 percent
sanctioned the use of violence in varying degrees.* (See
chapter on "Rebel Without a Cause" for tables presenting
data on attitudes toward violence.)

Later investigation into the pre-Labor Day jitters indicated that members of the white community—more than
those in Negro areas—were most concerned about the possibility of a Houston riot. There was a greater amount of talk
by white people about the "threat" of violence, and more
white people purchased guns.

But nothing happened. One reason might be that despite
the word-of-mouth rumors about impending riot, no public
spotlight was placed on the community by news media, located in Houston or elsewhere. There was no asking of Houston Negroes if they felt conditions warranted a riot. There
was no public "suggestion" that the city was on the verge of
violence. In fact, the one reference to any Labor Day trouble

---

*Although the "natural dialogue" interview technique seeks to put "poll-
ing" in a conversational context and to minimize biased responses that
may be obtained by questionnaire-type surveying, any opinion sampling
must be interpreted with the recognition that what a person says does
not necessarily establish what he is going to do, or has done.

came from Mayor Louie Welch, who took to television and
said that despite 500 "leads" phoned into police, none had
proved to show that anyone in Houston was planning trouble and that citizens should go about their business and enjoy
the holiday.

Whether or not the mayor's disclaimer of potential violence had an influence on the fact that none occurred will
remain a question. What is known is that the public did not
fulfill any word-of-mouth prophecy in this instance.

Perhaps Houston Negroes, unlike those in Oakland, did
not know—because of lack of spotlight—that they were "expected" to riot. None of this should be interpreted to mean
that the news media should ever refrain from zeroing in on
conditions and attitudes that do in fact exist. It is meant to
suggest that attitudes, expectations and postures can be
shaped—even created—by the public spotlight. By mid-
August 1967, there still had been no community rioting, but
the city did receive attention twice, during the late spring
and summer for limited outbreaks of collective violence.
These will be discussed in detail later, although it should not
be inferred here that the spotlight was responsible for the
violence. The spotlight, which today is most powerful from a
national television level, is just one "sead" factor of unrest.
Now let's explore another. Since it has already been suggested
that expectations seem to play a major role in the level of
dissatisfaction in a given Negro community, the focus will
shift to this factor. What are the kinds of expectations that
Houston Negroes have and what are they based on?

Expectations

"You can't miss something you never had."

This was one Negro's way of explaining the acceptance
that he thinks many black people in Houston show toward
their lot in life—at least, on the surface. It would be a mistake to assume that they desire nothing better than what they
have. But desires are measured by relative indices.

> What if your world has been limited to a small East Texas town
> and to a rent house in the Fifth Ward in Houston? How much
> better off you think you are—and how much better off you think
> you can be—are going to be influenced by what you remember of
> the small town and what you have seen or experienced that is any
> improvement in Houston.

The observer, an articulate heavy machine operator who

makes $27.10 a day, grew up outside a little town 50 miles
northeast of Houston. He came to the city at the age of 16
and lived with relatives in a four-room house that rented for
$10 a week in the lower Fifth Ward. By the age of 18 he
had a regular job with a large construction company. Five
years later, when the company opened up its machine operator training program to Negroes, he qualified for one of the
first classes. After six months of attending school on Saturdays, on his own time, he graduated as an apprentice in heavy
machine operations. It took him three more years to work up
to his present wage level.

Meanwhile, he had married, and after his first child
was born, he and his wife and baby moved to a four-room
house, also rented, in a better area of the Fifth Ward. Two
years later, after the birth of their second child, the couple
bought a small home in Kashmere Gardens, an area just
north of Fifth Ward. (See Figure 1 for various neighborhood
areas and other sections in Houston.)

When Mayor Louie Welch of Houston appeared at a
"Meet the Mayor" program in nearby Trinity Gardens, the
machine operator went to hear him talk. The mayor asked
how many had ever lived in a small town or "out in the country." The vast majority of those in the audience, including
the East Texas, small-town Negro, raised their hands. The
mayor said life was different in the country. There was no
need for sanitary service because the bathroom was "a little
house in back." There was no need for water lines because
water came from wells. There was no need for garbage
trucks because any food left over was given to the hogs and
trash was burned or buried. There was no need for parks because children had all the room they needed for play right
where they were. And there was not a great deal of concern
about roads so long as the one that went by a person's house
was good enough to get him to town and back once a week.

Members of the audience, mostly people from 35 to 60,
nodded their heads with understanding. The mayor, who
came from a small town (Slaton) in West Texas and knew
about outhouses, seemed to be speaking their language. He
also was telling them that in a city that has grown as fast as
Houston, the sewers, the water lines, the garbage service, the
parks and the streets were not what they should be in many
areas. He said the city had grown faster than its ability to
provide all the services it should.

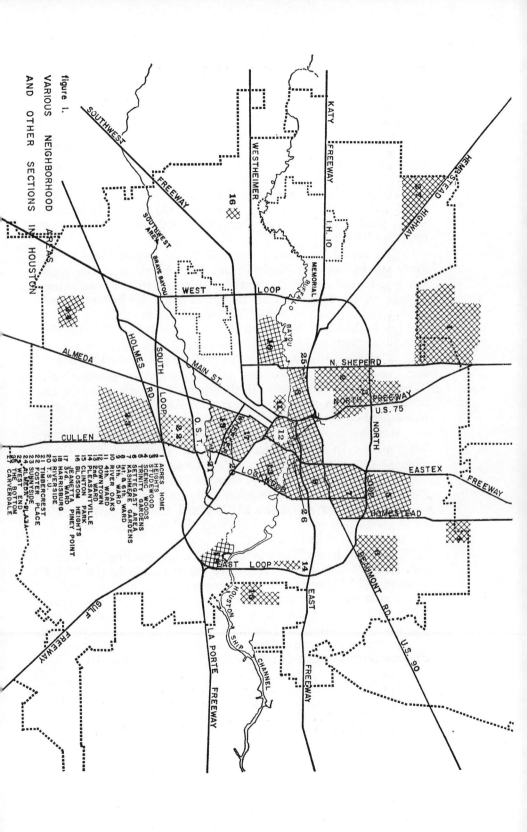

figure 1.
VARIOUS NEIGHBORHOOD AREAS
AND OTHER SECTIONS IN HOUSTON

1. ACRES HOME
2. HEIGHTS
3. STUDEWOOD
4. SCENIC WOODS
5. TRINITY GARDENS
6. SETTEGAST AREA
7. KASHMERE GARDENS
8. 1st. & 6th. WARD
9. 5th. WARD
10. RIVER OAKS
11. 4th. WARD
12. DOWNTOWN
13. 2nd. WARD
14. PLEASANTVILLE
15. CLINTON PARK
16. BLOSSOM HEIGHTS
17. JEANETTA PINEY POINT
18. 3rd. WARD
19. HARRISBURG
20. RIVERSIDE
21. FOSTER PLACE
22. TIMBERCREST
23. SUNNYSIDE
24. ALMEDA PLAZA
25. WEST
26. THE BOTTOM
27. CARVERDALE

Afterwards, the machine operator said he knew that many Negro areas needed improvement. But he himself lived on a paved street, he had sewer and water service and garbage pick up. He wished there was a park closer for his growing children, but the civic club he was a member of was working on that at present.

Neither the mayor, nor the machine operator, painted life "back on the farm" as "the good old days." Independently, they agreed that coming to the city provided greater opportunity for a better life.

The machine operator recalled the two-room "shack" he grew up in back in East Texas. He remembered the mud when it rained and the unpaved roads and the cold outhouse in winter. He compared all this with what he had now and he decided he was better off. Most of all, he thought about the job he had and compared it with farm labor. He thought about his wages and compared those.

"Don't get the idea that I'm strictly for everything staying the same for me, or any other Negro," he emphasized. "I'm for every civil rights bill they pass. I'm for better schools here in Houston and for integration. And I'll stand up and be counted on these things."

But, he went on, "I don't know anything about life in River Oaks [a high income area] or anywhere like that. They're just names to me, and I've never even been on a construction job that's taken me close to them. That's why I say you can't miss something you don't know anything about."

He did know about the Fifth Ward and Third Ward. He knew that there were homes in the Third Ward immeasurably better than those in the Fifth.

"But the Fifth Ward is where I've always lived in Houston. If I get dissatisfied or get to know people in the Third Ward, maybe I'll want to move there someday. But not now."

These were the "expectations" of just one Negro—a man whose world had been limited but who was surprisingly articulate for the amount of formal education he had.

A white city councilman, whose district in Houston includes a large number of Negroes, took a different position.

I have seen a great change in expectations, even among Negroes who have never lived anywhere but in the poorest sections. The change has been greatly accelerated by the mass media, particularly television. Like all of us, they have come to think there is some kind of American standard that includes a large, comfortable house, two cars to a family and a high-paying job. Their demands, from a politician's point of view, indicate they expect that standard to be theirs.

This politician said he did not care how far back in the "piney woods of East Texas" Negroes came from—"they have a mental picture of that standard."

Many of Houston's 300,000 Negroes came from rural areas of Texas or Louisiana, or were born and reared in Houston. In a random-sample survey conducted in 1966-67 among 600 Negroes, it was found that 35 percent had been born in Houston, 36 percent in a small Texas town or rural area, 19 percent somewhere in the Deep South, 9 percent in a large Texas city other than Houston and 1 percent in various other parts of the United States.

This survey was conducted among people in shotgun houses renting for $8.50 a week as well as among the relatively few owning homes valued from $85,000 to $100,000.

As an example of just how big an influx of Negroes there has been from the kind of areas already named, the city gained 24,843 Negroes 15 years of age and over in the single decade between 1940 and 1950.[11] From 1950 to 1960, Harris County—which contains Houston—increased its Negro population by 65 percent.[12]

Although rural areas have served as a source for a large number of Negroes in Houston, it should not be assumed that their world is so limited they cannot even imagine what they are missing. It may be true that many, such as the heavy machine operator, have never personally lived in more than a few places in their lives, but there are other links to the outside world, as the city councilman suggested.

And as TV reaches into more and more homes (9 out of every 10 Negro homes have sets in Houston), the effect on expectations will undoubtedly increase. Couched in the language of Marshall McLuhan, black people are becoming "steeped in the software environment of affluence images. The discrepancy between the old and the new images enrages the victims."[13]

The black man, then, and the poor of any color, are "enveloped," McLuhan says, "in images of physical splendor." Just as the child is bombarded with adult programs on TV and tries to bypass childhood and adolescence, "the poor quite naturally decide to bypass the bureaucratic maze that denies them cornflakes." The rise in expectation is concerned not only with images of affluence, but also of freedom from "second-class citizenship." As the National Advisory Report on Civil Disorders noted, the success of legislative action and the courts "led to intensified Negro expectations and resulting dissatisfaction." Houston Negroes have received "legal freedom." It is the level of expectations toward affluence that is in question.

Television is not the only link to images and expectations of affluence. In a survey made of the Houston Negro's exposure to news media, it was found that 77.3 percent of Negro homes regularly received one or more of the city's daily newspapers, and 46.2 percent took one or more national magazines.[14] Pictorial magazines are the most popular, with *Ebony* ranking high on the list. *Life* and *Look* also have heavy subscriptions.

Negro newspapers also get to many homes. The survey showed that non-dailies, such as *The Forward Times*, the *Informer* and the *Pittsburgh Courier*, were regularly received by 71.4 percent of the Negro families in Houston.

But radio reaches more homes than any other media. Nearly all families, regardless of how low the income bracket, have a radio.

Exposure to the world outside of Houston by newspaper, magazine or radio is clearly not the same as personal experience. But, in the opinion of the white city councilman, such exposure does raise expectations. The question is: What happens to the expectations once adaptation is made to conditions that become a part of one's everyday existence? When a person's movement within the city where he lives is limited, his vision of what he is missing elsewhere is likely to be narrowed, not broadened. A number of Negroes who come to Houston live lives largely confined to specific areas they start considering their own. A number who were born in the city live similarly.

These points were brought out in a random-sample survey of approximately 800 subjects that was made in 1966-67. There were 48 percent who said they had moved only once or twice out of the general area where they were born or had spent most of their lives. There were 36 percent who reported from three to five moves beyond their "own general neighborhood." The remaining 16 percent had moved more than five times.

By staying in one or two areas, a person's expectations often take on the coloration of what he has lived around the longest. It would be unfair to say that he "expects nothing better" and wants to live in the same conditions the rest of his life. But as we have seen, it would be a mistake to assume that lack of direct contact with better living conditions does not play a part in expectations. For many people impoverishment cripples both motivations and expectations, but in other cases it goads individuals to high attainment.

One Houston Negro, who had been active in civil rights causes, observed:

> You have to remember that a lot of Negroes have very little contact with white people. Sure, they may do some work for them or even hold a job where the boss is always a white man. But they have little opportunity to see how a white person really lives. This may not be true of domestics who go into white homes during the day to do maid work. But even there, the kind of contact is not the same as a white person looking at the big home of another white person and building up expectations of owning one like it later. Negroes simply look and feel frustration. They don't see any means by which they can get what the white person has.

Misconceptions about the kind of life white people lead, and how "comfortable" it is, may result from the very lack of direct contact that the Negro observer was commenting on. Just how limited the contact really is was brought out in a random-sample survey made in Houston among 533 Negroes in the summer of 1966. A large 46 percent said they had no contact at all with white people; 29 percent reported four hours or more a day exposure by reason of their jobs; 17 percent said they had under four hours a day contact and 4.5 percent gave no answer. The social "isolation" the black person feels in a predominantly white society can contribute to his potential for participation in riots, according to H. Edward Ransford. He found that Negroes who had the least contact with white people—such as visiting in their homes—were more willing to use violence.[15]

A Negro woman teacher in Houston commented on the misconceptions that also result among white people about Negroes as a result of the minimum exposure:

> Most of them know so little about us—have been exposed to only a certain class. I'd like to see the races acquire a better understanding of each other. You can't legislate love. As I heard it said once, 'I hope we haven't started hating whites by the time they've started loving Negroes.'[16]

What Negroes think of whites and whites think of Negroes clearly influence expectations of black people. This applies not only in terms of anticipated behavior but also in the
sense that some, perhaps many, Negroes seem to keep themselves from building up hopes, as long as they are imbued
with negative self-images largely derived from the white
man's view of them. (See Chapter 5.)

One Houston observer noted that this building up of
hopes, has been noticeably blocked by limited opportunities
to take advantage of a higher standard of living.

> There are many of the better things in life that Negroes don't build
> up expectations for, because they simply aren't in reach as long
> as our pay is smaller, and our standard of living is lower. This
> goes for opening up hotels and restaurants to Negroes. You can't
> take advantage of the right if you don't have the money, and you
> won't have the money as long as your education is inferior and
> there is discrimination in employment. You can't really tell what
> it's like to live better without some opportunity to sample it.

All of these factors affect expectations. But they do not
kill expectations, nor do they necessarily mean that a person
cannot see beyond his own horizon or wish for anything better. There are activists and militants in Houston who lead
activities designed to improve the Negro's lot in life. Most
have lived elsewhere at some time in their life. In 1967,
they included Rev. William Lawson, formerly of Texas Southern University, who was instrumental in a school boycott and
march in Houston; Rev. Earl Allen, former director of community development for the Harris County Community Action Association and founder of HOPE Development, Inc., and
Rev. F. D. Kirkpatrick, who was area co-ordinator for the
Student Nonviolent Coordinating Committee at TSU before
rejoining the Southern Christian Leadership Conference.
Such men represent a definite level of expectations for black
people.

Another Negro, who considers himself more nationalistic
and militant than those three and disagrees with their "nonviolent" tactics, objects to the idea that exposure to other
parts of the country is associated with higher expectations.

> It all depends on the kind of expectations you're talking about.
> If you expect to integrate into a rich neighborhood like River
> Oaks, then it helps to know that fat cat Negroes in some place
> like San Francisco have shown that this kind of integration is
> possible. It helps if you have seen it for yourself or believe what
> you've seen on TV. But if you have realistic expectations about

improving the black man's lot, you don't need to know about any place but home. All it takes is exposure to the right kind of teaching—teaching that tells the black man to establish his own black power in a black community and forget all this crap about integrating, which is just a sure-fire way of diluting your strength.

But there are many who stay in the black community and never gather strength from it. A Negro city detective, who grew up in the Fifth Ward and still lives there, notes that "people get to know their surroundings and, almost by reflex action, they keep going back to the same hole every night. They don't ever move or try anything better." Many are unmotivated, he says, and passive.

In contrast, a fairly high degree of activism and militancy could be found among urban-bred youths, particularly those who belong to such organizations as the Student Nonviolent Coordinating Committee, which had headquarters at Texas Southern University, a predominantly Negro college. Of 20 interviewed, 15 SNCC members were born in Houston and five others came to the city at an early age. Surprisingly, there were 14 who expressed general approval about living in Houston but had some specific complaints. There were six who said they liked nothing about the city. When the entire group was asked what they disliked about living in Houston, five answered "everything" and nine named such items as "slums," "lack of zoning" and "too little understanding between the races." Three said they did not like the laws. The remainder named no grievances.

The same urban-bred SNCC members expressed strong disapproval of the mayor and of the governor. They had a good opinion of a Negro woman lawyer elected to the State Senate, but even in regard to her, five expressed disapproval.

Now, applying all this to our factor of expectations—how well a person likes or dislikes living in a city is a function, in part at least, of his expectations about the place. The evidence seems to suggest that many Negroes coming from East Texas found conditions better than those they left but that they did not bring with them excessively high expectations toward Houston. From interviews in Watts, I found that Negroes moving to California, on the other hand, looked toward it as promising much more than it could deliver. I think the same can be said about Harlem and Chicago, particularly in past years.

In "Space City, USA," expectations cannot be high when 60,000 families live in substandard dwellings. No one who lives in a four-room house renting for $10.50 a week without hot water is likely to expect too much out of life in Houston. The word gets back to people in rural East Texas and Louisiana that "if you can't make it in Houston, you can't make it anywhere," but at the same time the word also says "don't expect any paradise here because even if you get a regular job, you probably won't find decent housing."

The expectations that are most likely to be converted into potentially violent action, in Houston or any other city, are represented by people who have had just enough of a taste of a better life to want more, but seem unable to get it. Their frustration is fed by an unwillingness to stay in their "place" and by a lack of further power and additional resources to gain the better life they know exists but seems out of reach. They do not want to be like adolescents having to search for definition in society. They want an identity of their own; an adult identity with the power and the recognition of an adult. Some find their identity among black nationalists and militants. Others join nothing, but seethe with a fierce frustration of not being able to hurdle the fence between them and the greener grass they see on the other side. Such was the case with this 29 year-old Negro waitress in a hotel restaurant:

> You tell me that all the laws have been passed to make me a first-class citizen. For every 500 white people I see pass through the lobby of this hotel, or eat in the coffee shop, there's maybe one Negro. You don't think my husband and I would like to stay in one of those suites upstairs and let our kids swim in the hotel pool? You don't think we'd like our daughter to be able to eat in the fancy restaurant here with candlelight on the table? We've got all the ambition but none of the means. I make more money as a waitress here than I can as a kindergarten aide in a Negro school. What am I supposed to do the rest of my life? Be satisfied with waiting tables and watching other people treat their families to a nice vacation in this hotel? These people aren't rich, but they can save a little money and live the kind of life my husband and I'd like to have. My husband is a deliveryman for a big department store. It's a fancy store just like this hotel is. His store and my hotel are as close to status as either one of us is ever likely to get. I wanted to go to college, but I didn't even get to finish high school because I had to go to work. The same thing happened to him. We're both willing to work night and day, but we really remain 'nothing' in terms of an identity we want. We can't see that the system is going to open up to us so that we can enjoy some of the fruits of it and find the status we want.

If it takes rioting to open the system up, then I say Negroes need to riot. I need to riot. My husband does. If we rioted, maybe somebody would notice us. As it is I'm just a waitress and he's just a deliveryman. We want a chance to be more, but we're too busy working and paying bills to start all over and buck the system for something better.

This woman was born and reared in Houston, as was her husband. Her story is a clear contrast to the one of the machine operator, who felt he was accomplishing as much as he could expect in life. He had his identity. Expectations have deep psychological roots, and the question of identity is one of them. When the expectations cannot be fulfilled, they may generate severe identity problems—such as a waitress feeling she is "nothing" because she feels she cannot fulfill the expectations she has for herself. An inner conflict over expectations can be coped with by denying them or repressing them, and this may lead to a blandness in attitude and an inarticulation in expression that often are misleading in terms of understanding what the person really feels. Expectations, of course, can influence attitudes, just as the "sead" factor of the spotlight can affect both. All the "sead" factors are interrelated, and they are being dealt with separately here only to suggest how each play a part in urban violence and unrest.

Before taking a look at the "sead" factor of attitudes, it should be recalled that what we have been examining are findings obtained from surveys in the Negro community *before* any violence occurred. In the following section, we will get into findings *after* violence and consider the important impact that an upheaval limited to a Negro campus has on the entire black community.

Attitudes

It has been said that Negroes have "more fortitude" for coping with unfavorable conditions, such as overcrowding.[17] Paul Gillen, who has made such an observation, says he does not mean that Negroes "enjoy" their living conditions but that when the Negro migrant considers moving to urban centers that are already densely populated, "overcrowding does not appear to deter him."

Whether the Negro has "more fortitude" or simply must adjust to what he finds is an open question. The Negro may have no choice in moving to the city—that may be the only place there are jobs. As to what he says about the conditions, once he settles in the city, he may not be able to articulate his feelings and this is a point that must be considered in any survey of attitudes. This is particularly true in the case of surveys among lower-income Negroes, who may well have difficulty verbalizing their feelings and who may show a reluctance to attack or criticize what little they do have. Even in a natural dialogue, "conversational" approach, what people say may reflect more what they have adjusted to rather than what they feel should exist. They may well be aware that conditions should be better but until they feel some power to improve them, their expressed attitudes may suggest an acceptance of what is—particularly in terms of their own personal life.

The "what is" in Houston—as measured by objective yardsticks—needs to be presented as a backdrop to the findings from attitude surveys that were conducted in 1966-67. Housing, income, and education will serve as examples of what kind of conditions prevail. No attempt will be made at this point to present detailed findings. What will be done here is to take a brief look at some of the conditions that prevail and, more importantly, some of the possible reasons for the attitudes expressed toward them.

But do conditions that involve bad housing, low income and poor education affect attitudes, and contribute to social unrest? The answer seems to be an emphatic "yes." What Alvin Schorr has said about bad housing would seem to apply to inadequate income and unsatisfactory education as well: " . . . the evidence is overwhelming—extremely poor housing conditions perceptibly influence behavior and attitudes."[18] Schorr believes poor housing is viewed as "a symbolic extension of one's self," and increases "stress" and feelings of frustration, as well as contributes to poor health. He thinks child-rearing practices, housekeeping, study habits, all are affected by housing. He sees other effects in terms of the type neighborhood that poor housing is usually found in and what kind of conditions breed there.

If it is accepted that attitudes, if not behavior too, are affected by a person's living conditions, then what are the objective facts concerning housing, income and education in Houston?

Housing, by an index, needs improving for Houston Negroes. Although it is possible to find high-income Negroes living in houses costing from $35,000 to $125,000 on "Sugar Hill," and Timbercrest (see Figure 1 on Page 19), the number

of substandard dwellings is high. In 1960, Houston ranked
fourth in the state in the percent of houses considered un-
sound or without proper plumbing facilities.[19] The percent
was listed as 47.49. A total of 48,978 families were reported
living in substandard units in Houston.* Most were Negroes.
More recent estimates place the number of substandard dwellings at 60,000 with 10,000 having no indoor plumbing. One
reason for the high number of substandard dwellings is the
lack of a housing code. A housing code would require that
landlords keep the houses they rent to people up to minimum
standards. Without any housing code, landlords can charge,
even in slum areas such as the Fourth Ward, $14.50 a week
and keep renters in the units without making any improvements. The reason few people move out is that with 60,000
substandard dwellings across the city, there just isn't any
better place for the tenant to rent for the same price. (See
Figure 2, on Page 30, showing the extent of substandard
housing.)

Economically, the 1960 indices listed Houston as having
18.8 percent of its population with income under $3,000 a
year.[20] About 13 percent of white families made $3,000 a year
or less, compared with 41.9 percent Negro.[21] (Nation-wide,
18 percent of white families and 55 percent of Negro ones
were below the poverty level of $3,000 in 1960.) In a study
done by the Houston-Harris County Economic Opportunity
Organization, using 1965 data, it was reported that Negroes
made up 53 percent of the poverty census, "anglos" 36 percent and Mexican-Americans 11 percent.[22] Figure 3, on Page
31, shows the areas in Houston where 25 percent or more of
the people have incomes below poverty guidelines. As can be
seen by comparing these areas with those where Negroes live
in Houston, which is shown in Figure 4, on Page 32, there is
considerable overlap. Poverty persists despite the fact that in
December 1968, the unemployment rate in Houston dropped
to a record low of 1.5 percent, with an estimated 5 to 7 percent
being the average in Negro areas.† Many of the unemployed

---

*"Substandard" is considered as including any of the following housing
problems: deteriorating with all plumbing; deteriorating lacking hot
water; deteriorating lacking other plumbing, and dilapidated. "Dilapidated" is considered by the Census Bureau as being a house in worse
condition than one that is "deteriorating." Both are "substandard."

†Nationally, the rate of unemployment was 3.3 percent, a 15-year record
low.

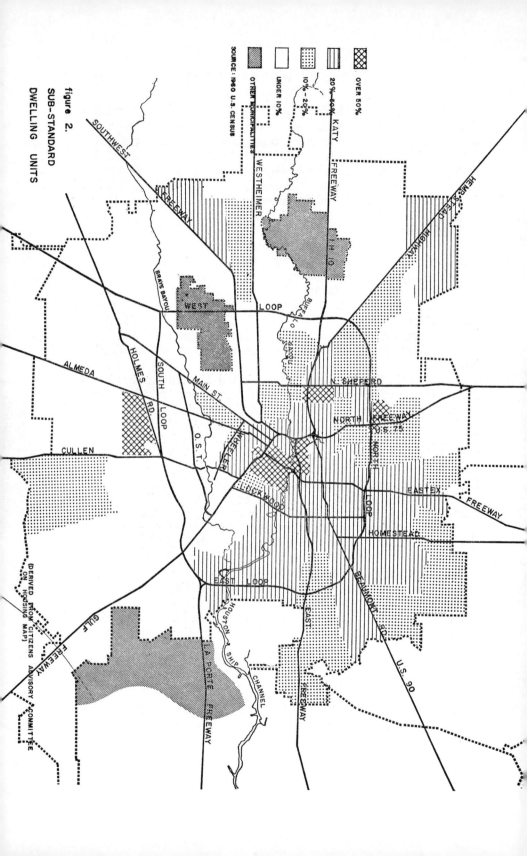

figure 2.
SUB-STANDARD
DWELLING UNITS

SOURCE: 1960 U.S. CENSUS

OTHER MUNICIPALITIES

UNDER 10%

10% - 20%

20% - 50%

OVER 50%

(DERIVED FROM CITIZENS ADVISORY COMMITTEE ON HOUSING MAP)

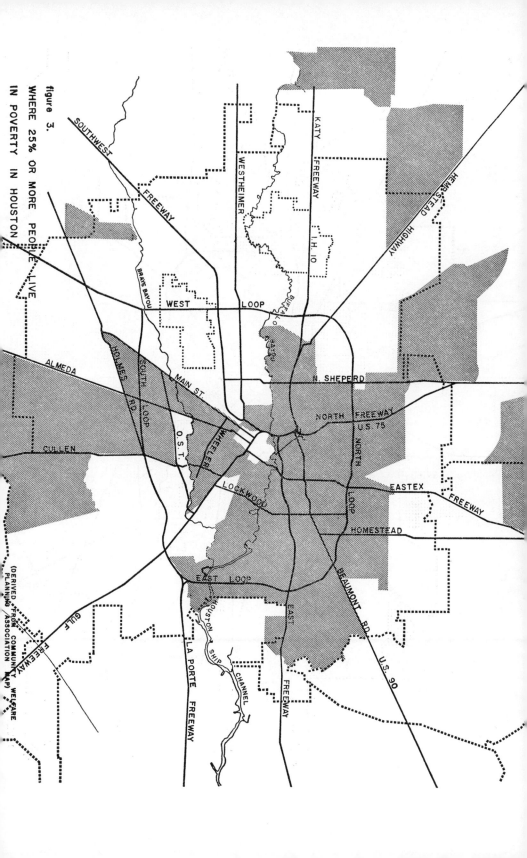

figure 3.
WHERE 25% OR MORE PEOPLE LIVE
IN POVERTY IN HOUSTON

(DERIVED FROM COMMUNITY WELFARE
PLANNING ASSOCIATION MAP)

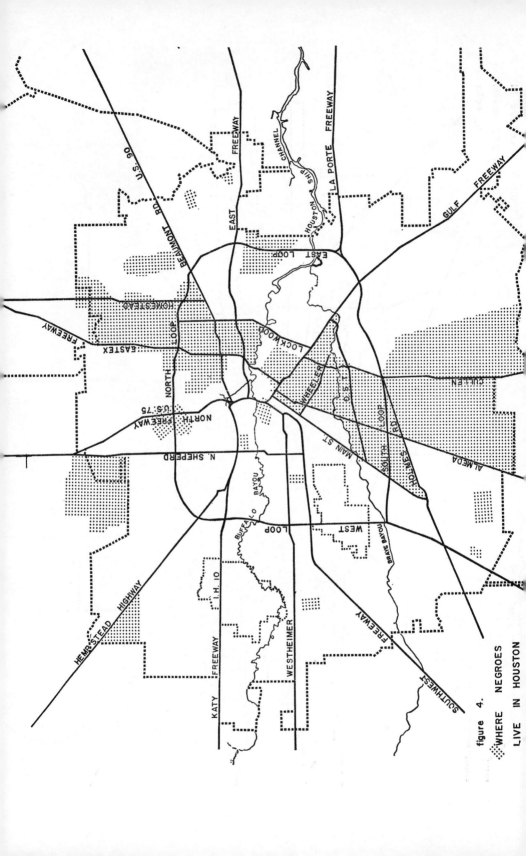

figure 4.

WHERE NEGROES
LIVE IN HOUSTON

are unable to work because of serious illness, senility or some other handicap. "Underemployment" is regarded as a bigger problem. Underemployment exists when a person works but cannot make enough money to support him or his family.

Educationally, deficiencies are also acute. Median education for white adults 25 or older in Houston has been computed at 11.3 years of schooling completed and for Negroes at 8.9.[23] About 50 percent of the white persons in Houston, as compared with 37.4 percent of the black, were reported in 1960 to be high school graduates.[24]

But what do Houston Negroes themselves say about their housing, jobs and schools? At first glance, there is the impression that a blandness pervades the opinions of Negroes toward their conditions. This impression may mislead authorities who want to believe "all is well." For instance, a random sample of opinion—conducted by formal questionnaires—was made among 572 Negroes in 18 distinct neighborhoods in the summer of 1966 with the following results:

Jobs—65 percent expressed satisfaction with their present employment, 14 percent dissatisfaction and 21 percent had mixed feelings. In the sample, only 6 percent said they had white collar or professional jobs. Unskilled workers outnumbered all others interviewed.

Schools—55 percent of the 572 interviewed expressed general approval of the school in their neighborhood. Forty-one percent disapproved of the quality of the schools, but only 1 percent of the total sample expressed their disapproval on the basis of racial discrimination. Three percent expressed no opinion.

Housing—52 percent classified housing in Houston as "fair," 39 percent as "bad" and 7 percent as "good." The remaining 2 percent gave no answer.*

When the 572 Negroes in the random sample were asked about the problems they considered most pressing, the results were: Twenty percent said housing, 21 percent named schools and 57 percent said job opportunities. (Miscellaneous problems made up the balance of responses.) Housing may not have received greater attention as a source of complaint because of the comparatively high percent of Negroes who own homes in Houston. It is important to note that when the interview subjects were asked a general question about "the

---

*Since opinions on housing were not asked on the questionnaire used in the random sample survey made among 572 Negroes in the summer of 1966, these figures come from 2,206 natural-dialogue interviews.

main problems of Negroes living in Houston," jobs were mentioned by a large majority, followed by schools and housing.
What is significant here is that people seem inclined to give
more conservative answers to questions bearing directly on
their own problems and living conditions—their own housing,
jobs, and schools. But when asked to comment on problems
in general, they feel less reluctance to name the very things
that confront them in their own lives.

Such a conclusion seems to be borne out by 2,026 "natural
dialogue" interviews conducted later in 1966 and in early
1967 by a different Negro survey team. As has been mentioned, the natural dialogue approach places the flow of question and answer in a conversational context. A number of the
interviews, conducted by trained Negro men and women,
ranging in age from 21 to 56, took place on street corners,
buses, in bars, outpatient clinics, washaterias—and any other
place that people had time to talk. Again, a moderate expression of attitudes prevailed when people were asked about their
own jobs, housing and neighborhood schools. But in commenting about conditions in general, they would open up and become quite critical of problems Negroes have in employment,
housing and with schools.

It is important to emphasize here that interpretation of
survey findings is often difficult and involves several consid-
erations: (1) Using the natural dialogue approach, it is only
after the subject "warms up" to the conversation and is allowed to express random feelings on general causes of racial
tension that he will name discrimination in employment,
schools and housing as serious problems. As long as he is
questioned on opinions toward his own job and housing, he
will tend to take the option of a middle-of-the-road response
suggesting a "things-could-be-worse" attitude; (2) Psychological surveys done in the black community suggest that
many Houston Negroes "hold back" their deepest feelings and
let moderate attitudes come out as presenting their views.
This may constitute a dichotomy between what people think
—as expressed by attitudes—and what they feel. Or it may
represent a "blocking" that occurs when questions hit too
close to home. Surveys in other cities have shown the shift
that occurs in responses when people are brought to a discussion of problems right within their own neighborhood. Interviews conducted by John Kraft, Inc., in Harlem showed a definite need for public housing, but when subjects were asked

about problems right in their own neighborhood, they did not play up the condition of their own tenements;[25] (3) Attitudes can be largely shaped by what a person adapts to. If he adapts to chronic failure, his attitude is going to reflect an outlook of defeat, and hopelessness. If he adapts to a day-to-day life of uncertainty, having a job one day and not the next, his attitude is going to be cautious and probably ambivalent. All of this is embedded in the problem of interpreting survey results.

But regardless of what may influence the kind of response a person gives in an interview, the important point here is how much does his stated attitude change once violence has occurred. The violence in this instance was the one-night upheaval at Texas Southern University, and it profoundly influenced the attitudes expressed by members of the Negro community in all parts of Houston. This finding, I think, has significant implications for all cities in terms of how far-reaching an impact even campus violence can have on the climate of race relations in a community.

Attitudes Before and After Violence

The autopsy report on Case 67-1219 read:

> This 25-year-old white man was a police officer of the City of Houston Police Department who was shot during rioting on the campus of Texas Southern University at 3200 Wheeler Street at approximately 2:20 AM on May 17, 1967. He died at Ben Taub General Hospital at 8:30 AM on May 17, 1967.

Officer Louis Raymond Kuba had graduated from the Police Academy only the month before. He and his wife were expecting their first child in three months. A lead bullet weighing 49 grains was removed from his brain. It was never established where the bullet came from that killed Kuba.

A time-table of events for the night of May 16-17 at Texas Southern University, as put together by police, included the following:

> 8:15 PM, May 16—Fifty students are observed milling around in front of the TSU Student Center Building.
>
> 10:15 PM—Crowd increases to approximately 150 persons. Five subjects approach the crowd stating: 'They killed a six-year-old child out near the Scenic Woods School. What do you intend to do about it?' [Scenic Woods is an area in Northeast Houston, where members of the TSU chapter of the Student Nonviolent Coordinating Committee had been demonstrating in front of a junior high school. The report of the shooting was false.]

10:20 PM—'An object' is thrown at observing officers, and strikes Unit 191 on the hood.

10:30 PM—An armed Negro subject is arrested on the TSU campus. The pistol recovered was found to be stolen property.

10:45 PM—Crowd continues to grow and more inciting statements are made. Rocks, bricks, and other missiles are thrown at police vehicles.

11:00 PM—Sporadic firing from men's dormitories begins. Officers observe armed subject running toward the Student Center.

11:30 PM—Officer Blaylock is wounded by sniper fire from the TSU campus.

11:35 PM—Police reinforcements arrive at the scene and snipers continue to fire from TSU dormitories.

The clash between police and students at TSU came after three months of tension on the campus. As mentioned earlier, a number of nights had been spent on the scene trying to reduce tensions and mitigate problems—problems that included blocking the thoroughfare running through the campus, chaining doors to campus buildings to keep students and teachers out (this was done on one occasion), ransacking two cafeterias and overturning tables in protest of bad food, and a long list of other grievances toward the school administration. Two marches from TSU to downtown Houston also had been staged. Most serious, however, was a series of incidents involving the throwing of bricks at cars driving along Wheeler Street, the thoroughfare that runs through the campus. One weekend, a flurry of brick-throwing occurred and several motorists were injured. A number of cars—including a few driven by Negroes—were damaged.

Rev. F. D. Kirkpatrick, leader of the campus Student Nonviolent Coordinating Committee and founder of the Deacons for Defense in Louisiana, was sought out and was asked for his cooperation in trying to prevent the brick-throwing. He agreed to organize a group within SNCC to "police" the campus at night and stand guard against any outbreak of brick-throwing. This arrangement worked for about three weeks. Then, on the day preceding the gun-battle between police and students at TSU, one of Kirkpatrick's lieutenants pulled out of the arrangement and moved his activities to Northeast Houston, where some black students had received longer suspensions from a junior high school than white students with whom they had been having fights. The Northeast Houston activity pulled other students away who had been

helping prevent brick-throwing on campus. While they were
in the Northeast part of the city, yet another contingent of
SNCC people and TSU students went to a dump in the south
part of town to join a group of preachers picketing at that
site. This left the TSU campus uncovered as far as Rev. Kirkpatrick's having anyone to help him exercise control over
students. And on the night of May 16, the lid blew off. Before
police moved in, efforts were made through Rev. Kirkpatrick
and other embassaries to dissuade students from further
firing, but their terms were that Wheeler Street be closed.
The mayor, by mobile phone, said the street must remain
open.* While attempts at negotiations were being made, con-
struction-site building materials and barrels of roofing tar
were dragged onto Wheeler to block the street. Police were
then ordered to remove the obstruction. Exchange of gunfire
resumed.

The clash at TSU followed violence that had already
struck Negro campuses in other parts of the country. In
Nashville, Tennessee, students had rioted three successive
nights after a speech by Stokely Carmichael. Carmichael
spoke in Houston April 14, 1967, at Texas Southern University, but the unrest on that campus did not explode until 32
days later, and his appearance had no bearing on the outbreak.

The primary question to be answered here is how did the
Negro community react to the four hours of violence in which
one policeman was killed, two officers and three students
wounded and 489 arrested? If it is possible to provide answers
to this question, some inferences might be made as to the
residual effect that a violent outbreak leaves in its wake in a
city. An immediate effect is the generation of widely varying interpretations on what happened, and the emergence of
groups that come forward with differing accounts.

One interpretation was that the campus violence really
was a community clash. For instance, the United Ministries

---

*In 1969, the mayor joined with officials from TSU and the University
of Houston in asking the state Legislature for funds to re-route through
traffic around TSU so Wheeler Street could be closed, or, at least, that
portion going through the campus. Before the TSU violence ever occurred, a master plan had been discussed between city and school officials, but the multi-million dollar cost to implement it was clearly going
to require state aid. Both TSU and the University of Houston are state
schools.

staff of the university—five clergymen representing their respective churches, Catholic, Episcopal, Lutheran, Methodist and Presbyterian—issued a statement saying:

> We believe this incident to be a city 'power play' in the local racial confrontation, Negro versus white . . . the incident was definitely a community and not a University affair. Our students were involved—but not as students, *per se*. The city, not the students, made the University an issue.

By the Sunday following the Tuesday night and early Wednesday morning when the gunbattle occurred on May 16-17, mimeographed circulars were being distributed in the area, including churches, by members of SNCC and various community people.

The "crisis fact sheet" opened with the statement that "it is evident that the white power structure in this state, and most specifically in this city, has declared war on the black community. . . ." Quotations then followed that were attributed to students who were arrested in the TSU dormitories:

> The police seemed to have been waiting for this for a long time. It was obvious that they herded us out of the dormitories, not so much to arrest us, as to get a chance to destroy our rooms. And they say that our rooms were in such condition when they arrived. That's a bare-faced lie. . . .

> When I woke up, two large German Shepherd (police) dogs were in the bed with me; one was tearing at the mattress and the other was biting me on the leg. I kicked the dog and suddenly was hit with a billy club and this white policeman said: 'Get up nigger, and get downstairs.' . . .

> I asked one officer if he were prejudiced; he replied to the effect that no, he wasn't prejudiced; he just didn't like people who 'did things wrong, and since all Negroes did things wrong, he just had to hate them all.'

> Until now, I didn't know what police brutality was. They hit us with billy clubs, pistol butts, rifles—whatever they had in their hands, they hit us with it. . . .*

Although both the statement from the university ministers and the "crisis fact sheet" complained that the news media were deliberately giving the public distorted information on the "TSU incident," particularly in terms of telling "only the police side," the reaction in the Negro community

---

*See Appendix B for position taken by the Harris County Grand Jury on action taken by the police. In brief, the grand jury said, "The law enforcement officers acted in the best interests of the community."

was swift and strongly negative toward law enforcement officers.

This reaction resulted despite survey evidence that a considerable percent of people in the widely-dispersed black community stated that they did not know what occurred the night of May 16-17. For instance, in a random-sample survey conducted by Negro interviewers using questionnaire forms, a number of questions about what happened at TSU elicited a high percent of "don't know" answers, as shown below:

Question	People Who Answered "Don't Know" %
1. What do you think started the trouble at TSU Tuesday night, May 16? (Nine percent of those surveyed in the community answered, "Police made arrests for no reason.")	70
2. How could the shooting from the dormitories have been stopped Tuesday night? (Fifty-four percent answered "let campus police intervene," which they had tried to do at the outset of the disturbance; only two percent said the "situation was handled the only way it could be.")	25
3. Do you think that students caused any of the damage done inside the dormitories? (Police and reporters on the scene who entered the dormitiories first stated students had "vandalized" rooms before officers entered; students said police were responsible for the damage. Twenty-four percent of the community people thought the students "may have caused some" damage.)	24

Added evidence that members of the Negro community were unclear on the sequence of events came from two questions of a "did-you-hear" nature (by television, radio or other means). The results were:

Question	People Who Answered "No" %
1. Did you hear that prior to the shooting (at TSU), a report was circulating that a Negro child had been shot by a white boy in the Northeast section of Houston?	47
2. Did you hear that a student fired a pistol into the air near the Student Union before the trouble began Tuesday night?	78

Although the details were not known as to what precipitated the exchange of gunfire, feelings already were hardening against police, as reflected in these results:

Question	Responses %
1. Before police moved full forces in, why do you think shots were fired across Wheeler Street from the men's dormitories?	
Optional choices were:	
Police should not have made arrest on campus	58
The first policeman who was wounded fired first	23
Students were only trying to scare people	15
Shooting was planned as part of starting a riot	4
2. Do you think students' attitudes toward city policemen have changed since Tuesday? In what way?	
Options were:	
Dislike them more	55
Hate them more	28
Still regard them as just doing their job	2
Don't know	15

The word spread swiftly that police had "invaded" the campus. There is no denying the police did move in mass on the men's dormitories after students started the trouble. Police thoroughly searched (the students say "ransacked") every room and marched all students out to lie on the ground. Police think they were justified in doing so, and at least three militants who tried to act as embassaries that night said at the time they saw no other alternative open to police. Whether the police were right or wrong, this fact remains: A significant percent of Negroes in the community said they did not know what caused the trouble at TSU. What they did know was that had the trouble been at a white school such as Rice University or the University of Houston they felt no such "invasion" by police would have ever occurred. Anger over the police action soon overshadowed the issue of what students were doing to cause officers to go to the campus in the first place. Contributing to the increased animosity toward the police, as a symbol of all white authority, was the charging of five TSU students in the death of the police officer who was slain during the gunbattle at the school. These students were accused of having "incited" the disturbance and, under the law, could technically be charged with murder. The reaction, however, to such a charge was extremely negative.

To resolve any question that the feelings about police

might not have had any relation to the violence that occurred
at TSU, a comparison was made of attitudes toward police
before violence with those after. A questionnaire survey on
police had been started in the Negro community three days
before the campus outbreak. After the violence, the survey
continued in the same census tracts among people of the same
age groups, the same socio-economic classes and educational
levels—and in the same proportions—as before the gunbattle.
A total of 287 interviews were completed in residential portions of Negro neighborhoods in six census tracts within the
city limits, with the following results:

Key Questions	Responses from Six Areas	
	Immediately Before TSU Violence %	Immediately After TSU Violence %
*1. In Houston, how would you say that the police treat Negroes— very well, fairly well, fairly badly or very badly,		
Very well/Fairly well	52	24
Fairly badly/Very badly	37	67
Don't know	11	9
2. What kind of job do you think the police chief is doing?		
Excellent/Good	30	8
Not so good/Poor	44	73
Not sure	26	19
3. Do you think the mayor is trying to improve police relations with Negroes?		
Yes	42	29
No	18	41
Not sure	40	30

As might be expected, the sharpest changes of all that
occurred in attitudes were recorded on the TSU campus itself.
The students reflected extreme hostility toward police. But
what about areas in the Negro community far removed from
the campus? The most distant neighborhood from the site of
the violence was Carverdale, some 15 miles northwest of TSU.
A before-and-after comparison of attitudes in that area was
made and the results are presented below along with the sharp

---

*All results presented in tabulations in this chapter are significant at
the .001 level, unless otherwise indicated.

changes that occurred in the attitudes of TSU students themselves.

| | Responses of Widely-Separated Areas | | | |
| | TSU Campus | | Carverdale | |
Key Questions	Before Violence %	After Violence %	Before Violence %	After Violence %
1. In Houston, how would you say that the police treat Negroes— very well, fairly well, fairly badly, or very badly?				
Very well/Fairly well	89	1	56	27
Fairly badly/Very badly	1	99	35	68
Don't know	10	0	9	5
2. What kind of job do you think the police chief is doing?				
Excellent/Good	70	1	17	5
Not so good/Poor	30	99	35	86
Not sure	0	0	48	9
3. Is the mayor trying to improve police relations with Negroes?				
Yes	50	24	39	5
No	10	69	17	24
Not sure	40	7	44	71

Clearly, the students' animosity was even greater than the hostility in the community. The morning after the violence, many students milled around, grouped together and discussed possible action. Some parents of students came and moved the young people out of the dormitories.

What can be learned from the effects of the kind of violence Houston experienced at TSU? Two points suggest themselves: (1) A single episode can cause striking reversals in attitudes. Before the exchange of gunfire at TSU, police were looked upon with a surprising degree of acceptance, apparently because of the restraint they had shown toward incidents on the campus that had spilled over into Wheeler Street, a public thoroughfare. In April 1967 when militants and student followers held a "block party" and danced in Wheeler Street, the police held off from moving in and making mass arrests, since it was known that the leaders wanted such a confrontation to gain support for their cause. The police also waited until the block party broke up before taking into custody three SNCC leaders who had been charged by university officials with disruptive activities on campus, including—in one case—knocking a woman teacher down. When Stokely Carmichael came to the campus two weeks later to speak, the police and the mayor's office were actually commended at the program for the restraint shown in dealing with the potentially explosive situation at TSU. This favorable attitude was completely reversed when the explosion occurred the next month; (2) The effects of collective violence carry to the far corners of a city. This point was well illustrated by results of surveys done in all parts of the widely-dispersed Negro community in Houston. Hostility toward police rose sharply in Negro neighborhoods 15 miles from TSU. Not only did the effects of the violence extend geographically, they also produced changes in attitude toward subjects other than police. Feelings changed, for instance, toward Cassius Clay and Carmichael.

Cassius Clay in Houston

In June 1967, Cassius Clay (Muhammad Ali) returned to Houston to face trial for refusing induction in the Army. There was considerably more sympathy for him and his cause then than there had been in April, before the TSU disturbance.

Clay fought two title bouts in Houston in 1967 and decided he liked it so well he would move his residence to the city. When he received his papers for induction into the armed forces, this meant that Houston became the site where Clay would either refuse to be drafted, as he said he would, or join up. His reason for refusal, as he and lawyers repeatedly pointed out, was that Clay was primarily a Black Muslim minister —his Muslim name being Muhammad Ali, and the only one to which he would answer—and not a boxer.* The draft board refused to accept Muhammad's claim for exemption and ordered him to report for induction on April 28, 1967, at the U. S. Army's Recruiting Station No. 1 in downtown Houston. Clay refused to take the symbolic step forward indicating acceptance of induction, and made frontpage headlines across the nation.

Considerable concern was expressed by both local and federal authorities over whether Clay's refusal to be inducted

*In April 1969, Clay's Muslim name, Muhammud Ali, was reportedly withdrawn by the Black Muslim organization after Clay made statements he would box again to pay his debts. "The Nation of Islam" also was reported to have expelled Clay from its "brotherhood" for one year.

would set off an outbreak of violence in Houston. Although
the night of May 16-17 was yet to come, it has already been
pointed out that TSU had experienced a string of incidents,
including brick-throwing and street blocking on the thoroughfare running through the campus. Police repeatedly had to
stop traffic from traveling on that portion of Wheeler Street
bisecting the campus. The arrangement with Rev. Kirkpatrick to "police" the TSU campus had just been agreed upon
when Clay reported to Houston and refused induction. Pri-
vately, Kirkpatrick said in advance there would be a small
demonstration, which there was, but there would be no violence and he would be on hand to control the group, which
he did. Nevertheless, sheriff's deputies and city police were
standing by in case of trouble while U. S. law enforcement
authorities saturated the inside and immediate outside of the
federal building where the recruiting station was located.
When the boxer and his lawyers left the building, Clay was
greeted by a group of SNCC students demonstrating in his
behalf outside. Clay had paid several visits to the TSU campus, and had preached at the local Black Muslim mosque. But
he never urged students or the Muslims to adopt violence as
a tactic in protest of his treatment at the hands of the U. S.
Government or for any cause, racial or otherwise.

The first survey on attitudes toward Clay and Black
Muslim beliefs was conducted in key census tracts of the
Negro community in April 1967. Areas included in these
tracts were (see Figure 1 on Page 19) Third Ward, which
contains the heaviest concentration of Negroes; Fifth Ward,
which is second in terms of Negro population and has a lower
average family income; Kashmere Gardens, which is north of
the Fifth Ward and contains more home owners; Clinton
Park, a section near the east city limits and just north of the
Houston Ship Channel; Studewood, a relatively confined but
rather heavily populated neighborhood in North Houston
which is surrounded by both white and Mexican-American
families; and Sunnyside, a sprawling section in the south
part of the city that contains an uneven mix of fairly decent,
occupant-owned homes, a number of apartment houses of
varying quality and quite a few cheap rent houses. Interviews
also were conducted on the Texas Southern University campus, which had consistently registered more militant attitudes
(than the Negro community) in nearly all previous surveys,

particularly since the visit of SNCC leader James Forman in October 1966.*

The second survey on attitudes toward Clay and Muslim principles was made in June 1967 in the same census tracts as before, with the same number of males and females represented as in the first questionnaire poll, together with the same proportions of persons in various age ranges, socio-economic groups and educational statuses. When Clay's trial was held in June, H. "Rap" Brown and James Forman, leaders of the Student Nonviolent Coordinating Committee, were in the city to speak at a rally, but no disorder ensued.

Clay was convicted June 20 in federal court in Houston for his refusal to be inducted in the Army. The second attitudinal survey was conducted June 23-29, 1967, among 321 subjects, the same number as in the first sample. A comparison was made of attitudes toward Clay *before* major violence at TSU, and *after*. In June, people showed much greater sympathy for Clay as shown in the results below:

	Combined Responses of All Areas	
Question	Before TSU Violence %	After TSU Violence %
Do you think Cassius Clay— Muhammad Ali—should be allowed to stay out of the Army because he says he is a Black Muslim Minister?		
Yes	39	61
No	43	22
Not sure	18	17

There were other questions that confirmed the shift that had occurred in the attitudes of community people. The people were not only still hostile toward police specifically, but they also were antagonistic toward all symbols of white authority such as the federal courts.

When Clay was assessed the maximum penalty of five years in prison and a $10,000 fine, (which is still being appealed) 60 percent of the community people said the sentence was unfair. Fifty-six percent said the trial was also unfair. People's attitudes also were changing in favor of another black spokesman, Stokely Carmichael.

------

*In 1969 Forman was leading a demand for $850 million in "reparations" from U.S. churches.

"Follow-Up" Reaction to Stokely Carmichael

Although Carmichael spoke in Houston April 13-14, 1967, a month before the upheaval at TSU, it was assumed that the campus violence might change people's attitudes toward the Black Power leader. A follow-up survey was done in June on reactions in the Negro community to Carmichael and his brand of Black Power. The survey was timed with the arrival in Houston of Carmichael's successor, H. "Rap" Brown, who was accompanied by James Forman, the new "international director" of the Student Nonviolent Coordinating Committee. Both gave talks at a rally in a Third Ward church. James Washington Ware, who later made national news during the long, hot summer when he was arrested in Nashville and the State Department revoked his passport for having gone to Havana, was another SNCC leader present.

The rally was held 34 days after the TSU outbreak. Carmichael had spoken 32 days before the campus gunbattle. So in terms of making a follow-up survey, there was approximately "equal distance" in point of time between the first random sample and TSU violence and the second set of interviews. What Brown and Forman did was to echo many of the points made by Carmichael when he was in Houston. At the time Brown and Forman spoke in June, Carmichael was making news of his own, having been jailed in Alabama. The June survey in Houston, then, focused on Carmichael himself and the points he had made in his talk in April, which were echoed two months later by Brown and Forman. Since the results had already been obtained on his April talk in Houston, the June survey simply went back to the same census tracts and asked the same questions of community people. With the TSU violence having occurred between the time the two surveys were made, a marked change in attitudes was noted, as indicated in the results below:

From the results, it can be inferred that Carmichael received more support for himself and his position from what happened in Houston *a month after* his visit in the city than from his own appearance in April. It cannot be proved that the violence at TSU was responsible for the sharp shift in sentiment in his favor, but the evidence points in that direction.

The potentially provocative effect of the visits by Brown and Forman, whose talks helped provide the opportunity for

Question	Responses of Negro Community	
	Before TSU Violence %	After TSU Violence %
1. Which best describes Carmichael—		
Greatest champion of Negroes/Speaks truth to whites	53	66
Rabble-rouser/Dangerous man who causes riots	47	34
2. Would you like Stokely Carmichael to come back to Houston—he was here in April—and stay all summer?		
Yes	32	46
No	68	54
3. Could Carmichael start a riot in Houston?		
Yes	36	53
No	63	19
Not sure	1	28
4. (a) Should Negroes "disrupt everything" for freedom?		
Yes	30	47
No	56	33
Not sure	14	20
(b) Agree that white people are not civilized?		
Yes	19	30
No	67	49
Not sure	14	21
(c) Agree that white people made this "nation of thieves?"		
Yes	40	45
No	41	35
Not sure	19	20

doing a follow-up survey on Black Power, is discounted as having a major influence on changed responses in the Negro community toward Carmichael. When community people were asked if they knew that the two national leaders of SNCC were in Houston, only 37 percent replied "yes," whereas 63 percent said "no."

In summary, it appears that one residual effect of violence is that a strong shift to a highly vocal Black Power personality may occur in the Negro community, particularly in situations where white authority is considered as having wronged other black people—even those with whom members of the community formerly disagreed, such as militant students. Before the TSU disturbance, in random-sample interviews done among 2,271 community people, there were 19 percent who said they had never even heard of Black Power;

46 percent said they were against it, and only 35 percent expressed favor of Carmichael and his program. After the violence, people were not only more aware of Black Power, they were much more in sympathy with its leading spokesman. The fact that they felt it would be easy for Carmichael to start a riot if he returned to Houston seemed to reflect an awareness of the increased level of hostility.

Continued Hostility Toward Police

It was clear that as late as July, police continued to be a main focus of hostility in the Negro community. The lingering antagonism was possible to measure objectively since three different questionnaires on police had been completed prior to the May 16-17 campus outbreak. It was possible, then, after the violence to survey attitudinal changes over an extended period, by asking people the same questions as before. The same measuring instruments were employed after the violence as before. The same census tracts were used for the "after" studies as for the "before" surveys and the same proportions of people were included in terms of age groups, socioeconomic status, and educational level. A total of 300 people were in each sample. The heightened hostility in July was registered despite the fact that no further clashes had occurred since the TSU gunbattle. While the July survey on police was in progress, there was the demonstration on the main street of the Third Ward in which six store windows were broken and two Molotov cocktails were tossed into the street. (See Introduction.) Dissidents used a bullhorn to try to rally neighborhood people to riot, but the community did not respond and the police held back from any confrontation with the demonstrators. Community people were asked in a series of interviews about their reaction to police holding back. Fifty-three percent agreed with the action, 25 percent said they were "not sure" if they agreed and 22 percent said arrests should have been made.

Going back, then, to the questions asked in March about police and then repeated in July, it appears that the increased hostility that lingered was linked to the TSU disturbance. The results from the "before-and-after" surveys were:

Key Questions	Responses of Negro Community	
	Before (March) TSU Violence	After (July) TSU Violence
	%	%
1. Have you ever seen an act by police you would regard as abusive or maltreatment of Negroes?*		
Yes	39	55
No	55	39
Not sure	6	6
2. Have you yourself ever been abused or mistreated by police in Houston? (Both physical and verbal abuse was counted)		
Yes	16	30
No	84	70

With almost an exact reversal of attitudes occurring between the two samples, it became fairly clear that the "fallout" from the violence had not diminished with time. Just as nuclear radiation from an H-bomb blast can cause radioactive particles to "float" to distant sites and continue to settle on them months later, so apparently can an outbreak of violence also produce lingering effects. The results indicated that after violence, people were much more inclined to recall acts by police that they now interpreted as abusive. They also were more likely to say that they themselves had been subject to police abuse. Violence, then seems to have marked effect on perceptions.[26] Accusations of "police brutality" become more frequent with the change in perception.

As to distance of the areas affected, the third survey on police—as well as the previous two samples—included neighborhoods at least 10 miles from TSU and some 12 miles from one to another. An area known as Sunnyside, which is an extensive Negro area starting some three miles south of the TSU campus, produced the greatest increase in negative responses. Part of the increase may have been due to a controversy with City Hall over a dump in the area. This contro-

---

*When this particular random-sample survey was conducted in Houston from March 27-April 3, 1967, this question was chosen so a comparison could be made with answers that the John F. Kraft opinion research firm of New York obtained in asking the same question of Negroes in Watts in January 1966—*four* months after the big racial explosion there. There was no information given in the Kraft results on sampling technique (other than Negro "peers" were used as interviewers) or size of sample. Findings, however, from the Watts survey were as follows: Witnessed police brutality or maltreatment—51 percent said "Yes," 47 percent said "No," and 2 percent were "Not Sure."

versy was going on at the same time that the TSU explosion occurred.

As in the other two surveys, the total results for all the neighborhoods combined showed the most heightened hostility to be among the younger age group (15 to 29 years old) and among males. But the hostility of members of the black community, regardless of age, did not extend to all issues and concerns. The violence affected attitudes on only certain subjects.

Selective Effects of Violence

What is the nature of the concerns and issues affected by violence? The assumption might be made that the effects of violence would release latent anger across the board. But the effects can be more limited than this. In Houston, as we have seen, police became a target of heightened hostility, Black Power gained in favor, strong feelings developed over black people gaining their "freedom," and more black people began regarding whites as "uncivilized." Also, sympathy increased for both Carmichael and Clay. All these issues were of an emotional and volatile nature and contained the seeds for producing more violence. The potential for triggering additional violence seems to increase as a function of violence that has already occurred. A case in point is Detroit. As William Serrin points out:

> Detroit is a city in trouble. Hit in 1967 by the most costly Negro riot in American history, and the scene in recent months of a series of clashes between police and Negroes, the city simmers in a kind of armed truce.[27]

If violence is massive enough, it undoubtedly can infect the attitudes of a whole city on all issues of concern to the black community. On the other hand, the effects can be more selective, focusing on the most emotional issues—such as police—and leaving attitudes relatively unchanged toward less volatile concerns such as jobs, housing and schools.*

---

*In early 1969, several developments moved the issue of schools toward a volatile position in terms of community tensions: (1) A 71-year old retired white man was appointed to replace the only Negro on the board, who resigned and moved out of the city; (2) The U. S. Department of Justice filed suit against the school district on grounds that the district's desegregation plan was not working, and (3) Free lunches for indigent children were cut back and restored after much controversy and picketing. Free breakfasts also had an uncertain future.

This, in fact, was found to be true when findings from 1966—before violence of any racial nature occurred in Houston—were compared with those from 1967, after violence occurred. A random-sample survey of 300 Negroes in eight Negro areas was conducted August 14-21, 1966, and repeated August 9-16, 1967, with these results:

Questions	Responses	
	August 1966	August 1967
	%	%
1. What is your attitude toward your present job? Do you look upon your job as being a good one, a fair one or a bad one?		
Good	39	40
Fair	48	48
Bad	13	12
2. Do you think most jobs are open to you?		
Most	11	16
Some	54	49
Few	35	35
3. Do you think salaries for Houston Negroes provide a decent living?		
Always	9	16
Usually	66	60
Never	25	24
4. What is your opinion of housing for Negroes in Houston?		
Good	18	15
Fair	57	51
Bad	25	34
5. What is your opinion of the quality of Houston schools?		
Good	10	16
All right	58	48
Poor	32	36
6. Do you think the general integration of society is too fast, about right or too slow?		
Too fast	4	4
About right	39	38
Too slow	57	58

Even a cursory examination of these findings strongly suggests that no significant differences in attitude occurred between August 1966, and one year later. There was some increase in negative opinions toward housing, but a somewhat surprising result was the more favorable attitudes relating to employment. It might have been surmised that the violence during the summer of 1967 would lead to increased dissatisfaction with the pace of integration into white society. But, again, the results did not confirm this. What the "one-year-later" results did confirm was the emergence of more sympathy for Black Power, stronger feelings toward use of violence, increased antagonism toward police and a greater likelihood to be influenced by riots occurring elsewhere. The results were:

Questions	Responses	
	August 1966	August 1967
	%	%
1. In what situation is violence justified for Negro rights?		
Always opposed	49	22
If attacked	36	39
To gain attention to cause	9	8
Only way to get results	6	31
2. What do you think of police in Houston and their treatment of Negroes?		
Fair	19	11
Some okay/Others are not	55	56
Abusive	26	33
3. What is your attitude toward Black Power?		
Against	45	51
In favor of	7	20
Never heard of	48	29
4. How have riots elsewhere affected racial tension in Houston?		
Not at all	39	19
Somewhat	42	60
Very	19	21

One finding obtained during the survey of August 9-16, 1967, may provide some glimpse of how people cope with violent or angry feelings during periods of increased tension. A question about "how important is religion to people today" was included in the 1967, as well as the 1966 sampling. The findings were:

	1966	1967
	%	%
Religion is very important	33	53
Religion is not so important	54	35
Religion is not at all important	13	12

It is doubtful that these results mean more people are returning to religion. They more likely represent a wish that religion could help people cope with periods of violence and with feelings of heightened hostility.

Now, as to the question of why didn't the heightened hostility explode into a city-wide riot in Houston in the summer

of 1967, there are a number of answers that could be given.
There were programs launched that undoubtedly had something to do with heading off violence. One was a police-community relations program. Details will be provided later. But
there is also the "sead" factor of *dispersion* to be considered.
The distribution of people in space can have an important
influence on what happens from the buildup of tension in a
city. Let's now examine this fourth and final "sead" factor
and its effect.

Dispersion

Houston has the distinction of being a city that has been
described as both exceptionally well-planned and almost totally unplanned. Whichever it is—and the truth probably lies
somewhere in between—there is little doubt that geographical dispersion is a significant characteristic of the Negro community in Houston. This does not mean that there are no
heavy concentrations of black people clustered in the city. It
simply means that outside of the Third Ward, which is as
concentrated and clustered as Watts, many other Negro
neighborhoods exist—some in proximity to each other but
sharing little solidarity. The Fifth Ward, for instance, which
is north of Buffalo Bayou (Third Ward is south), is splintered
into a number of neighborhoods that have their own names
and make their own attempts at doing things together. In
many, the people in these neighborhoods have a sense of "territoriality"—a sense that "this turf is ours." From the standpoint of those who feel Houston's 300,000 Negroes should
band together on concerns transcending local neighborhoods,
this "terroriality" may seem less desirable.

"Houston is a kind of jig saw puzzle with a lot of little
boroughs and subdivisions," observed Rev. William Lawson,
who led a march on the local school board and has tried other
organized attempts at action.[28] "You've got some people who
have a Harrisburg feeling, some who have a Piney Point feeling, there are Fifth Warders who wouldn't come south of the
bayou, there are Third Warders who wouldn't go north of it.
. . . There are all sorts of little provincialisms." (See Figure 1
on Page 19 for location of areas named.)

One of the main reasons for the "jig saw" and the subsequent dispersion is the long period in which city planning
was absent in Houston and a shorter one in which planning
was sporadic. This means that uncontrolled subdivisions of

land were common and that a pocket of people would spring
up in one area, cut off from another pocket right in the same
section of town. It was only in 1940—103 years after Houston
was founded—that the city formed a planning commission
that has managed to stay in existence since.

Further, Houston is the largest city in the United States
that has no zoning ordinance. The lack of zoning has had subtle but significant effects on the Negro community. It has
meant that a number of neighborhoods, particularly low income ones, have developed a "mix" of stores, shops, plants,
houses. This is important in terms of both social support and
employment. It is important to people who have no cars and
cannot drive to a friend's house to visit or across town to
work. In a mixed neighborhood, he can do his visiting by
walking to the corner grocery and he may also find work
within walking distance. For neighborhoods of people with
middle and high incomes, Houston has a well-planned system
of land use control, including deed restrictions and rigid requirements for the development of new subdivisions. It is in
the outlying areas within the city limits where middle-class
people largely live, and do so in a manner that places shops
and stores in one area and homes in another. But in older
areas, where there were no subdivision planning requirements
and deed restrictions to begin with—and no zoning—there
has been an interesting pattern develop of heterogeneous land
use.

The lack of zoning has been regarded as a mark against
the city by portions of the federal establishment. Houston had
a hard time convincing the federal government that it should
be awarded a Model Cities planning grant, which would lead
to a multi-million-dollar development of low-income areas
with a population of 141,000 people (64 percent Negroes, 21
percent Mexican-Americans and 15 percent "anglos"). Houston's argument was this: Zoning is a concept growing out of
the 1930's when middle-class people in America decided they
would like to have their homes in one part of town, their
shopping facilities in another and their places of employment
also somewhere else. This is fine for people who have cars and
are mobile. But there are non-middle-class people who are not
mobile and do not want to live that way. They should not be
required to do so by zoning or any other system of land use
control—such as deed restrictions, which require that property designated for a family dwelling must be used for a home

and not a business. A city should be flexible in terms of land-use control devices, and Houston has this flexibility. After presenting the Department of Housing and Urban Development with files on 2,300 cases in which the city legal department had intervened in the last three years in deed restriction violations in middle-class areas, a number of them racially mixed, the federal government consented to re-examine its position. And, after more meetings and appeals to Washington authorities, Houston was the last city in 1968 to be picked for the Model Cities program.

All this detail is provided to point up the unique position Houston is in from the standpoint of ecology and how people make use of the space they live and work in. The federal establishment finally recognized Houston's uniqueness in this respect and agreed to a proposal that a study be made to determine objectively whether Houston is any better off or any worse off than a city of comparable size that has zoning.

As Roscoe H. Jones, director of city planning, noted: "Houston is a natural laboratory for the study of the effects of no zoning in a large metropolitan area." He added, "This lack of zoning may have played a distinct role in race relations here." One role it has played has been to help turn all the city's "jig saw" pieces into the separate little boroughs and townsites that Rev. Lawson commented on. Once a cluster of houses formed in any part of the city, there was no reason that grocery stores, bars, barbershops, nightclubs or even factories could not move into the same area.

With mixed land use found in so many Negro areas—shops and stores next door to houses and apartments—self-contained subcommunities have been characteristic. A Negro secretary in Los Angeles who is from Houston commented: "I lived in Clinton Park and one thing I liked about Houston was that you had everything you want right in your own neighborhood—including nightclubs." Within some of the subcommunities, there seems to be a warmth and a "soul" that are absent in the sanitized suburbs. It is true that people have strongly identified with circumscribed areas and may largely remain within them. Some of the areas, perhaps the majority, have been populated by black people as long as anyone can remember.*

---

*For a statistical profile of what life is like in two of the oldest Negro neighborhoods, see Appendix C, which tells how people spend their time as well as what they would like improved.

Since there has been a historical background of "territoriality" in many cases, it might be expected that organized gangs would have formed. On the contrary, a random-sample survey turned up almost no one who had knowledge of organized gangs anywhere in Houston. Only 2.5 percent of the 300 Negroes interviewed, in January, 1967, said they had ever heard of any gangs in the city. Since organized gangs have been known to lead looting and burning activities once a riot breaks out in a city, their number and strength are a consideration in community violence. Authoritative sources agree that Houston has been free of any organized gangs for some time.

The "sead" factor of dispersion is important not only for the reasons already discussed but also for the fact that cities which riot often are cities with extreme crowding. The whole field of human ecology is now beginning to examine the corrosive effects that crowding has on behavior.[29] The clustering of people and the congestion they must put up with may well contribute to producing the heat that often leads to violent activities, including rioting. Just as there is a critical mass necessary for an atomic explosion, there may also be a certain degree of "squeezing" and "stacking" of people as a factor in producing the climate for a riot.

The dispersion factor also has had other implications for black people. It has provided a wider number of areas for migrants to live in when they move to the city. Because subcommunities for Negroes have grown up all over Houston, the traditional transition zones that produce slum housing have been only one source of residence for low-income black people. Negroes migrating to Houston have not had to wait for the inner core of the city to deteriorate to find housing. For years they have had a number of areas to choose from. This is not to say that the housing has been any better than in the core of the city or that the "outer" areas have escaped slum classification. All substandard housing, no matter where it is located, needs to be upgraded—and, to a considerable degree, will be if the Model Cities program and other proposals are carried through to completion. The problem Houston faces in housing is that with 60,000 families living in substandard units, there is no place for low-income people to move to find better quarters. And without a housing code that requires existing structures to be kept up to a minimum standard, people pay much more than they should for what they get.

But not all areas are made up of tenants living in sub-standard dwellings owned by absentee landlords. Forty-six percent of Houston Negroes own their homes and many are in the outlying "sub-boroughs" that have developed. There has been a natural reluctance to leave them to join in any massive efforts to unify all Houston Negroes in an attack on city-wide problems. Black militants deplore this lack of city-wide unity, but if improvements can be made on a neighborhood-by-neighborhood basis, better living conditions can still be brought to people and they are more likely to have a hand in the upgrading. Each area and neighborhood has its own prob-lems—and often its own neighborhood association that sends spokesmen to City Hall or visits with representatives of the mayor's office out in the community. (See Chapter on "Bar-gaining With 'The Power Structure'.")

Although there are some 96 neighborhood associations in Negro areas, it should not be concluded that all these areas are neatly organized into neighborhood groups and people within them work together. Some areas—such as the huge Third Ward—are too big and have too many socio-economic differ-ences within them for the people to all join together. The Third Ward, for instance, has its own "bottom," a slum at the northernmost edge. At the southernmost edge it has a "top," an area with large two-story brick homes that range in price from $35,000 to $125,000. These homes, in Timbercrest, were previously occupied by white families in the Riverside and MacGregor areas along Brays Bayou. Negroes who occupy them today have their own residential and subcommunity identity. They do not consider themselves to be on the south edge of the Third Ward. Instead, they make plain that they live in Riverside or Timbercrest, or, as their disparagers put it, on "Sugar Hill."

Because there is substantial gradation of income and housing within Negro areas, such as the Third Ward, one effect has been to leave people on the bottom some sense that there are better homes and more material comforts that Ne-groes *can* acquire in Houston. This is not to say that equal opportunity has been achieved for the man on the bottom to move up if he wants to, but at least he can see that other people have done it.

As for the relatively small percent who *have* moved up, and are in big homes in Riverside and Timbercrest, deed re-strictions are again a factor in the ecology. Deed restrictions are keeping spotty portions of these sections as residential. But in adjacent sections, the restrictions have expired, and nightclubs, bars, and restaurants and apartment houses have moved in. Here, such establishments have not contributed to any community social support, because people able to live in the expensive homes can afford to go outside their areas for a "night out." They do not need neighborhood gathering places. They complain of the transients who occupy the apartment houses that have cropped up in the neighborhood, and of the nightclubs that were once fine homes while deed restrictions were kept in force. Said one Negro homeowner:

> It's demoralizing to see one of the big homes in your neighborhood cut up into multiple apartment units or converted into a nightclub. This was once an area where Negroes could aspire to move once they made enough money. Now, we are stewing in our own juices. We have made the money, but we have no protection against property deterioration. We didn't get the deed restrictions renewed, and we should have. We should have formed a neighborhood association and kept the deed restrictions in force.

Along a number of streets south of Brays Bayou, as well as some north, the deed restrictions have been kept in force. Residential neighborhoods are still residential, and upwardly mobile Negroes are still buying—usually at prices much too high. Immediately south of the Bayou is an example of an integrated neighborhood, where some 300 Negro and white families live side by side in homes ranging from $30,000 to $100,000. White families who have been determined to stay in their neighborhood despite "block busting" efforts have had to put up signs in their yards reading: "This is my home. I do not want to sell." Said one white home owner:

> Real estate agents keep coming by making offers. They keep saying that Negroes are going to 'take over' the area and lower property values. They say to move out while there is still time to get some return on your investment. Those of us who want to continue to live where we are have found that Negroes make good neighbors and they are just as interested in keeping up the beauty and values of the area as anyone.

In a reverse twist of "discrimination," the Negro and white home owners in 1967 successfully fought off the conversion of a nearby apartment project into public housing. Their integrated civic clubs banded together to argue before the Houston Housing Authority and Mayor Louie Welch that putting public housing so close to the high-priced homes

would lower property values. But the Negroes and whites
alike emphasized that they were not against public housing
per se. "We just need to have more time to stabilize our own
residential area," said a spokesman, "before we give real
estate agents any added argument that we'd better move out
because public housing is moving in. It's hard enough as it is
to find financing for homes in our integrated area. If the
apartments we're talking about were converted into public
housing, the mortgage companies would have just one more
excuse to refuse financing to any home buyer in our area."
So, for the time being, the Brays Bayou integrated area maintained its own enclave—in this case, an enclave of economic
class rather than a racial one.

The racial enclaves, as we have seen, constitute towns
within towns and villages within villages. In the Third Ward,
for instance, there is little overall unity among the 30,000
Negroes clustered in the concentrated area of approximately three square miles. There are invisible walls throughout the
Third Ward, even though few neighborhoods can be identified
by name outside of Riverside, Timbercrest, "the area around
Texas Southern University," and the "Third Ward bottoms."
Said a tavern owner deep in the heart of the Third Ward:

> There's an area of about four square blocks that make up a little
> town in this part of the Third Ward. The people go to the same
> stores, to the same taverns and to the same street corners to talk.
> What is beyond certain streets is not theirs—it's just another
> little town.

People cross from one side to another physically but not
psychologically. A Negro cab driver said:

> It all gets back to wanting to have something to identify with—
> even if it's a block of shotgun houses where your house is just as
> bad as all the others. You don't own it, you take no pride in it,
> but it's where you live. And when you gather in a bar to let your
> hair down, you meet with people living in the same kind of houses
> in the same area. You understand each other.

The invisible walls, then, disperse people—and inside
them, there are activities that divert them. The dispersion by
the walls is compounded by a large geographical spread. In
1969 Houston was a city of 453.7 square miles. It was second
in area only to Los Angeles (457.9) until Oklahoma City
reached out with a huge annexation of bare plains and now
claims 644.7 square miles within its city limits. (Jacksonville,

Florida, came along later to outdo even Oklahoma City in taking in miles of unpopulated area.)*

Houston, then, has "towns," "villages," and "pockets" of Negroes living 30 to 35 miles apart—from Carverdale, northwest of a rich white community called Memorial on Houston's west side, to Clinton Park, along the ship channel on the city's far east side. The pockets of people are separated from each other by geography, and within each cluster they may be separated by artificial walls. In the lower income areas particularly, there also may well be suspicion to add to the separation. But in recent years, civic clubs and neighborhood associations have been organized in even the low-income sections, such as the Bottom (now Swiney Addition). Involvement, however, on the part of a number of residents is not yet substantial. (See Chapter on "Bargaining With 'The Power Structure'.")

"Don't take this to mean massive apathy," said a Negro neighborhood leader in one low-income area. "People are busy working and trying to keep their homes and kids together, and they don't show up at a lot of meetings. But they can be stirred."

How much it takes to "stir" them is not only a function of their grievances but also of diversionary factors such as work. Their work may not be satisfactory as far as providing the means for a decent living, but as long as there are jobs, they are occupied and busy. In many families, both husband and wife work—sometimes at more than one job. The high employment rate in Houston has been credited with keeping racial unrest from growing. In December 1968, as we have noted, it was at a low of 1.5 percent for the city as a whole, and estimated at 5 to 7 percent for Negroes. There are some people in Houston who think the relatively high employment rate constitutes the one and only reason that the city has had no community riot. It is *one* reason but certainly not the only one involved in a question as terribly complex as social unrest and collective violence. Taking such a position completely overlooks the effects of expectations and other "sead" factors of unrest.

It has been stated that Houston Negroes also have a high

---

*Houston has plans to annex approximately 135 more square miles in 1969. In terms of added population, it will probably pass Detroit as the fifth largest city in the nation in the early 1970's.

percent of their children enrolled in school or working at jobs open to teenagers. If this is true, school attendance and adolescent employment are additional influences in terms of keeping people occupied. As will be discussed later, the city has held three Job Fairs for disadvantaged youths and has a number of other employment projects, such as the Business Resource Development Center of the mayor's office and the Concentrated Employment Program, as well as services directed at hiring and training unskilled adults and the chronically unemployed. The National Alliance of Businessmen is an example of an intensive effort made in the field of hiring and training the hard-core unemployed.

All of this is mentioned here because in discussing dispersion, the concept needs to be extended beyond geography to the question of how the *efforts* and *energies* of people are "dispersed"—how they are allocated among activities, such as work and school. Both the geographical and energy kind of dispersion help to account for the many small-group efforts of neighborhoods and the constructive siphoning off of any massive build-up of collective aggression. It can be seen, then, that dispersion plays an important role as one of the "sead" factors in the level of unrest of a city—not just Houston but any large urban center.

There has been no attempt in this chapter to spell out what Houston, or any other city, has done to alleviate unrest, regardless of its level. As indicated in the Introduction, other chapters will go into detail on some of the programs that grew out of all the interviews and surveys in the city, and out of an analysis of what the more pressing problems are. It will be seen that City Hall alone cannot solve such problems of employment and housing and that a wide range of community resources must be brought to bear on them. The reason for attempting to solve the problems, of course, goes back not only to mitigation of unrest but also to what is right in terms of human decency.

For now, it is important to recognize that not all unrest is collective and not all problems of Negroes are group problems. The deep frustration that can be found in the lives of many ghetto dwellers often does not wait for collective social unrest to express itself. It is manifest in the ever-growing problem of crime. And no consideration of violence in the city would be complete without examining what some of the breeding grounds are for crime. I say "some" because I do not consider frustration to be responsible for all physical aggression and crime. I want to make this position clear, for the next chapter looks at crime on the basis of a frustration-aggression hypothesis. I recognize that this hypothesis is not the whole story, but it is a big enough part to warrant public attention.

Before moving to Chapter 2 and "Rebel Without a Cause," the first list of points pertaining to principles of belief will be presented. As mentioned in the Introduction, these will follow each chapter and are offered for consideration of what is right, just and true on the general question of race and violence in American society.

WHAT SHOULD WE BELIEVE?

POINTS TO CONSIDER—I

A. Let's recognize that material deprivation is not the whole cause of riots. Because of racial discrimination, many black people have been deprived for centuries. Many have also been subject for centuries to insults and indignities. But all sorts of additional influences have converged to produce riots, and the influences vary, in large part, according to the "sead" factors of unrest: the signals and stimulation transmitted by the spotlight of mass media; the gap between people's expectations and realization; the attitudes people adopt—and the adaptation they make—toward the conditions of their daily lives, and the breathing room that the dispersion of their physical environment provides or fails to provide.

B. Let's consider the possibility that there has been unprecedented community violence in the 1960's because people have been over-stimulated, over-promised, over-directed and over-crowded as never before. This is not to excuse inaction on problems that have been crying for action for years. It is only an attempt to set the record straight on the question: Why violence now?

C. Let's make up our minds that true opportunity for everyone to live decently in this society can be provided without violence, and that those who insist that this country must undergo another American Revolution or a modern-day counterpart to the French Revolution in order for black people to gain freedom from colonial status are mostly theorists who look upon death and destruction as an interesting subject to study—from a safe distance.

*D. Let's recognize that along with providing genuine oppor-
tunities for everyone to improve himself materially, the people who over-promise results should exercise restraint and
those who predict apocalyptic doom and failure should re-
consider.*

*E. Let's acknowledge that loud voices do affect what people
believe and how they act and that messages sanctioning violence can come from a whole host of visual and auditory
cues: persistent images of people acting out anger; dogged
attention focused on those who insist that violence is the
only language America understands.*

*F. Let's recognize that violence may have shock value and, in
the opinion of some, galvanize a city into action, but it also
increases the potential for more violence. It infects a city
with tension and an atmosphere of animosity that make constructive action harder. It makes it harder because communication, if not cooperation, between people is required for such
action, and if they are hostile toward one another, they are
not likely to communicate, much less cooperate.*

*G. Let's recognize that white society has kept in the front
lines certain symbols of authority that have acted as "catch-
ment basins" for the hostility of black people, but the anger
heaped on these symbols—which include police and City
Hall—stems from the behavior of all white society toward
Negroes, as well as from what police and City Hall may or
may not do.*

*H. Let's acknowledge the fact that feelings toward police are
often such that regardless of what move they make in a volatile situation, they frequently end up in a "damned-if-you-do"
and "damned-if-you-don't" position.*

*I. Let's recognize that the very rhetoric of "white" and
"black" has obscured the individual differences that exist
among all human beings and that black and white alike
should stop categorizing and stereotyping without ever getting to know people as individuals. Let's also recognize that if
we believe "institutional racism" is so rampant that white
people are already known only too well by black people, then
we are denying the system can work and that equal opportunity is possible. So do we destroy the system, fold our tents
and steal away, or decide that the system can and will be
fixed?*

*J. Let's start recognizing that not all ghettos and slums are
the same and those that have squeezed and stacked people*

the worst have probably produced the most deleterious effect. On a national basis, let's consider how we can help disperse *people and give them breathing room, as well as how to rehabilitate the areas where people want to continue to live.*

K. Let's recognize that not all the people who call themselves militant, or get described as militant, are violent. This is just as important as the difference between feeling angry and acting out anger.

L. Let's face up to the fact that the acting out of rage is violence, and no society has ever stayed intact where people went around acting out all their angry feelings. Let's remember that it is in childhood where people should learn they have complete freedom to think whatever they feel, and to feel whatever they think, but that freedom does not extend to what they do. *The freedom of a man to swing his fist stops at the end of another man's nose.*

M. Let's recognize that an intact society does not mean an unchanging one. Assuming that we believe necessary change can be made without violence, then let's work swiftly and surely at giving every person an opportunity to develop his full potential and to make of his life what he himself decides.

CHAPTER 2

REBEL WITHOUT A CAUSE

The slum spawns more than the conditions that lead to collective violence. It also is the arena for producing individual violence. Its shabby streets see a higher rate of murder, rape, armed robbery and assault than any other section of the city. Violence becomes a way of life for many. A riot just provides one more opportunity to lash out with a mindless fury that comes from nowhere—and everywhere.

There is a psychological premise that states: "Aggression is always a consequence of frustration."[1] For the rebel without a cause, the aggression is chronic and criminal. He strikes out at others or their property. He hits for the sake of hitting. It is his form of release, of expressing a reaction against a whole host of conditions that characterize his life— and usually have from an early age. The rebel without a cause is, as Robert Lindner says, a revolutionary without a program.*

Why does he do it? "There is every reason to believe that as long as the Negro is discriminated against in employment and is forced to live in ghettos where there is considerable social disorganization, criminality among them will be high," says E. Franklin Frazier.[2] This offers some clue as to high crime rates in general among Negroes. Gunnar Myrdal adds another factor: "The Negro's hatred of whites." Myrdal says that "a significant number of crimes of Negroes against whites are motivated by revenge for discriminatory or insulting treatment. Such a crime may be emotional, as when a Negro suddenly feels that he has stood enough in the way of deprivation and insults and that he only desires to make white people suffer too. . . ."[3]

The position here will be that the rebel without a cause reflects not only "social disorganization" and a reaction against discrimination, but also an intense need to gain a sense of power and control in his life. The need may be based,

---

*See Page 81 for reference to Lindner's *Rebel Without A Cause.*

in large part, on social fragmentation and the personal devaluation that comes from discrimination. But the distinguishing feature of the rebel is that these factors do not lead to a general apathy or to withdrawal through drugs or mental illness. They generate a need to demonstrate power—power over someone else through violence.

What this power bestows is recognition from others—a sense of identity, a sense of being "somebody." Erik Erikson has noted that power is vitally related to the concept of identity.[4] Lee Rainwater has discussed the effects of "negative" identity in terms of the lower-class Negro child. He says the child is "constantly exposed to identity labeling by his parents as a bad person."[5] This serves not only to encourage "bad" behavior, such as exhibited by the rebel, but also to inculcate strivings for power or feelings to overcome helplessness. Rainwater also refers to the insulting treatment whereby one Negro may denigrate another by using the phrase, "nothing but a nigger like everybody else."[6] Being "nothing" or "nobody" connotes the lack of power or ability of an individual to assert himself as "somebody." The rebel without a cause, it will be contended here, sees violence as a means of becoming "somebody."

Lewis Yablonsky quotes a "nobody" as saying:

> If I could have got the knife, I would have stabbed him. That would have given me more of a buildup. People would have respected me for what I've done. They would say, 'There goes a cold killer.'[7]

Being recognized as a "cold killer" may be one way to gain identity. Yablonsky says that the "new criminal"—who is, in many ways, like the rebel—robs, assaults and kills for status, for a "rep." He is not necessarily interested in the victim's money or material possessions. He wants recognition, as this one did:

> My friends talk to me about what they gonna do. Like 'Man, we'll go out here and kill this cat.' I say, 'Yeah.' They keep on talkin'. I say, 'Man, I just gotta go with you.' Myself, I don't want to go, but when they start talkin' about what they gonna do, I say, 'So, he isn't gonna take over my rep. I ain't gonna let him be known more than me.' And I go ahead, just for selfishness. . . .[8]

In interviews with a group of 26 Negro men and women offenders, ranging in age from 17 to 35, there was a common theme that life offered nothing but feelings of having little or no control over anything. "You got to prove you got power or you ain't nothing," said a 25 year-old male who had committed armed robbery. This feeling of having to "prove yourself" may sound more typical of adolescence, but it was distinctly present in both men and women in the group who were in their twenties and early thirties.

One 27 year-old woman said: "Look, you live your life from the very beginning with everything and everyone controllin' you. You can't do nothin' but just take it. Then you start saying, 'I'm gonna start controllin'.' You control property by stealin', you control people by hittin'."

In the process of "hittin'," homicides occur. Alex Pokorny says Negro homicide rates are six times higher than

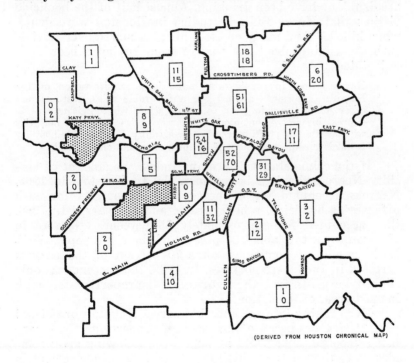

(DERIVED FROM HOUSTON CHRONICAL MAP)

figure 5

INCIDENCE OF MURDER AND RAPE BY GEOGRAPHICAL AREA

1968

those of whites.[9] The President's Commission on Law Enforcement says the Negro arrest rate for murder is almost ten times as high as that for whites.[10] Ninety-seven percent of the people killed by Negroes are other Negroes, according to Marvin Wolfgang.[11] Figure 5 on Page 67 shows where murders and rapes occurred in 1968 by geographical area. The top figure in each block represents the number of murders and the bottom digit, the number of rapes. By comparing this map with the one in Figure 4 (Chapter 1), which shows where Negroes live in Houston, it can be seen that black people are the greatest victims of such crimes of violence as murder and rape.

Much violence in the ghetto occurs between people who are drunk or have been drinking. Almost half of the homicide victims that Henry Bullock studied in Houston were drunk when killed.[12] And many of the killings occurred over trivials such as arguing about the change from buying a beer. Bullock stated:

> Negro crime, in considerable part, is a manifestation of the Negro's resentment against the unfavorable roles, statuses and other misfortunes imposed by segregation. Finding it unwise to express his resentment against the more powerful white majority who ascribe his position, the Negro actually displaces his hostility toward friendless persons of his own race and class. . . .[13]

If the crime statistics are any index, the amount of hostility Negroes displace is considerable. In Houston, in 1963, Negroes accounted for 47 percent of the arrests for such offenses as homicide, robbery, rape, and burglary.[14] In 1966, they accounted for approximately 55 percent. (Negroes in Houston constitute about 25 percent of the city's population.) Looking only at homicides, some 70 percent of the persons arrested in 1966 were Negroes. In 1968, the percent was only slightly lower. In fact, the figures are disproportionately high in most areas of the nation.

Even taking into account that arrest statistics are biased against Negroes because more whites, proportionately, escape being "booked" and jailed by police, the following gives some idea as to the relatively high degree of Negro involvement in situations related to crimes of violence:[15]

Arrests in 2,892 Cities With Population Over 2,500

	Negro	White
Murder and non-negligent manslaughter	2,593	1,662
Forcible rape	3,570	3,199
Aggravated assault	29,357	19,944

Since these figures may be taken as indicators of situations related to violent crime, just what are the breeding grounds of the problem? Some mention has been made of social disorganization, discrimination, and "unfavorable roles." What elaboration can be supplied on the antecedents?

The Breeding Grounds

Negro crime, Myrdal notes, "has periodically been the subject of serious debate in the United States and, at least since 1890, has often been the object of statistical measurement. . . ."[16] The day has long past when any informed person seriously believes that Negroes have an inborn criminal tendency. We are now in an era of trying to filter out all the multiple precipitants, and some attention will be given to broad "causes" before a sharper focus is placed on factors that seem to go into making the "rebel."

In any event, there will be no unilateral causation theories presented, regardless of whether the question is of Negro crime in general or of the rebel in particular.

In *Race Prejudice and Discrimination,* the point is made that, "the exact relation of economic factors to crime causation is still in dispute, but there is general agreement that they play an important role either as primary or associated factors. . . . Economic factors must not be considered merely in the restricted sense of the relation to crimes against property. Their ramifications extend into every sphere of life. There is the whole question of the effect of being born into a barren, dull, underprivileged lower-class household, of the effect of this upon the choices which a child can make, of the relation of this sort of environment to the personality, attitudes and philosophy of life which he will develop."[17]

On the relationship between economic factors and social disorder, many Negroes live in ghettos, "populated by people who occupy the lowest social and economic level. There is no moral order or a sense of community 'esprit de corps.' Vice, crime and social disorder become traditional."[18]

The slum, or ghetto, then, has been singled out as a significant contributing factor in Negro crime. "Compelled to live within a ghetto, the law-abiding Negro was given little choice in the selection of his neighbors. Where a white of sufficient means could flee to an area that contained a minimum of crime, the Negro . . . was usually condemned to raise his children in neighborhoods filled with inferior housing and populated by disorderly persons."[19] The ghetto often sanctions violence and militates against what control the family and other institutions try to practice. Where there is a decline in the social disorganization promoted by the ghetto, Frazier says there has been an accompanying decrease in Negro juvenile delinquency. Chicago is cited as an example. "The diminishing social disorganization was indicated by an increase in home ownership, a decrease in the number of adult criminals and a decrease in desertion and illegitimacy."[20]

Large cities favor ghettos and slums and the very anonymity of urban areas is another factor in the Negro crime rate. Former Attorney General Nicholas Katzenbach noted that "the bigger the city, the harder it is to deter crime."[21]

Yet Negroes continue to flock to cities (see the section in this chapter on "Mobility and Complexity"). And they are exposed to more massive breeding grounds for crime. For example, the rate for robbery in urban areas, as reported in 1965, was 88.6 per hundred thousand population, compared to a rate of 9.9 in rural areas. For aggravated assault, the rate was 127.7 per hundred thousand population, compared to 58.3 for rural sections of the country.[22]

What else happens in large-city ghettos that promotes crime? There is a loss of dignity or personal value. "If environment systemically deprived them of dignity and hope, closed most doors to self-fulfillment and left open only the door to despair, the white crime rate would soar."[23]

Roy Wilkins, executive secretary of the National Association for the Advancement of Colored People, has said: "I don't want to use deprivation as a blanket excuse, because I think people ought to have some restraints on their conduct, regardless of how much they suffer. Whether they kick you around or not, you ought to learn good from bad. But I do say that this kind of treatment has weakened those restraints among Negroes and made it easy for them to defy convention, to rob, to steal. . . ."[24]

And then, as Wilkins mentions, there is the type of justice that "doesn't breed respect for law. . . . If a Negro steals from another Negro that's no crime. If he kills another Negro, why that's just a misdemeanor. But if he kills a white man, why that means electrocution." Austin Porterfield and Robert Talbert have argued that when a crime is committed in a Negro district, the police "make a perfunctory inventory of the scene, go on about their business and never make any attempt to discover the perpetrator of the act."[25] Although there is good evidence that such practices are diminishing, and that equal justice under the law is also becoming a reality, the fact remains that many Negroes still believe that the police are not their protector and the courts are not fair.

The late Police Chief William H. Parker of Los Angeles, in discussing the kind of violence that erupted in the Watts riot of 1965, spoke of the "dislocation" of Negroes. He said: "You have this constant preachment that the Negro people are dislocated because of unfair treatment by the whites. This propaganda has been poured out all over America incessantly for the past several months—and these people [unemployed Negroes] are not occupied, so they are in a position to listen to it. If you tell people this story long enough, they will get to believe it. If you keep sowing the seeds of discontent—saying that the Liberty Bell never rang for the Negro and that sort of thing—eventually Negroes will look upon the white population as their enemy. . . ."[26]

So the factor of suggesting that Negroes should "rebel" is introduced as another possibility, particularly in terms of the violence found in riots. Since it has already been suggested that "aggression is always a consequence of frustration," what kind of summary can be made within this context of the factors that promote crime? Many undoubtedly apply to whites as well as Negroes, but because there is a disproportionate amount of Negro crime, any accurate summation must mean that the conditions are found more among Negroes than white people.

Factors of Frustration

In *Frustration and Aggression*, the authors suggest various conditions that seem to be correlated with crime, but they are cautious toward drawing conclusions until additional comparable observations can be made for "the non-criminal population." There is good reason for the caution because to draw conclusions on crime in slums, or anywhere else for that matter, suggests that specific "causes" can be neatly isolated and predictions made as to what individuals are going to become offenders. The factors that John Dollard and others have identified as playing an important part in the lives of slum-dwellers who become criminals will receive emphasis here. Equal attention will be given to why Negroes are represented by a disproportionately high percent, particularly in terms of violent offenses.

The factors that are discussed in *Frustration and Aggression* are incorporated in many other studies and observations on "the making of a criminal." For instance, in *The Challenge of Crime in a Free Society* report of the President's Commission on Law Enforcement and Administration of Justice, this position is taken on crime in low-income areas:

> Many slum residents feel overwhelmed and helpless in the face of the flourishing vice and crime around them; many have received indifferent treatment from the criminal justice system when they have attempted to do their duty as complainants and witnesses; many fear reprisals, especially victims of rackets.[27]

The commission also holds that:

> In a sense, social and economic conditions 'cause' crime. Crime flourishes, and always has flourished, in city slums, those neighborhoods where overcrowding, economic deprivation, social disruption and racial discrimination are endemic. Crime flourishes in conditions of affluence, when there is much desire for material goods and many opportunities to acquire them illegally. Crime flourishes when there are many restless, relatively footloose young people in the population. Crime flourishes when standards of morality are changing rapidly.[28]

Such "causes" are among the several factors that were isolated by Dollard. They suggest the kind of frustration that is believed to lead to physical aggression. They will be elaborated upon in the following list, which is derived from *Frustration and Aggression*.[29]

1) Vocational status—the unskilled are implicated in more crimes in proportion to their number than are any other kind of workers. ". . . persons who are forced into . . . less desirable kinds of work will experience, other things being equal, a higher-than-average amount of frustration and will therefore show a heightened tendency toward criminality."

2) Educational achievement—crime seems to decrease with the amount of formal education. "Measures of educational achievement usually include or imply not only training in the technological sense, which tends to decrease frustration (through increased earning capacity), but moral training as well, which makes for increased anticipation of pun-

ishment. . . . Deficient education is a source of frustration only at the adult level and then only to the extent that it leads to low income, inferior social status or other conditions interfering with the performance of goal-responses."

3) Economic status—as has been discussed, the poor are involved in crime at a higher rate than people of greater economic means. Low economic status, it is contended, is accompanied by "higher-than-average frustration." The poor also are less able to hire competent attorneys to make compensation for damage to property. Both these points affect who gets convicted and goes down on the record as an offender.

4) Marital status—"perhaps the most dramatic demonstration of all the roles of frustration in the causation of criminality is afforded by the data concerning the marital status of criminals as compared with non-criminals." Divorced men and women have significantly higher rates of crime than do persons with no background of marital breakups. "Loss of accustomed satisfactions through divorce is exceptionally frustrating, and it is therefore not surprising that divorcees—who are often more or less chronically maladjusted in other ways—should show an unusually higher crime rate."

5) Home conditions—incompatibility between parents, a broken home, working mothers, all have been described as factors that tend to promote frustration and a tendency toward criminal behavior on the part of the child subjected to such conditions.

6) Neighborhood conditions—the environment outside the home, as well as inside, has been found to be important. "Playmates and school associates exercise a strong leveling influence which is sometimes so great as to be a source of considerable conflict for families with high standards of conduct but lacking sufficient income to avoid low-standard neighborhoods."

7) Regional conditions—as already noted, less crime tends to be found in rural areas than in cities. ". . . when man encounters frustration in a rural environment his aggressions are more likely to be directed against hostile environmental forces than toward other men, as occurs in city life. . . ."

Each of these seven points has particular application to the Negro. A disproportionate number of Negroes are unskilled, have poor education, are economically deprived, have

fragmented families and homes of discord, live in neighborhoods where crime is higher and in congested sections of
cities where living conditions are difficult.

The factor of home conditions seems particularly pertinent. Though far from conclusive, research findings indicate
that anything in the family organization which diminishes
the moral and emotional influence of the family also increases
the likelihood of delinquency.[30] Relevant factors include the
absence of a parent, the nature of discipline, organization of
the family and the "female focus" that characterizes inner-
city families. Also, there is the important factor of parental
affection or rejection. As pointed out in the *The Challenge
of Crime in a Free Society*, perhaps the most important factor in the lives of many boys who become delinquent is their
failure to win the affection of their fathers.[31]

Both the Cambridge-Somerville findings and the Gluecks'
studies have emphasized the family environment as a central
feature in the making of the so-called sub-cultural criminal.
Sheldon and Eleanor Glueck found, in a cross-sectional study
of 1,000 boys, that relationships between parents and between parents and offspring were of primary importance.[32]
The Cambridge-Somerville study, using a longitudinal approach, confirmed the fact that parental rejection and discord significantly increase the chances of a slum boy turning
to crime.

These studies suggested that rejection by the mother is
even more damaging than neglect or indifference from the
father. Applying such a finding to Negroes, we can hypothe-
size that with so many Negro mothers traditionally bearing
the responsibility for making a living or contributing to the
family income and with so many having large families, children too often fail to receive the warm attention they need
from their mothers.

The factor of parental discord also ranks high in contributing to chances of driving a child to the streets and delinquency. Daniel Moynihan stated that ". . . the family structure of lower class Negroes is highly unstable, and in many
urban centers, is approaching complete breakdown."[33] Broken
homes were included in the Gluecks' findings and Cambridge-
Somerville study as contributing to chances of criminality.
Moynihan found that one-third of non-white children live in
broken homes.[34] Another finding from the Gluecks and Cambridge-Somerville study was that erratic discipline makes for

delinquency. Moynihan presents no figures on this factor, but he does state: "In a word, most Negro youth are in danger of being caught up in the tangle of pathology that affects their world, and probably a majority are so entrapped."[35]

When a child fails to find love, comfort—and firm but fair control—in the world that is his home, he frequently turns to the streets for acceptance.

When he finds an indifference and a dead dullness at home, he turns to the street for signs of life and thrills. In the words of Editor William A. Emerson, Jr.:

> Crime is positive. Criminals are a brotherhood and a criminal act is a commitment. Crime is a form of recreation and it is also a form of communication, and it helps overcome that 'invisible' or 'tuned out' feeling that destroys the black man living in the slums.[36]

When the streets represent a sub-culture of violence and crime, acceptance and "coming alive" mean becoming a delinquent. This is part of the "tangle of pathology" that so many Negro youths are caught up in.

One Example of the Tangle

In Houston, which has a Negro population of approximately 300,000, there is a section of the city that, until recently, was called "the Bottom." It was, in large part, a slum. Some people say it got its name from the fact that when you lived in the Bottom, you were on the bottom. Average weekly rent for the row-upon-row of shotgun houses in the area was $10-12, which included hot water. The Bottom was a congested island encircled by a freeway on the north, a railroad track on the east, a bayou on the south and deadend streets on the west.

Until 1966, when the city made the Bottom a demonstration area and began paving streets as the first project, dirt and dust were so thick that people kept their windows closed even during the hot summer months. Some 1,300 families live in the Bottom. In the heart of the area are rundown bars, grocery stores, a barber shop and other businesses that contribute to the tendency of the people to stay on their "island" and not leave it except to work. What follows is the way the Bottom was when the mayor's office decided to move in and try to help the people improve their neighborhood. (See later chapters for results of "Project Partner"). As it was then, the Bottom—now called Swiney Addition—illustrates what too often happens to young people in slums.

Crime is high in such areas. The Bottom is at the southern edge of the "Bloody" Fifth Ward. In the first 11 months of 1966, there were 394 offenses reported in the Bottom.[37] The majority of these were violent crimes, including six homicides, 15 investigations of other cases by the homicide division of the police department, plus rape, assault and armed robberies. All but three streets in the Bottom reported crimes during this 11-month period. In a six block stretch of just one of the streets, 73 offenses occurred from January through November.

In such a subculture of crime, Phil Fitch grew up.* There were no parks for him to play in (the city began constructing vest-pocket playgrounds in 1967). He went to an elementary school in the area that was so crowded that the wings of the building had to be extended right out to the street, completely eliminating the playground. Phil had three brothers and two sisters. His two older brothers were in the state prison before he ever got to know them well. One sister was a prostitute. His mother worked in a laundry and was gone when he left for school in the morning and was still not home when he returned in the afternoon. Phil was left to fend for himself on the dusty, narrow streets of the Bottom. He spent a lot of time "on the dump," a part of the Bottom that was once a city dump and still was littered with trash. He would sift through the trash hoping to find something of value that someone threw away by mistake. The most he ever found was a birdcage with a broken door.

Phil had no father—at least he never remembered having any. One of his sisters said that his father left home when Phil was 6 months old. His mother didn't go around with other men. She was too tired to do much of anything except come home, cook a late meal for whomever happened to be around and then go to bed. Mrs. Fitch wasn't cold and rejecting toward her children. She just didn't have any time or strength for them.

Phil turned to the streets early to find what he missed at home. There were no gangs in the neighborhood. People, even the youngsters, didn't trust each other enough to form any kind of organization. But there were boys he could pal

---

*Phil Fitch is a pseudonym.

around with. And when one named Leon, who was two years older, acted as though he was willing to be Phil's friend, Phil jumped at the chance. Leon was already smoking pot at 11. He broke into service station and grocery store vending machines at night to get money to buy marijuana from some older boys who grew it on the bayou outside city limits. One reason Leon befriended Phil was that a number of stores and stations had rear or side windows too small for the older boy to crawl through to loot the cigaret machines inside. Phil didn't need much encouragement to do the small-window jobs for Leon, even though the older boy took 90 per cent of what the younger one jimmied out of the machines.

The "partnership" continued for two years. At first, Phil used his small "earnings" to buy candy at school. He used to have no money for lunch and there was nothing at home to put in a sack for him to take to school to eat at noon. Now he ate candy. It gave him status even to buy candy. Most of the kids didn't have money for that sort of luxury. Phil had his first real taste of peer group approval. And he never forgot it.

At 11, Phil started smoking marijuana at the encouragement of Leon. Phil liked the feeling he got from pot, but Leon seemed to enjoy it much more. It was through marijuana that Phil began to meet other boys, who were willing to pal around with him, and when he told them of how little that Leon let him take of the loot from burglaries, the boys said he was crazy. They encouraged him to break with Leon. He did—but only after a fight in which Leon pulled a switchblade knife and slashed the boy's shirt to shreds. In the process, Phil suffered cuts across the chest and abdomen and had to be taken to the charity hospital for stitches. His mother heard about it the next morning and shook her head with resignation.

"First, Joey, then Charles, now you." Joey and Charles were the brothers in the state prison. Somehow, Phil's immediately older brother, Robert, had escaped the "tangle of pathology." He was finishing high school and was planning to work his way through college. He studied most of the time.

Phil began skipping school altogether. At 13, he was a fullfledged dropout. He hung around a bar and by 15 was drinking wine during the day and whisky at night. He continued to burglarize. He got picked up by police on one job and was given probation. He was picked up again a month later, but only for being drunk. He lied about his age.

Phil liked alcohol but not as much as the excitement he continued to feel from breaking into places and from getting into fights. At 18 he was a big boy and wore tight T-shirts to show off his biceps. He got into frequent fights and usually won. He enjoyed physical combat. Just as he was starting to get a reputation as a guy who could really take care of himself, he was talked into taking a slow freight train to Oklahoma. A new friend, whom Phil admired because he was older and carried a gun that he used for stick-ups, talked of a "big killing" to be made in Oklahoma.

There was no "big killing." Police picked the pair up almost as soon as they jumped out of the box car that had been their home for three days. Phil's friend resisted and in the process, police beat both of them up. After spending two days in jail, Phil was released and spent the next month drinking, fighting and robbing other Negroes by assault. He usually just beat them with his fists, but sometimes he threatened bigger ones with a switchblade knife.

From Oklahoma, Phil hopped another freight train for a larger northern city, where he ran into real trouble. He was by now regarding himself as "somebody"—meaning no one pushed him around. But in the slums of the big city, he met bigger and tougher "somebodies." One of them started singling Phil out for punishment calling him "that nigger from Texas." One night, after a long and bitter fight outside a slum bar frequented by both, the northern Negro literally made Phil eat dirt. He kept yelling, "you got no guts, Texas nigger. You're as gutless as a white man."

Bloody and choking back tears, Phil felt a frustration and bitterness surge through him with a fierceness he had never experienced before. He went home to the $2 a night hotel where he stayed and smashed his already-bruised fist through one of the few intact window panes on the second floor. A woman, who lived at the hotel, poured alcohol on the cuts from the glass. She tried to put her arm around Phil but he brushed her aside with contempt. "Git away from me, old lady. You ain't nothin' and you won't never be nothin' but a nigger." For some reason, she reminded him of his mother. She shrugged and went to bed.

The next day, Phil took $13 he had saved from assaults and went on a bus to a pawn shop across town. He bought a second-hand .32 caliber revolver. While waiting on the street corner for a bus to go back to the walk-up, the traffic light at the intersection hung and cars began to stack up. One of them, no more than three feet from the curb where Phil was standing at the bus sign, was a sleek Continental driven by a young white man in an Ivy League suit with a tab collar shirt and a rep necktie. As Phil stood and looked at the racy lines of the bright yellow car and the fashionably dressed white man, he was suddenly struck by a hatred and hostility he never knew was inside him. He hated the man for having the car and the fashion-plate clothes. Phil didn't care so much about the clothes as he did about what they represented. He knew they were expensive, and he hated the man for having the money to buy them. Phil had never had more than 20 minutes of consecutive conversation with any one white man in his whole life and that was with cops and judges.

But now he hated everything white. The next thing he knew he was jumping in the side door of the Continental and pushing the .32 into the ribs of the startled man. Phil felt a pleasure from seeing pain and fear, as well as surprise, cross the white man's face. "You gonna die, Whitey," Phil heard himself saying. The white man could only mutter the question, "Why are you doing this to me?" As soon as the traffic lights began working properly again, Phil started giving commands. He surprised himself with how forceful he could be. The .32 in his hand helped. He directed the white man out an expressway going north. Then, he changed his mind and directed him straight to the slum bar where he had the fight the night before. He wanted to show that guy who made him eat dirt just who it was who had guts and really was tough. It didn't take any trouble finding the guy. His name was Shad. Shad was outside the bar where the fight had occurred, leaning contemptuously against a light standard. Phil, with the revolver jammed even deeper into the white man's side, told him to stop across the street from where Shad was.

Phil hollered to Shad: "Come here, nigger, I want to show you somethin'." Shad looked up with disdain. "You achin' for another whuppin', Texas boy?" But the sight of Phil in the Continental was too much for Shad's curiosity to resist. He walked across to the car.

Phil baited him as he approached: "You think you're big, don't you, black nigger," Shad's step quickened. "I'll kill you, Texas boy." Phil locked the door and rolled up the win-

dow on his side of the Continental and laughed hysterically.
Shad stood outside seething. Phil yelled: "You want to see
somethin' you don't have the guts to do, nigger?" Shad just
stood there. "I'm gonna kill this white man just to show you
I'm more of a man than you'll ever be." A flicker of surprise
crossed Shad's face. "You're crazy, nigger."

Phil turned to the trembling man at the wheel and said:
"Tell him, Whitey, what I'm gonna do. Tell him I'm gonna kill
you." The white man was shaking all over and began plead-
ing. "Let me go. I'll give you my money, this car, anything."
Phil laughed.

Then he pulled the trigger, three times real fast. The
noise inside the closed car hurt his ears. He fired a fourth
and fifth time. By now, the white man had fallen over
against the driver's door and blood was seeping through the
expensive suit. Phil turned away, opened the door and stood
in front of Shad. "Okay, nigger, there's one bullet left in
this here gun. Let's see you shoot the white man." Shad was
visibly shaken. "You're . . ." He was afraid to say more for
fear that Phil would use the last bullet on him. Phil taunted
him. "Here's the gun, nigger. You got no guts?"

People, drawn by the sound of the shots, were looking
out of windows and doorways all up and down the block. But
none was coming out on the street. They saw the gun in
Phil's hand. Shad said: "You better beat it. That man's
dead." Phil kept laughing. "You admit I'm a bigger man?"
Shad began backing up toward the bar. "You better beat it."
Then he turned quickly and ran into the bar.

Phil laughed and laughed. He knew now everyone was
watching. He felt big. He walked slowly back to the Continental, opened the door and fired the last shot into the head
of the white man. Then he threw the gun on the floor-
board and nonchalantly walked to the bar. No one tried to
stop him. Those inside just edged back when he entered. They
knew he didn't have the gun any longer, but they feared him.
Phil knew they did. He felt big. Shad was at the far end of
the bar, a beer bottle in his hand.

"I don't want no trouble," he said. Phil laughed. "Who
said somethin' about trouble? You got no guts. I'm the big
man here and everyone knows it." Shad mumbled, "Yeah,
you're the big man." Then he went back to drinking his beer.
Phil looked around at the still-fearful eyes of the men in the
bar. He liked the feeling of being so powerful he made men

afraid of him. He began whistling softly and strolled out of the bar.

The police picked him up 20 minutes later walking down the street. He didn't resist arrest. He was a big man who didn't need to prove himself any longer. The "tangle of pathology" had completely ensnarled him. But Phil never knew it. He just knew that he had tasted power and control. He was a man with a "rep." He was somebody.

Why Violence?

Phil Fitch was exposed early to marijuana. He could have become a narcotic addict. He was exposed early to alcohol. He could have become an alcoholic. But he became a person who was drawn to violence and, as illustrated by his senseless aggression, was truly a rebel without a cause. It is not known just how much super-ego stunting there was in Phil's life. The evidence suggests there was considerable. But it can only be speculated what other problems he had in psychosexual development. Freudians would talk of pre-genital retardation, failure to resolve the Oedipus conflict, fixation of the libido and sexual energy at an immature level. All of these factors were important to Robert Lindner in his delineation of the "rebel without a cause," whom he considered as having a psychopathic personality.[38] Lindner described the rebel without a cause as "an agitator without a slogan, a revolutionary without a program: In other words, his rebelliousness is aimed to achieve goals satisfactory to himself alone; he is incapable of exertions for the sake of others."[39]

But the narcotics addict also achieves goals "satisfactory to himself alone." And so does the alcoholic. Why then become the rebel without a cause? The same questions are left dangling by other authorities in examining the breeding grounds of delinquency and crime. Thomas Pettigrew may have touched on the vulnerability of Negro youths to prove themselves through senseless violence when he observed: "Embittered by their experiences with men, many Negro mothers often act to perpetuate the mother-centered pattern by taking a greater interest in their daughters than their sons."[40] The sons, in turn, become embittered in their hunger for attention. Many turn to the streets and violence.

In addition to Moynihan and the Gluecks, other authorities have emphasized the role of the home life. One group of

researchers found that the non-delinquent in high delinquency neighborhoods comes from unusually stable, intact
families.[41] W. Mischel associated fatherless homes with promoting needs for immediate gratification.[42] O. H. Mowrer
and A. D. Ullman look upon the need for immediate gratification as critical in criminal behavior.[43]

Addressing himself specifically to the problem of Negroes and segregation, Pettigrew states: ". . . the type of
home life a Negro enjoys as a child may be far more crucial
for governing the influence of segregation upon his personality than the form the segregation takes—legal or informal,
Southern or Northern."[44]

The most important factor in affectional relationships
in the home "seemed to be the father's affection for the boy,"
according to the studies of the Gluecks in 1950 and of Audry
in London in 1957.[45] Many Negro youngsters apparently fail
to receive affection from fathers but also are never around
them. It has been reported that 21 percent of Negro families
in 1967 were fatherless.[46] Not all fatherless boys go bad or
not all slum neighborhoods are without informal means of
male adults exerting discipline and control over youths in
the area. But the fact remains that if the home is broken or
in discord, the chances for criminality increase. Thirty-eight
percent of delinquent youths in the lower socio-economic
class in New Haven were found to be from broken homes,
compared with 24 percent of non-delinquents.[47] In Los Angeles, one study showed that significantly greater numbers
of delinquents come from "disorganized" homes, while the
Gluecks found 60.4 percent of delinquents with broken homes
as compared to 34.2 percent of the non-delinquents.[48]

Thomas Monahan did a study in Philadelphia in which
he determined that among 44,448 delinquency cases, 62 percent of the Negro delinquents and 36 percent of the white
ones were not living with both parents.[49]

In an interview with Daniel Moynihan, it was pointed
out that "fewer than half of all Negroes reached the age of
18 having lived all of their lives with both parents. . . ."[50]

All of this re-emphasis on conditions of home life is presented here to point up the question that was raised in the
case of Phil Fitch: Although an unfavorable home life may
predispose a child toward delinquency, why does he try to
cope with his frustration through violence instead of some
other avenue of expression—narcotics addiction or alcohol-

ism or aggressive behavior that is not anti-social? "The tangle of pathology" that Moynihan talks about, breeds a variety of social and personality problems. The frustration that Dollard and co-workers stress as the basis for aggression also leads to other forms of anti-social or deviant expression, or it may produce behavior that is driving and forceful but accepted by society. The theory summarized by Edwin Sutherland and Donald Cressey on "differential association"—an excess of learning experiences conducive to law-violation—is one way to try to account for why two individuals in similar environments go in different directions.[51] But, as Seymour Halleck notes, the theory is too broad to account fully for why some people who are exposed to an excess of criminal associations become criminals, while others do not.[52]

Phil Fitch had a brother who did not become a criminal—the only one of three sons who went another direction. Few known theories—whether biological, sociological, psychological or psychiatric—at present can accurately predict the future of each individual from emotionally impoverished homes, slum neighborhoods or discriminatory environments, although probabilities for groups of youngsters can be stated with useful accuracy.*

As to the question of what form of anti-social behavior may become characteristic of an individual, distinctions can be drawn primarily on a personality basis between "the rebel," the narcotics addict and the alcoholic.

In the case of narcotics, statistics show that Negroes constituted 54 percent of the addicts in the United States in 1963.[53] There were eight times more narcotics users in Central Harlem in 1961 than in New York City as a whole.[54] Central Harlem is the same area where the estimated illegitimacy rate in 1963 was 434.1 per 1,000 live births for nonwhites.[55] Statistics based on later studies, reported in 1967, showed that "maybe as many as 40 percent of Negro children in the nation were illegitimate."[56]

In regard to alcoholism, there is little doubt that drinking is disproportionately high in Negro slums and broken homes. Muriel Sterne found drinking a common practice

---

*Recent studies, such as by the Gluecks, indicate criminal behavior in individuals has significant predictive probability, but the problem still remains in accounting for—and predicting—why one brother in three, such as Robert Fitch, fails to follow the path of his siblings in a broken family and slum subculture.

among 94 percent of teenage Negro boys and 91 percent of girls in urban areas.[57]

And so it goes. Alcoholism is high, narcotics addiction is high, rates of schizophrenia are—and so is crime. But why does someone like Phil Fitch turn to violence instead of drinking or drugs or psychosis? And is there anything peculiar to the frustrations of the Negro slum dweller that distinguishes him from the impoverished white person? Most studies indicate there is. The tangle of pathology seems more serious if for no other reason than white children do not get buffeted by the discrimination against blackness. Moreover they do not have a heritage of matriarchal family systems that contains its very own seeds of instability and deterioration.

It is easier to explain why lower-income Negroes, as compared with whites, should have higher rates of social deviancy than it is to tease out the factors responsible for the choice of crime over alcoholism or addiction or schizophrenia. But it must be recognized from the outset that no "pure" choices of deviancy are made. The violent ghetto-dweller may also be an alcoholic and a drug user. Some statistics on this question have already been quoted, showing the high rate of Negro homicides that involve alcohol. Claude Brown says that in 70 percent of 588 cases of Negro homicide, drinking played a part.[58] The violent ghetto-dweller may also be involved in narcotics, although it is highly likely that the violence displayed is a function of attempts to get money to buy drugs or to find a source to procure them. In fact, it is suggested that in the case of both the alcoholic and the narcotics addict, these are distinct from the personality that prefers violence.

There are some physical and physiological reasons for such a position:

1)   The objective in drinking and drug abuse is to incorporate something into the body—either alcohol or narcotics—that will make the person more comfortable with himself, give him a greater sense of well being or take the edge off the frustrations in his life.

The person who practices violence, though he may have similar needs to satisfy, must project himself onto his environment and those in it, rather than to modify the state of his central nervous system through oral means or injection. He works directly on the "outside" rather than the "in"—on trying to change the outside world to meet his own inner needs.

2) The person who expresses physical aggression is motoric. His satisfaction comes in part from direct use of gross muscle systems. The alcoholic may become aggressive, but first he must feel the cerebral effects of his liquid drug. His primary muscle action is limited to the mouth and elbow. His *real* concern is with his nervous system, not with the muscles that it activates. In the case of the drug addict, here again muscle action—such as crawling up in a corner or "going on the nod"—is secondary to altering the central and autonomic nervous systems.

3) Although these points are clearly in the form of theory, they coincide in some respect to the homeostatic model suggested by Lindner and with the emphasis that the Gluecks place on physique and delinquency. Lindner took Walter Cannon's classic description of the need for the human body to find internal equilibrium and applied it to rebels without a cause. He suggested, in effect, that the rebel experiences an internal buildup of pressure that he must discharge through violence in order to restore homeostasis.[59]

Now, moving from gross physical behavior to personality, some finer points of distinction can be developed, as related to why a person "chooses" violence in response to his role and conditions as opposed to some other form of expression.

Various possibilities present themselves, among them:

A) One central feature to the needs of the man who turns to physical aggression is to demonstrate to himself and others that he can exercise control over some part of his life. His background is one of being controlled, not controlling. He rebels against a sense of powerlessness.[60] This sense of powerlessness can be expressed not only in crime, but also in riots.[61]

B) As long as he feels he has no power to cope with life, he feels he is nothing. He knows no identity. He begins to equate power and control with defining himself and being somebody.

C) Like Phil Fitch and the "new criminal" described by Yablonsky, those who "choose" the violent option have deep needs to establish a "rep" and to be "big." In psychoanalytic terms, it could be argued that their sense of power-

lessness and insignificance is so great that a reaction formation takes over.[62]

Each of these three themes was expressed in the personalities of 26 young Negro men and women I interviewed as
subjects who had demonstrated, by police records, that they
practiced violence. They talked about "nobody pushing me
around" and about "busting heads" of people who got in their
way. They spoke with contempt of the fears they once had as
young children—fears of a hostile world, a dog-eat-dog neighborhood. Then, they "grew big" and learned that the key to
control was to hit before being hit.

A number in the group, which totalled 20 men and six
women, admitted drinking "regularly." But none was a skid-
row alcoholic, or could be labeled a defeatist. Why hadn't
alcohol become their coping mechanism? It was true that in
the backgrounds of most, there were strong dependency needs,
as is characteristic of the alcoholic. There was the drive to
demonstrate a self-sufficiency, which is so often the cover
that an early alcoholic uses to hide his dependency. There
was certainly a repressed rage that is frequently present in
the alcoholic toward the mother or parent who failed to satisfy needs to be dependent.

But there were distinctive features to the violent that
set them apart from the alcoholic. First, there was a decided
contempt on the part of many—including the "regular"
drinkers—toward alcohol. A "real man" never let alcohol
control him, any more than he let anything else control him.
He might drink, yes. He might get high. But he didn't let
alcohol control his life. He had only disdain for drunks and
looked upon them as "just somebody to roll—like queers."

Second, the alcoholic tended to be regarded as "a mouth"
—"just someone who talks a lot and says nothing." The
physically aggressive Negro sees himself as a person of action.
He is often not a very talkative person. Words do not come
easily. He had rather speak in action than words.

And, finally, there were few overt indications in the man
of violence of a despair that he had made a "mess of his life,"
and had humiliated his family. The alcoholic, particularly
when he is trying to dry out, often sees himself as worthless
and "not fit to kill." Even when he is drinking, he often
talks of what a burden he is to his family. There was little of
this in the group of the violent who were interviewed. The
absence of such feelings could be attributed to their all being

psychopathic personalities, the kinds of rebels without a cause that Lindner described. Doubtless, many could be so classified. But many also seemed to think that they found warmth and companionship once they turned to the streets and a life of crime. At least, they found others like themselves and some seemed capable of establishing close ties—something they never had at home and something the classical psychopath presumably doesn't even know the meaning of.

Little has been said here about the violent having modeled themselves after some adult in their home who was physically aggressive. Phil Fitch had two brothers in prison who had been violent, but he barely remembered them. Several in the group interviewed had fathers who were either criminals or who practiced violence toward others in the same household. The problem in placing emphasis on parents providing improper models is that, when it comes to violence, there is so much of it in Negro slums that a child doesn't have to see it in his own home to internalize aggressiveness.

A child who is physically abused in his own home may well get the idea that the whole world is that way and just live for the day when he is big enough to strike back. Two men in the group of 26 killed their own fathers. They said the fathers had beat them from the time they were old enough to remember. As teen-agers they were physically capable of being a match for their fathers and had little regret in beating them to death. Early physical abuse, then, may be an additional determinant in who takes up violence.

Now that some of the personality variables of the physically aggressive individuals have been explored and the influence of broken homes has been given particular attention, a couple of other *sociological* factors seem worthy of attention. At least they were found significant in lower income Negroes who expressed both a potential for violence and in those who had already committed assaultive behavior and were in the penitentiary as a result. These factors concern the effects of rootlessness and moving from rural to urban environments.

Mobility and Complexity

One of the most compelling changes in the lives of Negroes in the United States in this century has been the massive migration from farm to city, as has already been emphasized. The moving continues, not only from rural area to

urban area but from city to city and from one part of a city
to another. In five years, 1960 to 1965, the Negro population
in central cities in the U.S. was up 2,100,000, while the white
population was down 270,000.[63] "Today, three-fourths of all
Negroes are living in urban areas; a higher percentage than
for white Americans—and almost all Negroes outside the
South are in cities."[64] In the South, in 1967, only 54 percent
of all Negroes lived in that part of the nation, while in 1910,
almost 90 percent resided there.[65]

What has been the effect, from a psychosociological point
of view, of all this mobility? It can be assumed that identity
formation depends in part, at least, on calling some place
home. Loren Eiseley talks of man being a wanderer.[66] He
starts at the beginning—during that dim distant past when
man apparently came to a vague and gradual realization that
he could not rely on some built-in instinct to define himself
or his home on this alien planet. Foxes do not need to be
told about their holes, or birds about their nests. But, asks
Eiseley, what does man use as "radar" for directing him
home? Where is home? It is wherever he decides to try to
make it. For many low-income Negroes, the slums of cities
end up as home, but a very impermanent home. There is
usually considerable moving from one small rent house to
another, from one slum to another. And, as we have seen,
many who move to the city slum come from the more simple
environment of rural areas.

If violence is associated with a driving need to feel control and power, as has been suggested, then multiple moves
would seem to militate against fulfillment of this need and
only contribute to the potential for violence. A study in
Omaha, Nebraska found delinquency to be concentrated in
areas of high population density and mobility.[67] To investigate the effects of repeated moves, a group of 110 lower-
income Negroes were interviewed by the "natural dialogue"
technique on their attitudes toward violence, specifically as
it relates to obtaining civil rights.*

---

*The question on violence was: "Do you favor use of violence to gain
civil rights?" Elaboration was obtained to the point where it was possible to determine if the individual (1) opposed violence, both on an individual basis and collectively; (2) favored violence "if justified" but
would not likely participate; (3) favored violence "if justified" and
would participate, and (4) favored violence regardless, both individually
and collectively.

Twenty-five of the subjects opposed violence in any form. Thirty-two sanctioned it strongly—for use on an individual basis and collectively, and each said he would participate in violence if the opportunity presented itself. The remaining 53 subjects favored violence in lesser degrees. The tabulation below presents the association between the attitudes expressed toward violence and the number of moves each subject reported having made.

Comparison of Mobility with Attitudes Toward Violence

Degree of mobility	Sanctioning of Violence	
	None or little	Much
2 moves or fewer	35	11
3 moves or more	14	50
	—	—
Total Subjects	49	61

To make sure the relationship between mobility and violence was not just a question of chance, an analysis was made for statistical significance. It was found that there is a significant association between violence and mobility. A similar test was made to determine the influence, if any, of "complexity" on attitudes toward violence. By "complexity" is meant a move by age 13 from a rural to an urban environment. The following tabulation presents a breakdown on the number of subjects who sanctioned violence as a function of any move from a rural to an urban environment. Again, a significant association was found between violence and "complexity."

Comparison of Complexity with Attitudes Toward Violence

Shift from rural to urban environment	Sanctioning of Violence	
	None or Little	Much
No Shift	19	11
Shift	33	47
	—	—
Total Subjects	52	58

Violence, of course, may have one meaning and purpose to the "rebel without a cause" and another to persons expressing attitudes on the use of physical aggressiveness to gain civil rights. But if mobility and "complexity" are influencing factors on persons who sanction violence for a definite end, such as advancing the Negro cause, it would seem that the factors would certainly also be of significance in the behavior of the individual who uses physical aggressiveness to satisfy needs for power and identity. This point is borne out by studies by E. H. Powell, who found that a background of rootlessness, broken home and fractured relationships with other people constitute "the decisive variable" in criminal behavior.[68]

As a more direct indication of how mobility and complexity were central to the backgrounds of Negroes known to have practiced violence—as opposed to those who expressed an attitude about it—an analysis was made of the files on 108 Negro prisoners in the Texas Department of Corrections. Each was also interviewed. There were 19 in the total sample who were women. The offenses represented by the 108 inmates were as follows: Murder—29, assault to murder—25, rape—18, armed robbery—17, robbery by assault—15, sodomy—3, and failure to stop and render aid—1. Eighty-nine of those in the sample were recidivists. Mean age of the total group was 41.

In terms of mobility and complexity, 90 percent in the group reported four or more moves in childhood. Ninety-one percent had been born and reared in small towns or in the country, with 85 percent of this rural group having committed their violence in cities now considered their home. Mobility and complexity were particularly dominant in the backgrounds of those who had been convicted of murder, assault and rape. Ninety-six percent in this group reported four or more moves, and 92 percent of them lived in rural environments but moved to urban ones by the time they were adolescents. Recidivism rate among those convicted of such offenses as murder, assault, armed robbery and rape was a high 85 percent.*

A sample of 108 prisoners with non-violent records was matched with the violent group in terms of age, sex and economic class. It was found that 61 percent reported four or more moves in childhood, and that of the 82 percent who had been born and reared in small towns or in the country, only 60 percent had committed their offenses in cities.

Mobility and complexity, then, were significantly lower on a statistical basis among the inmates convicted of non-violent crimes.† These offenses consisted of burglary, theft, forgery, and passing of bad checks and fraud.

---

*Includes all crimes against person.

†For one degree of freedom, the difference is significant at the .01 level.

In interviews with the Negroes who had committed violence, the theme of identity problems was expressed repeatedly. There was the sense of no control or power over one's life, dating back to childhood in many cases. There were the memories of a broken home, of moving often and coping with environments that only increased the feeling of being "nothing." Just as the 26 "rebels" in Houston talked of wanting to be "somebody," so did the Negroes in the state prison.

Certainly, identity as it is related to violence cannot be expressed in all-or-none terms. What is being suggested here is that as the feeling of "nobody" increases as a function of having no power, no roots and a broken home, the tendency toward violence rises. It is possible for a person to feel a "nobody" to varying degrees. The same can be said of being "somebody." If a model was devised to illustrate the relation-

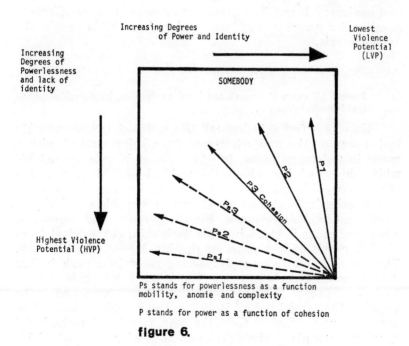

Ps stands for powerlessness as a function mobility, anomie and complexity

P stands for power as a function of cohesion

figure 6.

A Model For Identity And Potential Violence Using Mobility, Anomie And Complexity As A Unitary Influence.

ship that the "rebel" seems to express between his need to be "somebody" by demonstrating power and control over people through violence, the result might look like the diagram pictured in Figure 6 on Page 91. As will be noted, it is indicated that the feeling of having power and identity can increase as a function of the "cohesion" a person has experienced in his life. As the degree of cohesion that is experienced increases, the tendency toward violence is likely to decrease.

But "cohesion" can be discovered even by a person who has endured much mobility, anomie and complexity in his life. There is an individual difference in finding identity and inner power that no model is ever likely to capture. A Negro named James Norris discovered his identity and sense of power through a "self-thrust." His story is presented here as evidence that despite all the odds against the person born in a slum or ghetto, despite all the adverse influences of moving and having no home, it *is* possible to overcome these effects—possible for very extraordinary and unforgettable people like James Norris.

James Norris: A Case History*

> I went all sour. It wasn't too hard to do. The hate and rebellion had been building . . .

He was 5 feet 6 inches tall. He weighed 168 pounds. He had a scar on the upper left arm from being slashed with a razor in Coleman, Texas, in 1945. James Norris opened his white shirt and just above the webbed belt, there was another scar—this one from a knife plunged into his belly in Los Angeles in 1956. The worst scar was on his face but was hardly noticeable anymore. Plastic surgery had sanded it down and made it blend into his dark skin. It stretched from his left cheek to just short of the jugular vein in his neck. The wound came from a single-edge razor in a park in Los Angeles while Norris was supervising a bunch of kids at play. It was a case of mistaken identity. Norris happened to be wearing the same kind of jacket as the intended victim. The assailant, who attacked from the rear, tried to stop the blood flowing down his victim's face and neck when he realized his mistake. He paid $150 on Norris' hospital and doctor bills.

---

*Code names are substituted for real ones for both persons and places.

When a man's in solitary, he has lots of time to think. He thinks about things like this that have happened to him. He thinks about the bitterness inside him. He thinks about the bum rap he got. You don't think too much about the concrete that you sleep on, or the bread and water you get. You don't worry about the hole in the floor that is your bathroom.

What you think about is the bitterness that churns in your belly: Bitterness toward a wife you think has deserted you, bitterness toward the people you thought were friends and weren't, bitterness toward the home you never had, toward the father you never had, toward the moving and moving.

But most of all you taste and feel the bitterness toward a world and a system that you think has done you wrong. You think it is all 'their' fault. You hate the cops, you hate the judges, you hate the mulligans, you hate every goddamn son-of-a-bitch that you think is responsible for you being in this junkpile on an habitual criminal rap with a list of charges and convictions as long as your arm.

That is the storm and tempest that raged in this black man. His age: 41. First arrest: In 1936 for burglary. First offense: Stealing at the age of 6. First time drunk: When he was 7, on moonshine liquor. Family background: A father he couldn't remember and a mother who worked as a cleaning woman for white people.

When the storm passes and the rage recedes, a man goes on living and James Norris, Prisoner A3B150 in the Texas Department of Corrections, went on thinking.

I concluded that I could rant and rage and rebel all the rest of my life, but I wasn't going to change the world, or at least, that part of it that is my world—the prison system, the mulligans, the cops, the judges.

A man can sometimes see better in the dark than in the light. It came to me on that piece of concrete in solitary that there was one thing I could call my own, and that was me—myself. I figured it like this: I had been nothing. I had been worse than nothing. I had been a thing belonging to other people. I was just like somebody's knee when the doctor hits it with a hammer. I just reacted to what goaded me, and as long as I did that, I didn't have any control over my life, I didn't even have a life that was really my own. I didn't even have me. I was nothing, just a knee jerking this way and that like when somebody is using a slapstick on you and you're trying to get away.

So on September 14, 1962, the day I left solitary for the last time, I had it all figured out and I changed. I don't say I changed overnight. I don't say I stopped being a thing all at once. I don't say I decided the world had been right all along, and all I had to do was to get in step. That would be just another version of being a thing, a reacting thing, instead of somebody positive on your own. I didn't do any reforming. I just became me: Somebody who was going to have his own thrust.

By the time Norris came out of the darkness, where he had been placed for fighting, by the time he came out of the concrete block that measured 5½ feet by 8½ feet with a high ceiling and no window, he had a backlog of rebellion, of "jerking this way and that," that could match any other in the memory of the police and prison officials who knew him.

What he set upon doing on that September day, as he let his eyes get accustomed to the light again, was to gain a power he called "constructivism." He started with books. He had never had anything against books but he had never done any reading. Now he started as if the printed word had just been invented. He went through the Farley Prison Farm library in a matter of weeks. He asked for more. He stopped saying "ain't" and using double negatives. He picked up a fluency and a vocabulary that astonished prison officials. The "thrust" had been in him all along, he decided, but he was so busy "reacting" that he never let it assert itself. He had wanted a different life all along, and he remembered looking from the outside in—at people who had what he wanted but a way of getting it that he did not have.

> Even when I was in the free world, and I was knocking around getting a reputation for being a joker [a manipulator], I was listening with some part of my ear to guys that knew more than I did.
> I don't mean thugs or pros who got away with more than I could. I mean smart Negroes that I was around occasionally. They seemed to be able to get what I was after in life without using the means I did.
> These were the guys who seemed to know what it means to have a house with a yard and a wife who doesn't have to be somebody's cleaning woman and children who will run up to you when you come home and hug your neck and say: 'Daddy, daddy, you're home.' You think I didn't want those things? I wanted them all right. When you have them, you feel like you're wanted somewhere, you're important to somebody. At least somebody knows you're alive. You've got a face. I'm not saying that those guys I'm talking about really had all these things—they just seemed to me that they did. I'm not saying they knew everything there was to know. I am saying they had some education and I didn't.

By April 1959, Norris had done time in Minnesota, Missouri, California, and Texas. Finally, in the Travis County Court House in Austin, he was given a life sentence as an habitual criminal. When he entered "the walls" at Huntsville, he was tested for educational grade level. His E. A. (educational achievement) was 3.5—meaning he had the edu-

cation of a person who had completed 3½ years of school
and was just .5 above illiteracy, as defined by Texas law.

But once he discovered his "thrust," Norris began a
rapid climb from the brink of illiteracy. If he had to chop
cotton on the line during the day, he still studied at night.
He wasn't going to let anything or anybody, including fellow
convicts with their taunts, keep him from his books. In the
school program offered every Saturday to prisoners, he took
English, mathematics, algebra, history, government—the
whole works. On March 16, 1964, he was awarded a high
school equivalency diploma after passing all these courses
and a General Educational Development test.

Then he kept right on going. On June 5, 1965, he was
one of 57 inmates at Farley who became the first prisoners
in Texas ever to take and pass college courses given within
a state prison.

Norris became just as interested in the discovery of his
thrust as in his books.

> That thinking I did in solitary stayed with me. I knew that I
> could take anything if I had to and still be me. I got the control,
> not the world. I read Adler, James, Sartre and God knows how
> many others, and they all said to me: 'Do your own choosing.
> Be your own man.'

Norris tried hard to be his own man. But "asserting"
instead of "reacting" was not the easiest thing in the world—
not around recidivists in a maximum security prison unit. He
got taunted, he got accused of becoming an "inmate" (a
prisoner who cooperates with the administration), and he
still didn't react. He said he had left "reacting" behind in
the sleepy town of Coleman where he first stole but only got
cuffed by the sheriff who put up with it. He said he had left
"reacting" behind in all the shacks he knew as a boy and in
the innocence he lost early from watching his mother go to
bed with men whose faces he couldn't remember and never
knew. He said he left "reacting" behind in one big city after
another, where a black man can become the anonymity he
feels. He left it behind in jails stinking with urine and in the
concrete floors that broke off his teeth when he got decked
by the cops for being a "smart nigger."

But at Farley there was this one guy "who got all swoll
up at me and kept after me," Norris said.

> I told him: 'You want to kill me? Go ahead. But remember this—
> you're not going to get any satisfaction. You're only going to get

the time and the anger of watching me ignore you. You're going to
have to kill me to find out that I'm not letting you determine me.'

Meanwhile, Norris became interested in the "reacting"
of Negroes in the free world, of the civil rights marches, the
demonstrations. He laughed.

The way to beat the white man is to be your own man. Stop
acting like a mirror, reflecting back to him what he doesn't want
to see in himself.

Norris started thinking about what he could do in the
free world. It was not impossible that he might get released,
even as early as 1968. He figured he could find a face out
there because he was finding one in a tougher place right
where he was.

It became even tougher on August 13, 1965. On that
blistering day, James Norris, a very unusual man who found
identity in a very unusual way, got stabbed in the chest. His
adversary and chief taunter decided to take him up on his
offer. The man took a heavy screwdriver, issued on the construction line, honed the flat end into a sharp point and
plunged it four inches into Norris' chest.

With a toughness that exceeded even the time and the
place, Norris stayed on his feet, pulled the screwdriver out
and threw it at the feet of his assailant. Then he fell to the
ground, his blood staining the scorched earth. Those closest
heard him say something about being his own man.

The Rebel and Civil Rights

Since the rebel without a cause is viewed as a person
driven toward violence in a search for identity, civil rights
activity is clearly not his dominant avenue of expression. But
since riots have been linked to the thrust for civil rights, the
attitudes of the rebel in certain phases of the Negro protest
have relevance. This is particularly true in terms of the part
played by delinquents and gangs who moved into the Watts
riot in August 1965 to loot, vandalize and set up posts as
snipers.[69]

Attitudes on civil rights questions were explored in
Houston among 42 Negroes who were known by authorities
as "bad actors" and "repeaters," including the 26 mentioned
earlier who were interviewed on violence and their life histories. Attitude surveys also were conducted among 45 mem-

bers of the Student Nonviolent Coordinating Committee (see Chapter on "The Black Revolutionary"). A comparison will be made here between the views of the rebel without a cause and SNCC, an organized group (in 1967) with a cause.

The "unorganized" rebels were asked, as were the members of SNCC: "Do you think the riots in Watts helped or hurt the Negro's cause?" The results were:

	Rebel Without a Cause	SNCC
	%	%
Helped	40	66
Hurt	27	15
Both helped & hurt	27	19
No opinion	6	0

It might be surprising that a larger percent of rebels did not say they believed the Watts riot helped. But it should be remembered that the question asked if "the Negro's cause" was helped. The rebel, as indicated by other questions in the civil rights interviews, indicated little concern with causes and movements. By the very definition here of "the rebel," he has no cause. He may sympathize in one direction or another, but he is not likely to respond to his role as a Negro in American society by taking up civil rights activity.

Next came the question: "In what situations, if any, do you think violence is justified in defending Negro rights?" The results were:

	Rebel	SNCC
	%	%
General justification	35	80
Self-defense	49	9
Never	13	11
Defense of property	0	0
No opinion	3	0

For a group of people who make a habit of transgressing against the rights of others, as well as downright attacking them, the results may seem difficult to accept. But again, the question is in the context of "defending Negro rights." The rebel is not a defender, he is an aggressor. He is not interested in "rights," but in control and power.

To the question, "Do you think anything like a Watts riot could occur in Houston," the rebels also deviated from what might first be expected in terms of how they would answer. The results were:

	Rebel	SNCC
	%	%
Yes	17	71
No	38	23
Maybe	45	6

Although it is likely, as occurred in Watts, that the rebel would be attracted to a riot, particularly when looting and sniping began in earnest, it must be remembered that the violence this type of individual thinks in terms of is individual, not collective. He is not concerned with rioting as an avenue of response to "oppression" of the Negro. He oppresses others. He may be involved in a police incident that could very well trigger a riot, but it is not likely that he gives much thought to whether a collective outbreak of violence could occur in his city. He is preoccupied with the violence he commits as an individual.

One question that would seemingly be in context for the rebel to understand and appreciate was: "What do you think about the police in your neighborhood?" The results were:

	Rebel	SNCC
	%	%
General disapproval	44	32
Disapproval on racial grounds	12	40
General approval/neutral	39	18
No contact	3	10
No opinion	2	0

The low percentage of disapproval expressed in terms of the police being racially biased can be understood if one regards the rebel as a person who is not as much consciously concerned with the law on the basis of his color as he is with being caught. The relatively high percent of approval and neutrality expressed toward police may reflect a repression of just how much hate exists. It is true that "acting out" rather than "holding in" is more characteristic of the rebel, but when it comes to verbalizing hostility, true feelings may not be expressed the way they are in behavior. For instance in Watts, the John Kraft opinion research firm found that 47 percent of the people said in January 1966 that Los Angeles city police did an "excellent" or "pretty good" job. Forty percent expressed the opinion the police were "not so good" or "poor."[70] Yet only five months earlier, the police were the hated enemy to the people of Watts. And among adult rioters arrested, 64 percent had a police record.[71]

What all this amounts to is that people can express an

attitude in one direction and behave in another. It does not
necessarily mean deception or deliberate lying in answer to
a question. It can simply mean that persons who tend to "act
out" may gravitate toward moderate opinions when asked
their attitude on a subject, even a subject such as police.

SNCC members were asked about how trusting they are
toward someone when they meet him for the first time. The
question was also tossed to the "unorganized" rebel. The results were:

	Rebel	SNCC
	%	%
Trust	26	42
Caution	42	52
Distrust	32	6

Here the outright suspicion of the rebel seems to show
itself. In most cases, he has lived most of his life in the
"tangle of pathology" Moynihan talks about—in a jungle
where suspicion is learned early for survival. It is a question
of either taking or being taken, and the rebel learns he must
take.

Another question that appears to draw out what some
of the rebels see as a basic grievance was this one: "What
do you think are the main problems for Negroes living in
Houston?" The results were:

	Rebel	SNCC
	%	%
"Internal problems with Negro"*	0	38
Job opportunities	40	30
Housing	7	17
Schools	9	2
Relations with power structure	0	10
General discrimination	21	3
Negro apathy	5	0
Lack of Negro leadership	1	0
No opinion	17	0

A striking feature to these findings is that the rebel is
not at all concerned with his own need for self-pride, dignity
or improvement, as are members of SNCC. He is also much
more inclined to project the cause of Negro problems to "general discrimination." But in terms of what he probably knows
best, or lived with as a child—poverty—he clearly indicates
that "job opportunities" tops the list of problems. In the en-

---

*Includes issues of pride in race, need for negritude, black consciousness.

vironment in which he grew up, jobs were important to people, because even in "the jungle," the majority of residents struggle to be law-abiding, working citizens. There is much talk of jobs, and the problem of opportunities.

Last, how does the rebel feel about the progress of the civil rights movement? It has already been said that he does not take civil rights up as a cause and probably has little concern with it as such. But he is still a Negro who has knowledge that a push for greater civil rights has been underway. What does he think of the question: "In attempts of Negroes to gain their civil rights, have things been going too slowly, about right or too fast?" The results were:

	Rebel	SNCC
	%	%
Too slow	60	83
About right	39	11
Too fast	0	6
No opinion	1	0

The rebel is an "activist" in the motoric sense of the word, and just about everything might seem "too slow" to him, given a choice of answers such as above. The moderation in his replies—again attributable to his being a person who acts out rather than discusses problems—can be seen in the 39 percent who expressed an "about right" opinion.

The overall rundown on how the rebel without a cause compares in attitude with the SNCC member suggests most of all the difference between the two. Questions—even ones vital to Negroes—relating to people and events outside of the rebel's own life style have comparatively little meaning to him. At least, they do not capture attention and energy. The energy of the rebel without a cause has been too long diverted off into survival and a struggle for identity. His attitudes are more comparable to low-income Negroes in general, who are most concerned with the day-to-day matter of existence. The Phil Fitches and the James Norrises spent too much of their lives running, attacking and being attacked to be concerned with causes and movements.

Those who express concern are rebels of a different kind. Some are the revolutionaries in the city crisis. They are not lone pursuers of violence without an ideology attached. And though they may talk violence more than they practice it, the black revolutionaries play an important part in urban unrest, as we will see in the next chapter.

WHAT SHOULD WE BELIEVE?
POINTS TO CONSIDER—II

A. Let's recognize that every human being seeks some kind of identity in life, some sense of acknowledgement from others that he exists as an individual in his own right. Let's recognize that those who remain faceless and invisible are most likely to seek an identity through striking out at others. This gives them a sense of power, and with power comes a sense of identity and acknowledgement.

B. Let's also recognize that human beings are uniquely endowed with the ability to overcome even the most adverse circumstances and that self-thrust is not just some abstract concept. It is real and should be encouraged in people, no matter where they live. How can it be encouraged? Through the same means that ideas and messages are disseminated all the time—through parents, teachers, preachers, mass media and the leaders of this country who have a national forum.

C. Let's work on developing resources that can help buffer the effect of the baffling complexity that greets people moving into a highly urban environment. Consequences of the move can lead to feelings of helplessness and powerlessness in the face of a complex and baffling world. Out of such feelings the seeds of violence are spawned.

D. Let's also work on helping people gain a sense of roots in city life. For a child to move repeatedly is like transplanting him to new soil before he ever has time to establish roots. The effect of rootlessness can be a sense of no belonging, a sense of isolation, a sense of no identity—and a self-defeating attempt to overcome these things through violence. Let's work on helping more people own their own homes. Let's also attack all those conditions that contribute to broken homes. Let's disseminate among parents and teachers what is known about the need for "caring" discipline and consistent treatment of children, and let's try to make it possible for such discipline and treatment to be provided.

E. Let's use as "living witnesses" law-abiding people who grew up in slums under the most adverse conditions and never turned to crime as a way of life. Let them show youngsters still in slums that crime is not the only way of coping or attempting to prove manhood or gaining identity or ac-

quiring material benefits. Let's also use "turnabouts," people who once lived a life of violence and turned themselves around, getting along in the world without striking out at it.

CHAPTER 3

THE BLACK REVOLUTIONARY.

They are under a frequent focus of attention by intelligence units of city police departments. They make headlines with their fiery demands. They appear on television panels as the vocal representative of extreme militancy in the black community.

They are the black revolutionaries. They are watched, heard, discussed and despaired. Yet few people really know how they got the way they are or what kind of person becomes a revolutionary.*

A revolution is ". . . a form of social change distinguished by its scope and speed. It may, or may not, be accompanied by violence and temporary disorganization. . . . The essense of revolution is sudden change, not the violent upheaval which frequently accompanies it."[1]

Is there a Negro revolution going on in the United States today? There is, according to the social scientists who are following the action. Hardly anything is written on the Negro protest that fails to use the word "revolution" to describe the social change the nation is undergoing.

Even the classic pattern of such change seems to fit the current conditions. This pattern depends on a minimum of three basic requisites, according to Crane Brinton.[2] They are: (1) the society in which revolution most often occurs is prosperous but fails to find ways for equitably distributing its wealth throughout the population; (2) the government is delinquent or ineffective in adopting reforms (such as for minority groups); and (3) the intellectuals in the society

---

*Despite all the attention given the black revolutionary, he represents a distinct minority among Negroes. He may, however, verbalize many unspoken feelings of numerous Negroes and gain their tacit—sometimes overt—support, particularly among the young. In regard to young people, this chapter will be concerned more with the activities of the black revolutionary in the community than on the campus where a host of organizations have been established since the Student Nonviolent Coordinating Committee was formed and became the forerunner of many other highly militant groups.

that breeds revolution must have the leisure to focus a social consciousness on the problems of "have-nots." Regarding the last point, the present Negro revolution has received considerable impetus from the college-educated class, from professors and students alike.

Another condition Brinton considered important in the cultivation of social revolution is the absence of embroilment in war or international conflict. The fact that the United States is involved in the Vietnam conflict is openly decried by civil rights leaders as distracting the nation from the plight of the Negro.

If the classic pattern for revolution does fit conditions today, there is still the question of who the revolutionaries are. The group that first became the most vociferous is the Student Nonviolent Coordinating Committee (SNCC), which serves as a prototype for some of the newer organizations now making headlines.*

The Black Muslims also date back to an early advocacy of radical social change. Leaders within SNCC and the Muslims made it clear that violence is not a means to be skirted in pressing for this change.

Although a common orientation toward strong action was shared by SNCC and Black Muslims, revolutionary organizations do differ in purpose, method and structure. It is not even certain that all of the revolutionary groups can be called organizations. SNCC was described by Howard Zinn as "more a movement than an organization."[3] Whatever it was, SNCC had a history of moving increasingly toward radical positions. Kenneth Clark, in 1965, saw it as being "almost nationalistic in spirit."[4] Another observer, in the same year, believed it was gravitating toward "new styles in leftism" and that its "entire posture" was "at odds with the large part of the civil rights movement."[5]

The authors of both these observations only dimly perceived what was coming in 1966 when Black Power burst upon the scene, and 1967 brought community violence unequalled in modern American history. Since the most vocal advocate of Black Power was Stokely Carmichael, SNCC's leading spokesman, SNCC was indelibly linked with the

---

*Although the Student Nonviolent Coordinating Committee is not nearly as active now as in past years, it will be used in this chapter as a leading example of what a revolutionary group stands for.

phrase. No attempt here will be made to dissect all the various meanings that have been ascribed to Black Power. The
important point is that SNCC leaders became increasingly
nationalistic not only in spirit but ideology. By the summer
of 1968, Carmichael had become so nationalistic (in a Black
Panther sense) that he and SNCC parted ways. The central
issue was not necessarily nationalism, but Carmichael did
decide to cast his lot with the fiercely Afro-American Black
Panthers. In fact, he became the prime minister of "colonized
Afro-America," and H. "Rap" Brown joined in the exodus
from SNCC to become the Panthers' minister of justice.
There is no doubt, though, that SNCC, as well as the Black
Panther party, operated on an ideology of black nationalism.
In fact, one primary characteristic that all Negro revolutionary organizations have in common is a dedication to black
nationalism.

"Black Nationalism," Eric Lincoln says, "is more than
courage and rebellion; it is a way of life. It is an implicit
rejection of the 'alien' white culture, balanced by an exag-
gerated and undiluted pride in 'black' culture. . . . Black nationalism addresses itself not to an existent state but a state
of mind. But if there is no past or present black nation,
what is to prevent the projection of a Black Nation of the
future?"[6]

Among the groups that will be identified here as revolutionary, SNCC represents one that has definitely been dedicated to black nationalism as "a state of mind" but not necessarily as a separate geographical state. The Black Muslims
represent a movement that stands squarely for a separate
state not only in a figurative but also literal sense. There are
many differences between SNCC and the Black Muslims,
but in ideology these mostly revolve around the question of
how far one group, as compared with the other, has turned
its back on having anything to do with the white man.

The Black Muslims have gone all the way in rejection of
the white man, unless the position is taken that since they
are taught to work hard and live clean lives, they have
adopted the white man's Protestant Ethic. But even if this
position is taken, it can be argued that the rigid, personal
morality required of Black Muslims is not emulation of the
white man's way but as Philip Mason says, a "determination . . . to prove to white people that black people are superior

and actually practice behavior that whites only give lip service to."[7]

Some observers say the Black Muslims are losing strength. Others say that the Protestant Ethic orientation is so ingrained in the Black Muslims that the organization can in no way be considered revolutionary. The Muslims may not be making the headlines they once did in terms of violence, but the group still serves as a prototype for a revolutionary group seeking radical social change. The organization may not be increasing by the same percentage of growth it recorded five or ten years ago; in fact it may be even slightly declining in the face of competition from such guerilla-warfare groups as the Revolutionary Action Movement (RAM) or the Black Panthers. It may well be that the Black Muslims have suffered a decline because Allah has failed to "destroy North America" as promised and because the "Nation of Islam" remains split over the death of the fiery Malcolm X.[8] But the fact remains that the Black Muslim movement still has drawing power, particularly as long as it has among its members such personalities as Muhammad Ali (Cassius Clay). And it still provides a revolutionary outlet for Negroes who have a deep and abiding bitterness toward the white man. It is "revolutionary" in the sense that it not only represents an extreme "impatience" with white America but also a rejection, as Mason believes, of Western values.[9]

One of the underlying tenets to black nationalism is to instill pride in black people—by preaching a fierce respect for their color. This is a tenet that both SNCC and the Black Muslims share. It is also shared by all the smaller and more local movements that can be found around the country with a black nationalist base. What is not shared is any agreement on how much truck black people should have with white people. SNCC still retains a philosophy of challenge and confrontation of "the white power structure." Confrontation clearly requires facing whites and saying something to them. The Black Muslims have never made a pretense of being interested in demonstrations and confrontations. As Gary Marx notes, they have been "critical of the civil rights movement. They have accused it of being a trick and have called demonstrations ineffective and directed at what they perceive to be rather trivial ends. . . . They state that only token changes have occurred and in fact can occur until Negroes and whites are completely separated."[10]

But from the standpoint of the Negro seeking an outlet for expression, the Muslim movement provides one for "the angry, sensitive and disillusioned."[11] And, as Louis Lomax adds, "the Black Muslims, like the sit-ins and the freedom rides, are part of the Negro revolt. They are not aimed in the same direction, but they stem from the same unrest."[12]

Those who cannot follow their "apocalyptic language" and their belief in the coming Armageddon, as Marx describes it, have other black nationalist movements available. Some are more vocal in outright advocacy of violence. Gary Marx describes the leader of one, based in New York, as screaming during the Harlem riots: "I'm preaching violence . . . the Negroes must be free and the state must be completely and totally smashed. We'll have to kill a lot of cops and judges. No revolution was ever won by peaceful means, so we must fight and then set up a state of our choosing."[13]

As for violence, the Muslims say they do not seek it but that they do believe in "keeping the scores even, and they have warned all America that 'an eye for an eye and a tooth for a tooth' is the only effective way to settle racial differences."[14] In all fairness, though, it should be noted here that the Black Muslims were not involved in any of the limited violence Houston experienced in 1967, and a Muslim from Harlem whom I got to know even was proud of the fact that he had helped Mayor John Lindsay of New York "cool some of the brothers" during times of crisis there. None of this, of course, negates any of the basic philosophy or ideology of the Nation of Islam—or the fact that some Muslims favor violence.

And what about SNCC's position on violence? If its name could be taken literally, the question would never have to be raised. If one of its goals, as stated in 1960, could be accepted as characteristic, there would be no question of violence. At that time, SNCC said it was in existence to build "a social order of justice permeated by love." The Congress of Racial Equality, which was founded 20 years before SNCC, also started out with a philosophy based on non-violence. Its goal was to "abolish racial discrimination through application of the Gandhian philosophy and techniques of nonviolent direct action," according to James Laue.[15] CORE has probably moved toward nationalism almost as much as SNCC in its support of Black Power and Negro solidarity. Floyd McKissick, former CORE leader, largely seconded what the more vocal

Stokely Carmichael said, as has Roy Innis, present head of CORE. But if McKissick or Innis wanted to press the point, they could note that CORE was supporting armed groups such as the Deacons for Defense and Justice in Louisiana in 1965 when SNCC was still vacillating as to how much encouragement should be given to violence.

Whatever the original aims were of both SNCC and CORE, it seems undeniable that the character of goals changes in the Negro protest. SNCC, rather than CORE, will be focused on in this study since Carmichael has been played up as the leading spokesman in the swing to a more revolutionary stance on the part of both these organizations, and their successors.

Members of SNCC talked of "revolution" as much or more than black people in any other phase of the "revolt." Zinn says "they are prepared to use revolutionary means against the old order. They believe in civil disobedience. . . ."[16] And Carmichael, at least in the summer of 1967, believed that it was time to change the name of SNCC so its revolutionary orientation would be more widely recognized, if not represented. While in Havana in August of 1967, he suggested to the Cuban news agency, Prensa Latina, that he would recommend changing the name of the Student Nonviolent Coordinating Committee to the Negro Movement of Liberation.[17]

Both Carmichael and H. "Rap" Brown (real name: Hubert Geriod Brown) seemed to go out of their way in the long, hot summer of 1967 to cast SNCC in an image of violence and revolution. The reason for this can only be speculated on, but it should be noted that there was a distinct shift in "strategy" of SNCC starting about May 1967, when Brown succeeded Carmichael as SNCC chairman. Carmichael soon began making visits to points overseas—one of his longest being in Havana—and SNCC suddenly had a "director of international affairs" in the person of James Forman, a long-time member of the movement who has played a leading role in what direction the organization takes.

Before examining what Forman announced as part of his new job, and what the implications were for SNCC's involvement in "international affairs," the statements by Carmichael and Brown on the subject of violence and revolution should be considered.

The following are quotations attributed to the two during the summer of 1967.

Carmichael—Revolution is the only way for U. S. Negroes to get their rights.[18]

Brown—Black folks built America. If America don't come around, we're going to burn America down, brother. We're going to burn it if we don't get our share of it.[19]

Carmichael—In Newark [where rioting July 12-16, 1967, left 27 dead and 1,100 injured] we applied the war tactics of the guerillas. We are preparing groups of urban guerillas for our defense in the cities. The price of rebellions is a high price that one must pay. . . . It is going to be a fight to the death.[20]

Brown—After the Newark and Detroit rioting, Brown told 1,500 Negroes in Queens, New York, that the recent race riots were merely "dress rehearsals for revolution."[21]

Carmichael—"The Black Power movement," he told delegates to the Latin American Organization of the Solidarity in Havana, "is ready to help the cause of revolution from Tierra del Fuego to Alaska. We seek with you to change the bases of the world."[22]

Brown—in Washington, he said, "Violence is necessary. It is as American as cherry pie. If you give me a gun and tell me to shoot my enemy, I might just shoot Lady Bird."[23]

Carmichael—When you talk of SNCC power, you talk of building a movement that will smash everything Western civilization has created."[24] Carmichael defined "black power" at the meeting in Havana as a "union of the Negro population which is struggling to destroy the capitalist structure which is exploiting us."[25]

Brown—at a news conference in Washington on July 27, 1967, he exhorted Negroes to get their guns. "The honky don't respect nothing but guns. . . . Lyndon Johnson started the riots . . . I want Johnson to resign and go to Vietnam and fight and take his family with him . . . Johnson is a wild, mad dog—an outlaw from Texas. . . ."[26]

Carmichael—For 400 years we have been trying to make . . . conquests by talks and we have realized it is impossible to by just using petitions. The only solution is armed struggle . . . if all communities go into the struggle simultaneously, it will be impossible for the American government to control the rebellion. . . . If in the United States, the people were armed they would have taken a good bead on Johnson.[27]

Brown—after being released on $15,000 bail in New York August 22, 1967 (on charges of traveling by air from New Orleans to New York in possession of a carbine rifle), Brown spoke before more than 3,000 Negroes August 27 in Detroit and said rioters there "did a good job." He added that the Detroit riot would "look like a picnic" after black people unite "to take their due."[28]

Carmichael—After his Havana visit, the SNCC spokesman visited
Communist China, then went to Hanoi, North Vietnam. In
Hanoi, he was quoted by the official North Vietnamese News
Agency on August 31, 1967, as saying that United States im-
perialism is a "common enemy of the Vietnamese and Negroes
in America."

Carmichael's itinerary was somewhat parallel to the earlier travels of Robert F. Williams, who has been identified as
the founder of the Revolutionary Action Movement (RAM),
a small band of blacks in the United States (and perhaps at
some scattered spots abroad) with a reputation of being
highly violent. In 1961 Williams took up residence in Cuba,
and after a falling out with Fidel Castro, ended up in Red
China about two years ago.

A 12-page folder, stating it was published in Peking by
Robert F. Williams, found its way to bookshops in Detroit
that specialize in militant publications. The folder, called
"The Crusade," contained tips for clogging sewer lines, blocking highways, burning public facilities and smashing windows. Although this folder was sold at newstands in Detroit
in the heart of the area torn by rioting in July 1967, there
was no evidence that guerilla groups were behind the violence
there. It is undoubtedly true that such groups exist and distribute instructions on tactics and weapons but their support
of guerilla warfare has attracted only a relatively few followers. An example of the kind of instructions they distribute is
found in Figure 7 on Page 111, complete with illustrations on
making a Molotov cocktail.

Although the Revolutionary Action Movement has been
linked with the "colonialist coalition" seeking to unite black
people in the United States with non-whites in other parts of
the world, the leaders of SNCC took the lead in pushing the
new strategy. RAM came to the fore during 1968 while SNCC
seemed to be declining. The Muslims stayed about the same.
Only the future will tell what groups will emerge as the most
durable black revolutionaries in America. Certainly, Carmichael and SNCC have left their mark in taking the initial
steps. As to what strategy the revolutionaries may ultimately
adopt, that is another open question. Nathan Hare, a former
assistant professor of sociology at Howard University who
was one of Stokely Carmichael's teachers, talked of a "black
blitzkrieg" and "guerilla civil war" in the United States. A

FIGURE 7

LIST OF GUERILLA WARFARE INSTRUCTIONS*

How to Organize Your Guerilla Group

1. A group should consist of 3 to 5 members from your own neighborhood, preferably close friends.
2. All members should take a lot of practice in karate and judo.
3. Each member must have a rifle and a pistol. It should be the role of your guerilla group to obtain these weapons and ammunition any way they can as long as you do not harm black people themselves. . . .
8. All these groups must meet in complete secrecy and members must pledge never to give any information to police, the military, family or friends. Any member who breaks these rules will be brought up in front of the other members and put on trial. If this member is found guilty he must be killed, or punished according to the seriousness of the crime. Traitors must not be allowed to live. . . .

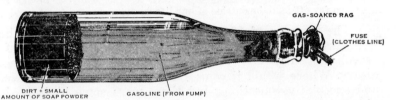

The Molotov cocktail should be used as much as possible, especially on moving vehicles, such as the type in diagram. . . . Here are a number of different formulas:
1. One-third motor oil, two-thirds gasoline.
2. One-third sugar, two-thirds gasoline.
3. One-third soap powder, two-thirds gasoline with a dash of oil.
4. One-third naptha (moth flakes), two-thirds gasoline. (This will result in a primitive napalm.)
A tampax will also do satisfactorily as the wick. The wick should be soaked in gasoline prior to ignition. The bottle should be as thin as possible.
(The guerilla should experiment with different mixtures.)

---

portion of an interview, published in question-and-answer form, went like this:[29]

Q. How would you define a black blitzkrieg?

A. It's sort of like a thousand giant Watts riots sweeping the country.

---

*Excerpted from an untitled handbook on guerilla warfare distributed in Northern ghettos.

Q. Do you still think that's a possibility?

A. Not a thousand Watts—that's exaggerating. But I think a great number of them.

Q. Do you think there is a serious possibility of guerilla civil war between whites and blacks in this country?

A. I don't see why it is so impossible in this country . . . what's so different about the blacks, as compared to other groups, that they would never come around to that if other means were not successful?

Q. How real do you regard the possibility of civil war—and how soon?

A. I regard it as very real. But it would not happen all at once. There has to be so much organization—and, before that, so much discontent and loss of faith by so many persons. So, if it's comforting to you, it's going to be quite a while off yet—though not so far off as to be outside of our life span.

The summer of 1967 seemed to set the stage for what Dr. Hare was talking about. But for a full-scale successful "revolution" and "civil war," outside support would seem necessary. Where would it come from? These are problematical and speculative questions, but there were some hints beginning to appear by the spring of June 1967, as SNCC leaders talked more of unifying non-whites the world over, citing the revolutionary successes of colonialists in Africa. Carmichael, an admirer of the French psychiatrist Frantz Fanon, views the "oppressed" Negroes of America as kinsmen of colonial classes who have been dominated by "imperialistic" powers. Fanon, whom Carmichael likes to quote, has written of the African colonialists and described the power inherent in the "lumpen proletariat."

> The constitution of a lumpen-proletariat is a phenomenon which obeys its own logic, and neither the brimming activity of the missionaries nor the decrees of the central government can check its growth. The lumpen-proletariat is like a horde of rats; you may kick them and throw stones at them, but despite your efforts they'll go on gnawing at the roots of the tree. . . .[30]

After Carmichael's talks in Houston in April, Brown and James Forman spoke in the city June 19, 1967, as mentioned in Chapter 1. Forman had also spent three days in Houston in October 1966 discussing Black Power before audiences at Texas Southern University and the University of Houston. It was not apparent in October, but it was in June, that SNCC had adopted a new strategy in terms of (1) making stronger, more open, statements advocating violence, and (2) seeking alliances with "non-whites" outside the United States to support black revolution within the country. Forman devoted nearly all his June talk in Houston to a long statement that SNCC had sent to all African and Asian missions to the United Nations. The statement said, in part:

> We reject the position of the United States government that intolerable racism in the United States is a purely domestic concern. We find this claim as hypocritical as the claim of the racist government of South Africa that its suppression of the human rights of 13,000,000 Africans is an internal matter, or a similar claim by the government of Portugal. Such claims are typical of people in the United States and are a matter of international concern. We are therefore addressing to you an appeal for your moral support. . . .[31]

Although Forman mentioned opposition to the war in Vietnam, it was not until five days later, June 24, 1967, that the local SNCC chapter devoted a rally to "Negro Freedom and Vietnam," comparing the plight of the people of Southeast Asia with the struggle of Houston Negroes. A circular distributed in support of the rally said:

> Vietnam is like an enormous ghetto. Slum dwellers and Vietnamese peasants all face death, destruction, brutality, poverty. The fight for peace in Vietnam is the same as the fight for freedom in Houston.[32]

St. Clair Drake regarded the linking of the Vietnam issue to the Negro struggle in the United States as an attempt by black people to act as a goad to the slumbering conscience of white Americans and as an effort to instill "more soul" into white people.[33]

But the SNCC policy of seeking support from other non-whites in the world seemed more plainly based on the often-repeated reminder (by black nationalists) that "we may be only one in nine in the United States but in the world, we outnumber the whites by five to two." (Sometimes the ratio is given as four to one or five to three.) By 1966, SNCC was already bearing down hard on the theme that no Negro American should kill his "non-white" brothers among the Viet Cong. When Forman spoke at the University of Houston in October 1966, he said: "We are killing the other man overseas, supposedly our enemies, when who we should be killing—and I know this will be blasted across the world—are the cracker legislators and white men that we have supposedly representing us in Congress."[34]

In late August 1967, Rap Brown visited United Nations headquarters as the guest of Ambassador John Malecela of Tanzania, who had been appointed chairman of a 24-nation "colonialism" committee. Four weeks earlier Forman, in his capacity as director of international affairs for SNCC, had spoken on apartheid, racial discrimination and colonialism at a seminar in Kitwe, Zambia, with Malecela presiding. Forman was quoted as saying: "We consider ourselves a colonized people in the United States. We will continue in the tradition of the late Malcolm X."

Although the stated definition of "revolution" may not require the prevailing presence of violence, popular usage has associated the two. Indeed, "rebellion" (which Carmichael and Brown used interchangeably with "revolution") is defined as "an uprising of more or less significant proportions intended to effect territorial autonomy or independence but not complete overthrow of the central government. . . . "[35] The same definition, however, permits "rebellion" to be synonymous with "insurrection and revolution" in a broad sense. The point here is that violence became openly advocated by SNCC leaders in the summer of 1967. As for the Black Muslims, the other prototype of the revolutionary organization, their public statements, as always, were practically non-existent. However, nothing that developed during the long, hot summer of 1967 indicated any change in their position, which has been stated by a number of observers as, in fact, standing for violence. Mason, in commenting on the "impatience" of the Black Muslims for the obliteration of "the white devils," says their position "needs to be seen against the wider background expressed by Negro imaginative writers."[36] He quotes from James Baldwin's *Notes of a Native Son*, where the point is made that there is:

> . . . no Negro living in America who has not felt, briefly or for long periods, with anguish sharp or dull, in varying degrees and to varying effect, simple, naked and unanswerable hatred; who has not wanted to smash any white face he may encounter in a day, to violate, out of motives of the cruelest vengeance, their women, to break the bodies of all white people and bring them low, as low as that dust into which he has been and is being trampled.[37]

Mason believes that the hatred and violence thus described constitute a main strand in the "psychological background of the Muslims." So if to be violent and to advocate rebellion is to promote revolution, then there seemed little doubt by 1967 that members of both the Student Nonviolent Coordinating Committee and the "Black Nation of Islam" were moving in that direction, and set the pace for newer groups to follow.

But how does a black person get started on the revolutionary path, as opposed to some other? Laue says it is more at the "personality level" that one finds why a Negro chooses the revolutionary avenue of expression to follow. The "candidate" may "need" violence or the threat of it in his life. But there is more to his choice than this. Perhaps by taking a brief look at the life of a member of SNCC and of the Black Muslims, the matter of personality and need-fulfillment will be illuminated.*

Henry Walls

The earliest memory he had of his mother was her constant doing something, her almost feverish activity. He could never recall a time when she was just sitting. She was always up in the morning before anyone else and was the last to go to bed in the four-room house that she was largely responsible for the family of five owning. The other striking memory he had of his mother was that she never believed anyone. But this was a characteristic that he later decided came just as much from her brother, who lived with them off and on. As for his father, he was at home every evening after work, but he had neither the drive of Henry's mother nor the doubting. He accepted life on its own terms, and the terms were never to his wife's liking.

Henry's mother worked at so many jobs he could not remember them all. It wasn't that she was constantly changing. It was that she always held several jobs at the same time. For instance, she clerked at a dry goods store in Houston's Third Ward and during lunch she ran a pawn shop that was in back of the store. She took a correspondence course in filing, and at home at night, she did the filing for both the store and the pawn shop. This was all in between her household work. She cooked, washed and tended to her husband and three children. Henry was the youngest child.

Mrs. Walls was a woman who spoke her mind. She spoke

---

*Names and places have been changed in the two case studies presented.

it to white and black people alike. She never hesitated to tell
the Jewish merchant who owned and operated the dry goods
store when she felt something was wrong. They argued a lot.
This tendency to challenge had cost her a number of jobs in
the past, Henry knew. But if his mother was outspoken, her
brother was an inveterate rebel and critic. If she never believed anyone, he never believed anyone or anything. Henry's
uncle never held a job for more than a month or two at a
time. He got into fights over his open disbelief toward everyone and all things. He spent time in jail. And gradually he
began to blame his color for the reason that he couldn't
"speak my piece" and get away with it. Henry admired his
uncle more than his father. His father seemed phlegmatic
and apathetic compared to both his uncle and his mother. His
uncle, who lived with Henry's family between jobs, spent a
lot of time with him teaching him to question and doubt.
"They'll tell you lies, boy, they'll tell you lies. Don't you believe what your teachers say and don't you believe what them
books say. All lies."

Henry's mother was a little more selective in her disbelief. She would not hear of the boy not going to school. She
was a big believer in education. When she was asked about
the "lies" in the books, she said Henry would just have to wait
and decide that question for himself after he got his education. She didn't believe everything her brother said and that
included what he said about the books being "all lies." She did
believe in facing people with what she called "the truth."

"Don't you be afraid of telling people your mind if you
think you know what the truth is," she would tell Henry. "I
don't care what color they are."

The dampening effect on the boy, though, was his father.
He said that "stirring people up" did no good and that if the
boy just went about his business bothering no one, he would
get along all right in life. The father held the same job as a
porter for years and unlike Henry's uncle, he was never in
trouble with the law. Although he was quieter than both his
wife and brother-in-law, his easy-going way seemed to influence Henry's older brother and sister more than did "the loud
mouths in the family." That was the way the older children
came to describe both their mother and their uncle. As soon
as they finished high school, they moved away from home.
They said they were tired of listening to "all that yapping and

griping." Both the brother and the sister married, had families and settled down to quiet lives in the Third Ward.

Henry was different. He felt that he couldn't count on his mother's approval, her love, unless he was just as busy as she was and adopted her questioning personality. He got as many jobs after school as he could. He delivered circulars, sold magazines, had a newspaper route. His mother did not talk up the race issue as his uncle did. She simply stuck to the reminder that "you are as good as anyone."

Henry's uncle, however, made him feel that he had to stand up to the white man "or you'll get pushed around all you life—like your father has." The first time Henry got into a fight with a white boy, the uncle said he was "real proud." He insisted that "White people are no good. You better remember that, son. They'll trick you if you don't trick them first."

Henry Walls entered college the same year that Black Power became big in the civil rights movement. He was impressed by Stokely Carmichael on television, and every time he heard the word "trick" as directed toward all white men, he knew his uncle was right. "They really will trick you. They have all along," Henry decided.

At Texas Southern University in Houston, where he enrolled, Henry spent much time reading the history of African nations and accounts of slavery in the United States. By the time James Forman, a national leader of the Student Nonviolent Coordinating Committee, came to Houston to speak on "black power," Walls was already sold on both SNCC and Black Power. He was convinced that the white man had sold the black man a "false bag of goods" and that it was time, after 300 years of oppression, for the scales to be tipped in favor of black people. He agreed that the whole economic and legal structure of "the white man's system" would not accommodate the black man's needs and that only a major overhaul would give black people what was due them.

Walls liked SNCC not only because it exposed the white man for his lies but also because it "did things." At TSU, he kept busy painting protest and picket signs. He demonstrated against the mayor when the chief city official came to speak on the TSU campus. He marched downtown in protest of "the racism against Adam Clayton Powell." He went to a Negro area called Settegast to demonstrate against "police brutality." He took part in another march downtown to protest against the "brutal" treatment of four Houston Negroes who had been "attacked" by white policemen as they were passing through a small town northeast of the city.

Henry Walls' real test came the night that gunfire was exchanged between students in dormitories at Texas Southern University and city police. Although Walls was not a resident of the dormitory, he participated in many SNCC activities held in "the pit"—a concrete-lined student gathering spot —nearby and in demonstrations that blocked the street running through the campus. On the night of the outbreak of violence, he helped stir students up with the report that a Negro child had been shot to death by a white boy in Northeast Houston (the report was false). Walls then joined a student in one of the dormitories.

When police entered the dormitories in full force, Walls fled to one of the rooms on the first floor. He was arrested, along with 488 other students, and spent the night in jail. However, when a statement was taken from him by an assistant district attorney, he neither admitted participating in the gunfire exchange nor knowing anyone who did.

He later told his uncle the full details of his activities that night and received unstinting approval. He did not, however, tell his mother or father. His uncle said he was proud of him. He told Walls' mother that her son was learning to "make the white man face up to his lies." The mother asked no questions about her son's possible participation in the events at TSU the night of the violence, although she knew he had spent a short time in jail. She assumed that since he was released so soon the next day, he had nothing to do with the trouble. She too was pleased with the way that the young man had learned to speak up for himself and to question anyone he doubted. She was not as concerned with how much challenge he directed toward the white man as her brother was. She didn't want her son to forget his studies at college and reminded him constantly that he had an education to get. The son began talking back to his mother, contending that "the education you get at a Negro college is just a lot of white-man brainwashing. The black man needs his own colleges." The mother said she didn't know about that but she wanted her son to get a degree. Meanwhile, Walls' father became no more than an object of disdain for the young man. He openly said that his father was a Negro, not a black man—the difference being that many Negroes have "white minds" as a result of brainwashing. The uncle laughed and agreed. Walls considered his uncle a black man.

What Henry Walls Accepts and Rejects

To gain a broader understanding of how Henry Walls found fulfillment in SNCC, an additional look needs to be taken at what he has come to accept and reject in terms of the Negro "revolution." By cataloging some of his own beliefs— and lack of them—there should be further light cast on just what a revolutionary is today and what he stands for, particularly in terms of contrast with others involved in the Negro "revolt."

Credo of Acceptance

The following is a list of beliefs accepted by Walls, together with references to leaders he agreed and disagreed with on points of principle:

1) The nonviolent tactic is now obsolete. He agreed with Rev. F. D. Kirkpatrick, coordinator of SNCC in Houston through the spring of 1967, who said: "There's going to be guerilla warfare if the yoke isn't taken off the blackman's back. We don't have anything to lose. We're not even citizens. Martin Luther King's nonviolence has run out, like a car out of gas." When H. "Rap" Brown spoke in Houston on June 19, 1967, Walls raised his arms in a Carmichael salute as the new SNCC chairman said black people would have to gain their freedom by force.

2) Black people have two basic conditions to get rid of —shame of being black and the reality of being poor. Walls thinks Forman was completely right when he said "being black has been associated with being evil, being dirty and doing wrong. Blacks must overcome the idea that white is the ideal."[38] As for being poor, the system must be changed to give the Negro "a piece of the pie."

3) The black revolution must take "the role of inferiority" and turn it on its head. As Thomas Pettigrew has said: "When you are supposed to be passive, you are aggressive. When you are supposed to stay out because you are not wanted, you go in—particularly because you are not wanted. You have group support for it. You get group reward for it. It is publicly done. It has every known major characteristic for maximal change in the individual."[39]

4) Black people must push white allies aside. In confronting the white power structure, blacks must be the leaders and not let white people take over. "White allies further white supremacy," Carmichael said.[40] If whites do the leading, if they even participate in projects to "help" Negroes, it gives the impression that there are no black people capable of doing the job themselves.

Economically, black people must also take over from the whites in Negro neighborhoods. This means that businesses must be owned by blacks. This point was driven home at a rally in Houston in August 1967 by Ernest Thomas, national vice-president of the Deacons for Defense and self-styled bodyguard of Stokely Carmichael.

5) Revolutions are led by a minority who are not afraid to lose everything, including their lives, but the masses must be aroused. As Edwin Berry has said: "The leaders are people who are riding the tide of expectation and are dissatisfied. It is the bird that gets out of the cage occasionally and finds out a little bit about the world outside that is the most dissatisfied."[41] Walls thinks SNCC has led many black people out of their "cage," and he helped in the liberation.

6) The young must lead the battle; no one will follow or believe older people. Many older Negroes—Walls considers anyone over 40 as "old"—have "sold out." They are afraid of losing their job or the home and car they have. They cannot be counted on in the black revolution except as bystanders who might offer encouragement—"if Mr. Charlie isn't watching."

7) "High class" Uncle Toms—as well as "old" ones— must be eliminated. Walls received a description of a "high class" Uncle Tom from his SNCC chapter. It said that one of the hallmarks of the "high class" Tom is that "he must be well educated, clean, neat, polite, obedient, subservient with dignity and willing to see problems worked out peacefully over a long period of time." The position was taken that "until the educated Tom is removed or changed, the race problem will forever be a sad one."

8) The black man must attain his "manhood" through the revolution now in progress. Walls found that every SNCC leader emphasized that the very crux of finding dignity in being black, of being proud of being black, largely concerns the manhood theme. Negroes must overcome the white man's

label of "boy" by direct confrontation and challenge of the white man.

9) Riots contribute to Negro manhood and to a sense of pride in being black. Riots mean action, and Walls stands for action. It does not mean that violence is to be actively sought. But if it comes, then it should be actively engaged in, not retreated from. A black man must stand up for his rights and his manhood even if it means losing his life.

10) The black man must look to Africa as his "homeland" and heritage. Africa serves as a reminder of the fact that on a worldwide basis, nonwhites outnumber whites. Africa serves as a symbol of black unity and black culture.

This is just a partial list of the beliefs of Henry Walls— as a young revolutionary. Just as SNCC changes, so does Walls, but he does not think he will retreat from these convictions. Neither does he believe he will stop rejecting certain positions on the Negro revolution. He feels as strongly about saying what he does *not* believe as what he does believe. And what are the negative positions of this revolutionary?

Credo of Rejection

Here is what black people should not do and believe, according to Walls:

1) Black people should not develop a "color-blind" identity. Walls, following the teachings of his leaders, rejects any suggestion that the black man should play down his color. Their position is strongly opposed to the "plurization" of identity based on color.[42]

2) The black man should not forget that his color has been a stigma. It should remind him of what the white man has done to him. He should use the stigma to cultivate group solidarity and, as Fein has suggested, wear it as a "badge of honor."[43]

3) The goal of the black revolution should not be integration. "The government has gone around the world saying integration is the goal of the civil rights movement," Forman said. "Integration means becoming part of the exploiting elements. It's a false bag of goods."[44]

4) The civil rights movement has not produced the kind of progress the black person needs. It is too slow, and it misleads blacks into thinking something beneficial is being done. Using the problem of jobs as an example, it would take until

1992 for black people to gain equal proportional representation among clerical workers and until 2005 among skilled workers in general, if the present pace continues.[45] Even after the Watts riots, conditions were the same for most black people there one year later, Carmichael said.[46]

5) Civil rights legislation and court action have not been of much benefit to most blacks and are just another white man's trick. Although there may be disagreement on this point, even among revolutionaries, Walls sides with Rev. Kirkpatrick in believing the Supreme Court decisions on desegregation, as well as subsequent legislation "for the Negro," has been "tokenism" and the white man's way of making the Negro think he is getting something when he isn't.

6) The news media are not to be trusted in reporting the black revolution and have deliberately distorted issues. Carmichael expressed particular bitterness over "distortion" of the Black Power issue.[47] Forman, when he spoke at the University of Houston, started out by saying he always brought his own tape recording equipment because the press could never be trusted to present accurate accounts of what he said. Both positions are in direct contrast to that of Kenneth Clark, who has credited television and the press with helping the civil rights cause.[48]

7) Intermarriage is not the answer to the black person's problem. Forman has said he does not want to marry any white man's sister and that most black people do not care that much for whites.[49] Peter Rossi has suggested that "the Negro problem" is looking brighter because intermarriage is increasing.[50] Black revolutionaries reject this position out of hand.

8) Middle-class values should not be a goal of the black revolution. Middle-class values are white man values and will simply be used to give more Negroes "white minds," in the words of Rev. Kirkpatrick. They are another "trick bag."

9) Working within the present economic and legal framework of the American system is not possible for the black man to obtain what is due him. Forman has said that the framework "must be thrown out."[51] Carmichael has said that "it's going to shake the economic foundations of this country if black people get a decent way of life. . . . When they [the whites] want to talk to me about a decent way of life, then I'm going to sit down and talk to them—but don't talk to me about nonviolence unless you want to be nonviolent in

Vietnam. And don't tell me that you can't hate anybody, because I want to know how many Americans love the Vietnamese they shoot. Just don't talk to me about that nonsense."[52]

10) Acceptance of the present "American democracy" is not possible for the black man, because it excludes him. Walls is convinced that there is no democracy since black people "share so little in it." He believes they are simply used as "gun fodder" to be sent to Vietnam to be killed.

Although all these positions, both the negative ones and the positive ones presented earlier, characterize the sort of thinking of the young revolutionaries who belonged to SNCC, they do not constitute a formal doctrine of that organization. There is (and was) not that much organization to SNCC. The Black Muslim movement, on the other hand, has a highly regimented program and dogma. But it has a different kind of person belonging to it than SNCC does. Here is a profile of one Black Muslim.

Silas 2X

He decided to join the Muslims while he was doing two-weeks in solitary. Prison officials had already suspected he was a likely candidate for the movement. So when the Watts riot came, he was rounded up with convicts already known to be Muslims and thrown into solitary confinement until the disturbance was over. Silas 2X still had his "slave" name then, which was Silas Hookman. He knew that the Watts outbreak had thrown fear into prison officials, who figured that if the black man was revolting in California it could have the effect of spreading clear across the nation—even to the "hell holes" known as state farms.

Hookman had a simple reason for becoming Silas 2X: Pure hate. He hated white people so much he could taste it. In solitary, he thought of Malcolm X and the hatred he preached. Hookman smiled when he thought about the plane which crashed several years ago, killing all those crackers from Georgia. He knew that Malcolm X must have delighted in announcing the crash at a mosque meeting and using it as an example of how the white man was being drawn closer to total destruction.

Before his current prison stretch, Hookman had visited a mosque a number of times. He never quite got to joining, however, because he did not want to subscribe to the strict discipline the Nation of Islam required. Now, however, he felt the discipline would make him harder and keep his hatred of the white man burning fiercely within him. If he had to give up drinking and women, he would. It would keep him from dissipating and help him prepare for the day when he could join his black brothers in a massacre of the whites.

Hookman knew that Black Muslims did not publicly preach violence toward white people. He knew that Elijah Muhammad even went to great pains to say that such violence was wrong and the Nation of Islam would not sanction it. But he also knew that underneath the official words from the leading teacher, there were mosque leaders and rank-and-file members who looked forward to violence and were adamantly preparing for it. Hookman now decided he would join them.

He had never had respect for authority, or any reason to have it. As a boy he grew up in slums and seldom saw a night pass without a police car arriving to take some member of his "family" away. He described his family as "loose," meaning that there was a succession of men who passed through his house living with his mother and aunt, but he never knew which one, if any, was his father. Most of the time when the police came, there was a fight—a bloody one. The man staying at the house didn't want to go quietly and many times the police seemed only too ready to hit him in the face with a slap-jack or knock him over the head with the butt of a revolver.

Silas would crouch in a corner watching it all. He saw his first killing, on the dirt street in front of his house, when he was 6 years old. One Negro, who had been staying at his house some time ago, came back and stabbed another, who was there at present. The dying man got stabbed three times in the chest and neck. The assailant was taken to jail, but Silas saw him back in the neighborhood two weeks later. It was only later that he learned that such a killing wasn't taken very seriously by authorities.

Besides the police, the only other white men Silas ever saw in his neighborhood were those who came to "nigger town" to shack up. One was a drug store owner and another was a school administrator. He hated them both because sometimes they came to his own house and would go into the one bedroom with his mother. He was told to get out of the house.

As he grew older Silas tried to spend as much time out of the house as he could. He found more companionship on the streets than at home. At home there were only the men he didn't know and his mother, who was either at work or in bed, and his aunt, who was often drunk on wine, and three younger sisters, who seemed to get more attention than he ever did. But on the streets he also found more violence and more hatred of cops and everyone else who represented authority. The truant officer was an authority Silas came to hate. The man would call him "boy" even after Silas was was 6 feet tall and 19 years old. By the time he was 19, he had long lost all interest in school and had not attended regularly for at least five years. But the truant officer kept hounding him and calling him "boy." Finally, Silas beat him up. He went to jail for it, but it wasn't the first time he had been inside a cell. And it wasn't the first time he got roughed up in the process. He had scars on his head dating back to when he was 12 and 13 years old.

As the police came to know Silas Hookman, they picked him up two and three times a week. Often there were good reasons. Silas began stealing when he was 8, he was breaking into service stations at 11, he hit a white man over the head and robbed him when he was 14. Other times—and these were the ones that Silas always remembered—he had done nothing but still the police picked him up, and, when he resisted arrest, he got "worked over."

It was after Hookman's first prison stretch that buddies began taking him to the Muslim mosque. He liked the idea of a separate state for black people. He liked the idea that the white devils were going to get what was coming to them. But he wasn't ready for the discipline of living a life without women or drink or even cigarettes. And he couldn't see himself wearing a tie and a suit. He didn't even have a tie and a suit.

Now, however, as he was finishing his second prison term, he was ready. He was more than willing to take the discipline in exchange for the power that he felt being a Black Muslim gave him. He felt the power came from belonging to an organization with a fierce dedication to triumph over the white man. The Muslims appealed to him because they did not preach just separation from the white man; they preached superiority. They didn't have to sanction hate—officially. He knew there was hate in the organization because he knew members who had it. And he wanted to share his with theirs.

So, three months after discharge from prison, Hookman was Silas 2X and attending mosque meetings regularly. He joined the Fruit of Islam to practice "defense." Actually, he was waiting for the day when he could unleash aggression against the white man, not stave him off with "defense."

Silas 2X began living an ascetic life in preparation for the day of "judgement." He cut off contact with his prison buddies and the slum neighborhood where he still had friends. Gradually he came to believe that his whole police and prison record could be blamed on the blue-eyed white devils who had subjugated his race to such conditions that they were bound to rebel. He mourned the loss of Malcolm X but he figured that the white man was behind Malcolm's murder. Silas 2X had always felt closer to Malcolm X than to Elijah Muhammad, but now he began giving his full dedication to the leading teacher.

He still couldn't feel close to his Muslim brothers who seemed to be in the movement more to "straighten up and fly right" than to prepare for the day to do the white man in. Fortunately, at his mosque, the "right-living" brothers were in a minority. The majority were willing to subscribe by the disciplines of the order but their deepest motivation for belonging was hatred of the white man.

Silas 2X cut off all contact with white people. He found a job working for a Negro who operated a junkyard. He went to the mosque every night and made it his life. He read the Koran as the leading teacher required and listened to records that Elijah Muhammad preached. He liked best the accounts about black superiority and the day of doom impending for the white man. He lived for that day. Until then, he particularly enjoyed the long, hot summer of 1967.

Can Revolutionaries Get Together?

It would be unfair to say that even most of the members of the Black Muslims are drawn to the movement from the sort of deep hatred that Silas 2X has of the white man. Just as young people joined the Student Nonviolent Coordinating Committee for different reasons, there are different motivations at work in the case of the Muslims. Whether or not a group like SNCC could ever join hands with the Muslims is an open question. The Muslims have shown little interest in civil rights, but as SNCC placed greater emphasis on the importance of black nationalism, it found more grounds for agreement with the Muslims.

Carmichael went on record saying that any "summit" meeting of Negro leaders should include Elijah Muhammad. His position was stated in the following terms: "I would think that that summit meeting would be important only if an invitation is extended to the Honorable Elijah Muhammad and the so-called nationalist groups. . . . Because I think that one of the things the white people were able to do heretofore was to isolate these groups from us and as far as we are concerned —SNCC is—we are not going to have it any more; we are going to move to sit down and talk to those people and unless those people are sent an invitation, it would be useless for SNCC to participate."[53]

However, when a Black Power conference was held in Newark, N. J., in July 1967, openly-identified Black Muslims were conspicuous by their absence. All varieties of splinter groups of black nationalists were there—from the Black Panther party members to the Revolutionary Action Movement followers. In terms of numbers, none of these groups can come close to the strength that either SNCC or the Black Muslims had at the time.

Although the Black Muslims have indicated little concern with other nationalist groups, particularly those interested in civil rights, this does not keep non-Muslim revolutionaries from getting together, as they did in Newark. The Black Panther Party could serve as one possible base of political operations for revolutionaries. SNCC was instrumental in forming the party in the South. Since then it has been established in other parts of the country, including California.

Huey P. Newton, the leader of the Black Panthers in California, openly advocates black people arming themselves and stopping the "imperialistic" machinery that he believes suppresses the world-wide revolution of non-whites. He says, "We can stop the machinery. We can stop the imperialists from using it against the black people all over the world. We are in a strategic position in this country, and we won't be the only group rebelling against the oppressor here."[54]

The Los Angeles Black Panthers were formed in March 1967, with the announcement that "Malcolm X is going to be our patron saint. Our political philosophy is black nationalism."[55] Carmichael has stated that political power must be used by black people to gain economic power. The Black Panther party would presumably operate to mobilize Negroes to vote for black nationalist candidates.

In July 1968, James Forman of SNCC announced that
his organization was forming an alliance with the Black Panthers. Planks in the platform of the Black Panther party,
according to the July 8, 1968, issue of *Leftist Notes*, include:

> We want all black men to be exempt from military service.
> We want an end to the robbery by white racist businessmen of
> black people in their community.
> We want an immediate end to police brutality and murder of
> black people.
> We want all black men held in city, county, state and federal
> jails to be released because they have not had a fair trial
> because they've been tried by all-white juries, and that's like
> being tried in Nazi Germany, being a Jew.

The "black leadership conference" in Los Angeles, where
the 1967 announcement was made establishing a Black Panther party, was sponsored by a nationalist group called "US."
This group is an illustration of the many nationalist organizations to be found in the United States. Most operate on a
local basis and seldom make national headlines.

One group that has made headlines but has not gained a
wide national following is the Deacons for Defense and Justice. It can be considered revolutionary on the basis of its
arms and preparations for violence with the white man. It
can be regarded as nationalistic in terms of advocating black
unity.

Rev. F. D. Kirkpatrick, who became Houston regional
representative of the Southern Christian Leadership Conference in the summer of 1967, formed the Deacons in Jonesboro,
La., in 1964. The Deacons broke into the news in the summer
of 1965 when they began standing armed guard over Negro
neighborhoods in embattled Bogalusa, La. Kirkpatrick visited
Bogalusa and told nonviolent Negro leaders: "You been led by
the tap-dancing Negro, the head-tapping Negro—in other
words, the plain old Uncle Tom. You got to forget about right,
because right ain't gonna get you justice."[56]

The Deacons in Bogalusa were present during the round
of civil rights marches and demonstrations there. They pa-
trolled neighborhoods with walkie-talkie radios, escorted civil
rights workers about town and engaged in target practice.

In 1967, Kirkpatrick said Deacons for Defense would
come to Houston to protect civil rights workers. To examine
the articles of incorporation of the Deacons, one would not get
the impression that the group's purpose is to arm members to

form a militia. The incorporating articles list such points as teaching minority groups about the Constitution and democratic way of life and the duties of good citizenship. The articles also mention "defense of civil rights, by honorable and legal means. . . ." When Rev. Kirkpatrick was instrumental in bringing a national leader of the Deacons, Ernest Thomas, to Houston to speak in August 1967, there was little talk of open arming. "Honkies" were told to leave the meeting, being held under an elevated expressway in the Fifth Ward. Though there was no attempt to recruit residents or others for "militia" purposes, the Deacons had already established some reputation with Houston police as being Negroes interested in guns. One of the "captains" of the Deacons who belonged to the SNCC chapter at TSU made little effort to conceal the fact that he carried a sawed-off rifle stuck in his belt.

But the Deacons, like SNCC "members" themselves, came and went in Houston. As one SNCC follower noted: "Man, you can't say who is a 'member' of the Deacons. They just start claiming they are Deacons and that's all there is to it."

So whatever the formal charter of the Deacons may say, it is subject to being something quite different in practice. If it sounds as though the group is an innocuous organization, it should be noted that other revolutionaries operate under benign names also. In Watts, for instance, there is an association that has denominational sponsorship and in 1967, a leader who described himself as "the most radical" in the eyes of the Los Angeles police department. His philosophy was definitely nationalistic in terms of advocating pride in blackness and looking upon the white man as "an enemy." He seldom spoke of religion and frequently of the earthly needs of the Negro.

It is the religious angle that sets the Black Muslims apart from other revolutionaries. No other major group lays claim to any religious philosophy. The Muslims claim to be a branch of orthodox Islam. They accept the Koran or the "Holy Qur-an," as Elijah Muhammad calls it. Muhammad says the black man was created 66 trillion years ago and the white man was created by an evil scientist named Yakub. Allah is now punishing the black people for the albino mutation that the evil black scientist Yakub created. Allah is letting the white man rule, but his days are numbered. What has weakened the Muslims, in the eyes of some observers, is that Muhammad keeps saying the white man's downfall is imminent but it still has not come. For instance, Muhammad said: "The years of 1965 and 1966 are going to be fateful for America, bringing in the 'Fall of America'."[57]

But even though the Muslims may be weaker than they once were, they are still regarded by some as the prototype of the revolutionary movement in the Negro protest. Daniel Thompson has even described the Muslims in these terms: "The modern counterpart of the slave revolts is the Black Muslim movement."[58] Whether other revolutionaries would agree is doubtful. But there are ties that bind the Muslims to the revolutionary movement, and these include:

1) Rejection of nonviolence. Thompson says that Muslims "openly advocate violence as one important means of gaining race pride and respect. Members of this organization have been involved in some violent incidents, and constitute a constant threat; yet, until now, most of their protest has been verbal. Certainly they have not attempted bold, organized revolts comparable to some engaged in by slaves."[59]

2) Insistence on black unity. The Muslims may insist on it to a point that other revolutionaries do not accept, but they agree that separation from the white man can come in stages. "The economic and political links, for example, need not be severed immediately—but all personal relationships between the races must be broken now."[60]

3) Emphasis on pride in being black. The Muslims were preaching this probably before any other nationalist group took it up in recent years. Muhammad has said "the white man was still living in caves in Europe and eating meat raw while our forefathers lived in luxury in flourishing civilization on the banks of the Nile."[61] The Muslims borrowed the black superiority theme from Marcus Garvey, whose "back to Africa" movement came much earlier, but nevertheless stimulated Negroes to "a fierce pride of race by urging the rejection of everything the white man stood for."[62]

4) Deep distrust of the white man. "There is none a black man can trust," the leading teacher has said.[63] As has been noted, other nationalist groups are also playing up this theme. Carmichael has said white people not only cannot be trusted but that "we have found you out. You are rotten through and through."[64]

5) Appeal to the Negro "masses." Although revolutions may be led by leaders from the middle-class, they seek involvement, commitment and support from the lower-class. Few

people dispute that the Muslims have their strongest appeal in the lower-class.

Gordon Parks told of a conversation about Black Muslims with a Negro cab driver in Harlem.[65] The cabbie said: ". . . those Muslims or Moslems, 'ever what you call 'em, make more sense to me than the NAACP and Urban League and all the rest of 'em put together. They're down on the good earth with the brother. They're for their own people. . . ." Parks remarked: "Some people say the Muslims hate all white people." The cabbie replied: "Well, I don't know about that. But if they don't they should. . . ."

It was the cab driver's conviction that "the only thing" that is going to change the white man is "some lead in the belly."

Silas 2X is one of the Muslims who would like to change the white man by placing "some lead in his belly."

Comparing Attitudes

What Henry Walls, as a member of SNCC, and Silas 2X, as a Black Muslim, stand for in the terms of being revolutionaries in the Negro protest has already been discussed. But since there are differences among members in both groups, how close do attitudes compare in terms of any sample taken of a cross section of SNCC people and Muslims in the same city? There are broad points of agreement and differences among black nationalists that have already been outlined. But getting down to the opinion of individuals, do the points of agreement and differences hold? And is there more agreement than difference?

It was possible to complete questionnaires among 45 SNCC members and 22 Black Muslims in Houston. The interviewing was done by separate teams of young Negro men and women. Not all questions were answered and, in some cases, SNCC members answered questions that Muslims did not and vice versa. Where the same question was asked in random surveys of the Negro community, the results are presented for comparison. It must be emphasized that the results presented here were obtained from SNCC members in February 1967 and from Black Muslims and the general community in the summer of 1966. The first outbreak of disturbance occurred on the Texas Southern University campus, where the local SNCC chapter was located, in March 1967. The exchange of gunfire between students and police, and the mass arrests that followed, did not occur until May 1967. Thus, the findings that follow do not reflect changes in attitudes that affected both the general community, as well as SNCC and the Black Muslims, as a result of the violence that broke out later in 1967. (Attitudinal changes occurring in the general Negro community were discussed in Chapter 1).

Several of the questions that were presented to SNCC and Black Muslim members, as well as the general community in most instances, asked about the effects of riots and the use of violence. One was:

"Do you think the riots in Watts helped or hurt the Negro's cause?"

The Results

	SNCC (N = 45) %	Muslims (N = 22) %	Community Sample (N = 487) %
Helped	66	77	31
Hurt	15	9	40
Both helped & hurt	19	14	29

Another question on violence was:

"In what situations, if any, do you think violence is justified in defending Negro rights?"

The Results

	SNCC (N = 45) %	Muslims (N = 22) %	Community Sample (N = 487) %
General justification	80	60	10
Self-defense	9	38	51
Never	11	2	30
Discrimination in general	0	0	9
Defense of property	0	0	0

The groups were also asked:

"Do you think anything like the Watts riot could occur in Houston?"

The Results

	SNCC (N = 45) %	Muslims (N = 22) %	Community Sample (N = 487) %
Yes	71	60	31
No	23	23	42
Maybe	6	17	27

On the basis of these three sets of answers, attitudes toward violence do not appear to differ markedly between the two militant groups in Houston. The Muslims sanctioned some forms of violence—either general justification or self-defense—to a higher degree and felt more strongly that the Watts riots had helped. In terms of a "Watts in Houston," both groups had 77 percent who said "yes" or "maybe" there would be one. In the general community, much more moderate answers were given in the three sets of questions, as would be expected.

A curious finding developed among the Muslims in terms of their attitudes toward police. Both revolutionary groups were asked:

"What do you think about the police in your neighborhood?"

The Results

	SNCC (N = 45)	Muslims (N = 22)	Community Sample (N = 487)
	%	%	%
General disapproval	32	35	30
Disapproval racial	40	5	13
General approval	18	30	37
No Contact	10	30	20

The response toward the police recorded by the general community presents no surprises except in comparison with the higher rate of "racial disapproval" than the Muslims admitted. The fact that the highest percent of "general approval" of police existed in the community sample could be anticipated.

In interpreting the attitudes expressed by Black Muslims, it may be useful to remember that although they gain many recruits from prisons, they also attract many lower-class Negroes who have been given pride in the neck-tie neatness and rigid discipline that the movement has enforced upon them. All are not like Silas 2X and have prison records. But to find 30 percent approving of the police leads to the suggestion that either this question was "hitting too close to home" and the respondents were "blocking" on it or they were simply misrepresenting their attitudes. The interpretation that they were "holding back" is somewhat confirmed by the small percent who were willing to base their disapproval on racial grounds. The finding of 30 percent claiming "no contact" could be interpreted as meaning that these particular Muslims were adhering assiduously to the Islam doctrine of living "separate" lives and having nothing to do with white people, including police.

In examining the SNCC responses, it should be noted

here that 22 percent of the 45 in the sample were from 21 to 25 years old and 20 were from 16 to 20 years of age. In contrast, 17 of the 22 Muslims fell in the 26-35 age group. Five were from 21 to 25 years old.

The age differences appear important since it seems fairly well established that the young are not only more verbal and forthright with their answers but also are more challenging in their behavior—even among revolutionaries. It has been suggested that most young people, such as those in SNCC, have strong hostility toward any kind of authority. And certainly the police represent authority.

In terms of other personal background variables, the SNCC members and Houston Muslims were fairly well matched. The majority in both groups were from Houston, the majority said their parents were living together and, somewhat surprisingly in the case of the Muslims, most claimed to have finished at least high school. There were, however, more college students among the SNCC members, and four Muslims said they worked at unskilled jobs. The majority of Muslims did not answer questions pertaining to occupation.

It has already been noted that both the SNCC and the Muslim movement teach a deep distrust of the white man. But what attitude of distrust or trust do members of both groups have toward people in general, regardless of race?

They were asked:

> "When you meet someone for the first time, what do you do—(1) Trust him until he proves to be untrustworthy? (2) Be cautious about trusting him until you know him better? or (3) Not trust him because he may take advantage of you?"

Again, the factor of age may help explain some of the differences in results, which were:

	SNCC (N = 45)	Muslims (N = 22)	Community Sample (N = 487)
	%	%	%
Trust	42	15	41
Caution	52	50	40
Not Trust	6	35	19

Although there are sharp differences in terms of initial trust or distrust, it can be seen that there is general agreement as to the cautious course that *most* SNCC members and Muslims said they use in their approach to people. It is not surprising that Muslims show more distrust since they are known to be drawn largely from lower socio-economic classes, where suspicion is often a way of life. SNCC members come more from middle-class backgrounds, although Henry Walls—who was not included in this sample—would not represent a trusting attitude despite his having been reared in something better than an impoverished environment.

As for the general Negro community, a smaller percent expressed attitudes of caution in approaching others than did SNCC members or the Muslims, although findings on "trust" were almost equal to those reported by SNCC. These results seem consistent since members of the community, though suspicious toward outsiders and whites, are generally accepting in regard to others.

The emphasis placed by both Muslims and SNCC on Negro initiative and pride was reflected in a question that inquired into "the main problem for Negroes living in Houston." In the random-sample surveys made in the Negro community at large in Houston—using both formal questionnaires and natural dialogue interviews—people responded to such a question by saying jobs, housing and schools were the main problems. This was not so with the SNCC members and Muslims.

Responses to the "main problems" question were as follows:

	SNCC (N = 45) %	Muslims (N = 22) %	Community Sample (N = 487) %
Lack of self-esteem and pride in color	38	50	7
Job opportunities	30	30	33
Schools	2	2	25
Housing	17	16	24
Relations with power structure	10	0	1
General discrimination	3	2	10

Lack of self-esteem and pride in color is, of course, a theme that the Muslims have preached from their very inception. It has been picked up by other nationalist groups, and has now been incorporated in the whole Black Power concept that SNCC started.

Although Black Muslims take no official cognizance of the civil rights movement, the ones in Houston gave answers close to those of SNCC members when it came to the question:

"In the attempts of Negroes to gain their civil rights, have things been going too slowly, about right or too fast?"

The Results	SNCC (N = 45) %	Muslims (N = 22) %	Community Sample (N = 487) %
Too slow	83	83	61
About right	11	17	25
Too fast	6	0	14

A surprising feature to these results is that there was anyone at all in SNCC who felt that civil rights were going "too fast" for the Negro. But in a sample of 45, six percent represents only three people. And one reason this analysis of attitudes has been presented was to show that there can be individual variations in opinion within an organization, although the group itself may seem firmly committed to a position.

The primary reason for the comparison, however, was to test whether similarities in positions of two quite different nationalist groups would hold when individual opinions were sampled. The overall results suggest that they do, particularly when contrasted with attitudes expressed by the Negro community at large.

This does not mean that in terms of responding to their role in American society, Negroes who are inclined to be militant have little choice when it comes to joining revolutionary groups. Each group fulfills certain personality needs, as indicated by the profiles presented of Henry Walls and Silas 2X. It is doubtful that either of these two individuals would have responded to their role in other than a revolutionary manner. But there were enough differences between them, just as there are between SNCC and the Muslims, for them to choose different groups for membership. SNCC did not make Walls a revolutionary any more than did the Muslims make Silas Hookman one. Both brought to their groups the material which each organization could finish shaping.

Although revolutionary groups find the campuses of Negro colleges a fertile source for recruiting members, the vast majority of black students do not actively affiliate with such organizations. At the same time, however, many students do take part in protest movements at Negro colleges. They may not belong to the group leading the protest, but they are often in sympathy with it. There are several psychological factors that contribute to the unrest on the campuses of Negro colleges, and these will be examined in the next chapter.

WHAT SHOULD WE BELIEVE?

POINTS TO CONSIDER—III

A. Let's face the fact that the black revolutionary is likely to be around for some time to come and will continue to attract attention. Let's not make the mistake of believing that his anger is not also felt by other black people—they may not agree with his tactics but they may share some, if not most, of his sentiments.

B. Let's listen to quieter voices from Negroes who are also concerned with the plight of people. They often run the risk of getting drowned out by the rhetoric of the revolutionary. The more attention that is focused on the non-violent spokesman or leader, the more likely that his tactics and approaches for change will gain support from black and white alike.

C. Let's recognize that not every black revolutionary is dedicated to the destruction of society, but that his anger can become an end unto itself and his real goal may well be to keep feeding his anger. Anger can reach a point of saturation, however, where the only step left is acting it out.

D. Let's not fall in the trap of believing that all Black Muslims are the same or all people associated with the Student Nonviolent Coordinating Committee or its current counterpart are alike. They are not. They are individuals and though they may subscribe to the general ideology of their organizations, they may differ widely in behavior.

E. Let's recognize that as one revolutionary group fades from the scene, another is likely to appear. The fact that SNCC and Stokely Carmichael are not heard from as much any more does not mean that other groups such as the Black Panthers have not come along to take up where they left off.

F. Let's not make the mistake of believing that the only way of addressing the black revolutionary is by using the same means he may endorse—namely, violence. His rhetoric is strong and strident and is designed to shock and stir. But this does not mean that there can be no communication with him, and that in a given situation he will not agree there are other ways of handling problems than through violence.

G. Let's not lose our cool over what the black revolutionary has to say about white people. To respond with anger is to play his game.

H. Let's also not forget that there are some black revolutionaries who never say anything—publicly. They have made up their mind about the need for violence in this society, and they are serious about perpetrating it. Whether it is guerilla warfare or some other strategy they choose, we can expect that there will be outbreaks of violence from this quarter, but we must not assume that what they do has the endorsement of 22,000,000 black people in the United States.

I. Let's recognize that guerilla tactics have not been responsible for most riots and that it is misleading to believe that conspiratorial groups using such warfare were to blame for community violence in 1967. Evidence suggests, however, that a sniper group set off the Cleveland riot in July 1968 and may harbinger future such violence.

CHAPTER 4

PSYCHOLOGY OF STUDENT PROTEST

The black campus furnishes a crucible for many of the emotional ingredients that go into riots. There is impatience with the way the world is, there is anger at "the Establishment," there is frustration over a feeling of too little control. There is confusion over identity.

The Negro college campus has provided the battleground for disorders that have spilled over into the black community and were the harbinger of long, hot summers across the land. The focus here will be on the dynamics of the individual students rather than on the activities of specific militant organizations on campuses.

The black student has increasing opportunity to enter the mainstream of American society, but he does not embrace the opportunity with unmixed emotion. The relatively small percent of young Negroes who attend college accept it with ambivalence. They want a better life materially, but they are tied in many ways to the all-black neighborhood, slum or ghetto they call home (one half come from families with annual incomes of $4,000 or less).

Some go back home and try to awaken the apathetic and defeated they have left behind. Some join militant movements that work in Negro communities. They preach Black Power, black pride and nationalism. They look upon all ghetto dwellers as soul brothers and try to forge campus with community. But so few Negroes leave the community for the campus that college largely remains a foreign word. In the area covered by the Southern Regional Education Board, only 15 percent of the 846,000 college-age Negroes attended an institution of higher learning in 1966. Of the white college-age people, 44 percent were enrolled.[1] It has been estimated that the minimum number of Negro young people who ought to enter college, to balance the ratio between blacks and whites, is at least three times the present number.

Those who do enter but drop out constitute a fairly high proportion, despite increasing efforts by colleges to keep them enrolled. Some leave for what they consider to be reasons of principle. Such was the case with a young woman attending Tuskegee University on a scholarship. She took the position that she was being used by "the Establishment," which she believed wanted to bar the average black person from college out of a sense that most Negroes are inferior. She had a friend named Sally who did not make it to college. She said:

> A Negro college student is stepping on a lot of black people . . . the reason Sally didn't go is because she wasn't smart. She was lazy and stupid and ignorant and they're using me to make that point because if I can make it, then there's nothing wrong with the system. It's just something wrong with Sally.[2]

This young woman said in regard to her scholarship— "The great white father gave me a scholarship for being the smartest nigger in Alabama." She was not grateful. She was angry with herself for leaving her less smart brothers and sisters behind—those who were "stupid and ignorant" because, she believed, "the system" never gave them the opportunity to be anything but that. Not unpredictably, this young woman became a Black Power advocate and joined the Black Panthers (see chapter on "The Black Revolutionary"). Steeped in the writings of Frantz Fanon, author of *The Wretched of the Earth,* she finally took up work among the black people of Lowndes County, Alabama.

One easy analysis that could be made of the attitudes and behavior of such young people would be to say they are driven by a sense of guilt about "stepping on a lot of black people." The "marginal man" who opens up new hope and horizons for himself through better education often does feel guilty about his success. And one way he copes with his guilt is by joining movements to make radical changes in the world—changes that would presumably bring a better life to those he left behind in the ghetto.

But if there is guilt in the black student, there is also anxiety and apprehension. He is faced with having to make good, to take advantage of the new opportunities open to Negroes. He must compete on the open market with an education that he is not at all sure has prepared him for the world. As Henry Bullock has observed:

> One of the subtle ironies of our day is the fact that the privileges that desegregation brings to Negroes expose their inadequacies with such force as to drive them back into the protection and security of the segregated world they have always known.[3]

And as a Negro physician points out:

Now that Negroes expect to have equal opportunities with white people, they are finding that the pressure to succeed is greater. More is expected of the person who truly is given equal opportunity to achieve. From the standpoint of demands on the individual and the effects these have on health, you could argue that there are disadvantages to having equal opportunity as well as not having it.[4]

Few young Negroes would argue that there are disadvantages to equal opportunity. In fact, many question whether opportunities are truly equal. But the fear of failure, whether admitted or not, is part of the pressure the black college student feels, and he is not all sure the white world is not stacked against him.

Some who graduate from Negro colleges undeniably do fail in the world beyond the campus, and they fail in disproportionate numbers. A National Industrial Conference Board report found that "personnel managers were critical of diploma standards in segregated schools and colleges. Some said it was necessary to discount by as many as two or three years the grade attainment of Negro applicants from such institutions."[5] Granville M. Sawyer, who became president of Texas Southern University in 1968, notes that the problem really begins with the fact that the Negro student is ill-prepared before he ever enters the black university. Dr. Sawyer has called for "compensatory education" that would establish on each Negro campus an instructional resources center to offer remedial teaching in reading, writing, speaking, listening and arithmetic. He estimated the initial cost at about $100 million.[6]

There is no way a student can hide from himself his lack of preparation to do college work. There is no way he can hide being unprepared for appropriate employment after graduation. He knows he will have to compete with persons who had an opportunity to become better equipped, and he must live with his apprehension to face the world beyond the campus. Anxiety over what the future holds beyond the campus contributes to the unrest on campus. Strength and security are sought in movements of protest, in an acting out of deep and troubled feelings about the world beyond. Dr. Bullock, longtime sociologist at Texas Southern University and now a professor at the University of Texas at Austin, believes the threat of failure in the outside world is a significant

factor in the "withdrawal to resegregation" that can be
found in Black Power ideology. Other observers see youths
being attracted to themes of black unity and separatism on
the basis of a search for identity. Whatever the inner forces
are, they are often expressed in unrest.

A protest environment is characteristic of college life
today. As Lawrence Davis, president of Arkansas AM&N, has
pointed out:

> The Negro student today is prone to protest because he has grown
> up in the midst of the Civil Rights movement and is saturated
> with the Negro's struggle to obtain rights and freedom.[7]

The struggle has become increasingly "violent and vin-
dictive" on the part of college students. Regarding Negro
student revolts, psychiatrist Gordon Blaine suggests two reasons for their stepped-up violence: (1) the civil rights movement has given to civil disobedience a degree of "honor" that
it never had before, and (2) Negro students have more justifiable causes today for complaint.[8] The first reason is related
to what is the "in" thing to do and to be on the Negro campus.
It is now more socially acceptable at many colleges to be a
member of a black nationalist group, or to give support to
such an organization, than to belong to a fraternity or soror-
ity or to be a top student scholastically. As to more justifiable
causes for complaint, it is a fact that students are increasingly aware of how much better the quality of their education
should be for them to compete successfully in the world beyond the campus. The problem here, however, often centers
on lack of massive funds necessary for upgrading quality and
offering remedial training. But many students are concerned
not only with quality but also with kind. They want courses
in black history and a curriculum that promotes black pride.
Black Power students view the administrations of many
Negro colleges as having sold out to the white world and as
having developed institutions designed to keep black people
in their place.

Nathan Hare, a former Howard University sociologist
who was appointed to a post at San Francisco State College,
says that Negro college administrators "generally operate
with an Amos 'n Andy approach, laboring under a system of
second-hand power manipulated by white remote control."[9]
The administration at Negro colleges is often branded by
militant students as being made up of Negroes with "white

minds." The administration serves as a symbol of authority on which the students heap hostility, much like City Hall often acts as a hated symbol for militant members of the black community off campus. Dr. Hare says:

> Black students on Negro campuses are merely rejecting the paternalism (some say 'materialism') of their administrations and, like the black race generally, seeking a new direction.[10]

The hostility of the students in seeking this new direction relates also to the frustration felt in a fragmentation of identity.* The Negro student does not want to be like the faceless ghetto dweller who is locked in a deadend existence. He wants to be part of a proud black people who have their own identity. But this identity has not yet crystallized. The white world still overrides, and it angers him to have to blend in with it. To do so, he feels, fractionates any sense of wholeness. ". . . the question of identity," according to one observation, "has become compellingly important."[11] Although this was said in reference to the Negro community in general, it is even more applicable to the black student. The same is true of these statements on the evolution of the search for identity:

> Since white America seems unready to assimilate the blacks, the new black-conscious leaders respond by rejecting white America. Even the term 'black' has become a badge of honor. . . . The rise of the new African nations was a revelation for Negroes weaned, like whites on 'Little Black Sambo' and cartoons of natives stewing missionaries in iron pots. . . . The Negro was searching for a past he could be proud of; the new Africa handed him one, and a future to boot.[12]

Although some of this analysis is questionable, the black student undeniably has embraced the search for a past with intensity. He does not feel an affinity with those of older generations that have accommodated to the white world, yet he has not worn his new African identity long enough to be sure of its lasting quality. James Farmer has this to say about the desperation with which black students in the United States are searching for an identity in roots abroad:

> I do not think that anyone can grasp the full meaning of the fierce energies driving black youth today except by seeing them

---

*This chapter is concerned with unrest on Negro college campuses, but the problem of identity applies also to black students at predominantly white schools.

as part of the waters of the tidal wave of nationalistic assertiveness that swept Asia and Africa in the wake of World War II.[13]

The student has tried to promote his Afro identity by wearing his hair "natural," dressing in African robes and professing an interest in Swahili. It is all part of "black consciousness" and, as Finley Campbell, who teaches at Morehouse College, has observed: "When black consciousness takes over, you eat your chitlin's with an air of ceremony. . . . When you sit down to take tea, you are losing your identity. Tea is not your bag, man."[14]

Saul Bernstein, in *Alternatives to Violence: Alienated Youth and Riots, Race and Poverty,* links the black youth's rebellion against acquiescence (see my chapter on "The Blue Minority") and his activities in civil rights to a thrust to be "somebody," and to achieve wholeness and identity.

Unchanneled, this thrust can lead to violent upheaval. Long before the student revolt at Columbia University in the spring of 1968, black campuses were experiencing "lockouts" as Black Power students blocked doorways to classrooms, raided cafeterias and staged confrontations with administrators. Participating students and the many more who supported "the cause" found an identity based on the power that comes from aggrandizement.

Such are too often the consequences when the student is left mostly on his own in his search for identity. Some observers believe the Negro college has done little too to help give students a sense of identity based on black pride and culture. I question whether black culture is the only source for finding an identity. But if it is, authorities such as David Riesman and Christopher Jencks, writing in *Harvard Educational Review,* are probably right when they say the Negro college has failed to "promote a distinctive set of habits and values in their students" and has not sought to "preserve a separate subculture" in which the student can take pride and gain a sense of unity. Instead, the Negro colleges have been "militantly opposed to almost everything which made Negroes different from whites, on the grounds that it was 'lower class'."

Riesman and Jencks, I think, do an injustice to Negro colleges and fail to understand the important role the schools have played in producing black people who have taken a lead in breaking down barriers in white society. The colleges they regard as "educational disaster areas" are the very ones, as Dr. Sawyer of TSU points out, that have developed the most expertise in working with highly unprepared and disadvantaged youths to help them take the step into the world beyond the campus. The schools have not had adequate resources to do as good a job with students as they could. In fact, the 35 Negro universities in the United States receive only 1 percent of funds going to higher education. They need greater support.

As for being opposed to "everything which made Negroes different from whites," most black schools have taken a very hard-headed view toward trying to offer training that will put money into the pockets of blacks, that will make them lawyers, engineers, doctors, teachers, as well as socially concerned leaders in the community. Black nationalists have preached the failure of the colleges to promote black pride and the subculture Reisman and Jencks favor, and the message of separatism has led to confusion on the part of many Negro students.

The student is caught between a drive for a black identity—which the nationalists say is to be found in separatism—and the serious attempts made by his college to prepare him for a place in the American mainstream. Out of the split and suspension in which the student finds himself comes rage, and out of the rage come protest and violence. The protest and violence can easily become an end in themselves, since they serve to establish a sense of identity for the student. Those engaging in protest and riot gain a cohesion and a unity, which stay intact as long as the rage keeps pouring forth.

It is simple to say that to be identified as a rioter or a person engaged in violence is self-defeating. But, as we have seen, such identification brings attention and recognition. As the kind of "invisible man" described by author Ralph Ellison, the Negro has little chance of gaining the acknowledgement of others and without this minimum recognition, an identity is impossible. The student feels this more acutely than anyone else, and unfortunately the way that he may seek acknowledgement is through violence. It is not difficult to disguise this search by using an "issue" as the reason for violence. The "issue" may in fact be real. But so is the need for attention and recognition that violence fulfills.

The Negro college student brings out in sharp relief the consequences that come from feeling that he must do something, something striking, to gain acknowledgement to and escape invisibility. What he may do is to adopt a "negative" identity. He may assume a hyperaggressive arrogance toward all white people and a superiority about being black.

Erik Erikson describes similar dynamics in young persons of any color who fail to find "a form for their adolescent powers." He said they may be "driven to despair, to making a totalistic choice, and to accepting a negative identity rather than a positive one that would be fragmented at best."[15] An example of a totalistic choice would be the acceptance of black nationalism, which psychologist Kenneth Clark, a black man himself, has called a "shoddy moral product disguised in the gaudy package of racial militance."[16] Black nationalism teaches a negritude that represents an attempt to establish a wholeness of person, a pride. But it goes beyond this to a philosophy of separatism and a totalism that brooks no alternatives. It is an inflexible extreme. And it requires an object of hate and rage, for such emotions help keep the negative identity intact. Hostile emotions have a unifying function in that all who share the passion that honkies are to be hated are provided with a common enemy. The cohesion is also reinforced by emotional rhetoric, by cries of "racism" to express irate rejection of all the circumstances and conditions that an individual simply does not like—regardless of whether they have anything to do with racial discrimination.* After two weeks of Negro revolt on the campus of Brandeis University in Waltham, Mass., in January 1969, President Morris Abram commented:

> The black students . . . use it [racism] . . . as an epithet, but it has no precise meaning. Generally, it means the world around acting upon them in a way they don't like. And they will admit at the same time that the university they label racist actually has treated them well; it has made incredible efforts to give them not only equality but preference. Yet they will still say it's racist. But when I use the word, I would mean something entirely different. I would mean malignant purpose: discrimination by word or deed or thought against people on account of race.[17]

The rhetoric of racism furnishes a cornerstone to much black nationalism, which is attracting increasing attention on college campuses. The strength of black nationalism cannot be measured solely in terms of how many students actively belong to nationalist movements such as the Afro-Amer-

---

*Because the meaning of "racism" has been so overextended, it has been used sparingly in this book.

ican Liberation groups which have followed in the wake of the prototypic Student Nonviolent Coordinating Committee. There are many students who share the sentiments of such groups who do not belong to any organization. The sentiments, and the sharing of them, serve to establish a common identity and give a sense of direction. In a 1967 survey made among Negro adolescents and young people in Houston, all of high school and college age, it was found that 66 percent said they favored Black Power, such as SNCC Black Power. The same survey found that on the campus of Texas Southern University, 67 percent of the students said they would participate in Black Power movements, although only a fraction of this number actually belonged to the SNCC chapter on campus. This survey was made two months before the campus upheaval of May 16-17, 1967. The percent favoring Black Power and black nationalism rose sharply after the disorder, both off and on campus.

But to infer that the TSU violence, or any other campus outbreak, was caused by Black Power or by the expression of "negative" identities is to miss the point. There is no single cause, psychological or otherwise. The psychological is being emphasized here because it is basic to the aggressive build-up that leads to the explosion. Not all the psychological factors have been explored, however. For instance, there is little doubt that some people get kicks out of violence, on or off campus. This is particularly true of young people. When a riot breaks out, John Spiegel has observed, young people display "an angry intoxication indistinguishable from glee," and a "Roman holiday" atmosphere takes over.[18] There was this "king-for-a-day" and carnival spirit at times on black campuses that were in turmoil in the spring of 1967. Rebellion can be a "fun" thing.

But a situation can go beyond "fun," and destruction can follow. As a crowd becomes destructive, it often is reinforced by the feedback it receives from the sights and sounds of the damage it is causing. As Elias Canetti pointed out in his book, *Crowds and Power:*

> The crowd particularly likes destroying houses and objects . . . It is true that the noise of destruction adds to its satisfaction; the banging of windows and the crashing of glass are the robust sound of fresh life, the cries of something newborn. . . . Everything shouts together; the din is the applause of objects.[19]

Although kicks may be a dominant feeling during the

course of destruction, on or off campus, a sense of power is also of primary importance. Power is related to "being a man," and manhood is important to people who have had little chance to achieve it through the long course of history. The driving need to be identified as "a man" can lead students to engage in dissent for the purpose of dissent, to display anger for the purpose of anger, to challenge any and all who would now hint that black people should not be assertive. Carl T. Rowan, syndicated columnist and first Negro ambassador (to Finland) for the United States, notes that "the least thinking elements on the campus" can intimidate all others just by branding them as unassertive Uncle Toms or Aunt Janes. "So when the chief campus revolutionary says, 'Black brother, are you going to be a real man and help us take over the administration building and break up some furniture?' he sees no alternative to participation than the awful fate of being called an Uncle Tom or a 'house nigger'."[20]

Negro students, then, more than any other group, are searching for full adulthood, for power and identity. They rebel against "boy status," and they may assert an aggressiveness that comes from rage—rage at the Negro's being non-assertive for too long, rage at themselves, rage at the compliance they insist on seeing in the administrators of their colleges, vis-a-vis the white world.

A professor and former dean of students at a Negro college says that what he hears from many black young people is this: They are not interested in joining society, they want to attack and change it—even destroy it, if necessary. They see today's society as self-serving, manipulative, lacking genuine concern and becoming too complex to work with. It is not rational, they believe, and their own actions may not be either—they feel and act before they think.

There are still other factors, of course, in the rebellion of the Negro college student. What adds to the complication is that on top of the race factors—the matter of identity, of manhood, the suspicion toward white society—there are also forces that are affecting all young people in the country today, regardless of color. The former dean touched on one or two. A few others will be added here to show how the unrest on the Negro campus is fed by currents that are sweeping all across the land, producing effects that represent both immediate and longterm consequences.

First, there is the influence of the automated age, the

second industrial revolution. The first industrial revolution introduced mechanical energy to replace manual labor. It developed machines that were operated by men. The second industrial revolution has developed machines that are operated by machines. It is the push-button, everything-is-automatic age. And it has had profound effects on both black and white college students. Each year the American economy can turn out the same amount of goods and services as in the previous year, but with 2 to 3 million fewer workers. The workers who get dropped or are stuck with deadend jobs are those with the least education and the fewest skills. The biggest percent are black, and all the civil rights laws put on the books in this country have not altered this fact. The black man has been told he should have self-determination, but how can a man direct and determine his life if he is faced with chronic underemployment or a deadend job from being a casualty of a highly-technical and complex economy? The black student recognizes the plight of the less educated, and it adds to his sense of unrest and suspiciousness of white society. He also realizes that this feeling of not knowing how to get at the levers of control in life is one that is found even among people who *do* have skills and an education.

It is felt, for instance, by students, both black and white. Many look at the vast "mega-machine" that characterizes the second industrial revolution and wonder how people can be anything but cogs in a giant wheel. The demand now is for technocrats, for people who can—and want to—shuffle papers in bureaucratic organizations, for persons with technical skills. All this means that people who aspire for affluence, and certainly Negroes do, must be better educated and spend more years of their lives in school. They are likely to feel during these years that they are remote from the levers of power controlling their lives, because if they are going to gain the skills necessary for the automated age, they are going to have to listen to teachers, keep their noses in books and put up with a feeling that they do not have much of a voice in what is happening.

The impatience and restlessness felt by young people, both black and white, has been influenced by yet another development—the enormous growth of television. Negro youths are part of the first generation to grow up with television almost from birth. Before members of the 18-to-25 generation ever reached the first grade, many had countless hours in front of the TV screen, watching the whole gamut of human behavior. Television gave them a greater awareness of problems than any other generation ever had. The awareness is of problems the world over. But television did not increase the power to control the problems. Awareness, without power or control, can produce frustration, anger, turbulent behavior. But the awareness brought by TV has not all been of problems. Television, as has already been mentioned, serves as a day-and-night carrier of messages for the affluent society. It flashes images and scenes of material comfort across the screen with rapid regularity. It provides systematic instruction in what comforts a person should have in this society. The commercials equate the comforts and conveniences with happiness and perennial youth. They project a mythology about a life without problems. And there it leaves the viewer hanging. It provides no systematic instruction in what is necessary to gain the material comforts it so grandly parades across the screen. It provides no reality to counter the myth that a certain brand of cigarettes is to be associated with sex, youth and the rugged virility of a tattooed cowboy. Television throws out a scrambled sequence of cues, signals and sensations that can leave the young viewer with a kaleidescopic picture of a confusing world. If the viewer is not old enough to bring order to the images himself, he is likely to come away with greater emotional stimulation than intelligible information about the world.

He is also more likely to be impatient with all the problems he has seen, and ready to act on them out of sheer emotion and sensory stimulation. On television, conflict is seldom resolved by means other than violence. Violence is quick and dramatic, and it leaves the impression that there are no other ways, longer and tedious though they may be, for conflict and disputes between people to be ended. Thus, TV leaves the image of a shortcut for resolution of problems that require time and effort if they are to be settled without violence. It encourages an acting out of feelings to "settle" problems.

A child who grew up in a home where little distinction was made between feeling angry and acting out anger can only be considered a greater candidate for engaging in violence after a daily diet of television. The contemporary campus, including the black campus, inherited the first generation to grow up on such a diet.

The campus also is currently confronted with the first

generation to grow up sharing the world's sense of potential total destruction. Many young people today have mental pictures of death and destruction in their earliest memories. The pictures were embedded there by fathers fresh from World War II, by the widespread apprehension that came with development of the H-bomb, by the sights and sounds of new wars carried into the living room by television from various corners of the world, by missile crises and ultimatums, by assassinations, and by riots in the cities—the burning and bloodshed that have been brought so close to home. But that is outside. Inside, no young person today can fail to sense his own potential for violence, for he shares with mankind the lethal forces that lie latent in all of us waiting removal of the restraint that holds them in check. Every man has the capacity to kill, to destroy, but few people face the painful fact that rage and fury are part of the human condition, and modified forms of both are expressed every day in more acceptable styles of aggressive behavior. As Kenneth Keniston has noted, members of the under-25 generation may well find that their greatest personal conflict will be over control of internal violence.[21] Both the stimulation and sanction of violence come from many quarters today. The decision as to restraint and control lies ultimately with each individual. Senseless wars may rage, injustices may continue, but once the individual taps his own reservoir of violence in forceful protest, he has made a choice that may be hard to reverse— because the acting out of rage can become an end unto itself. As already mentioned, it can bring a heady sense of power and control, it can bring meaning and identity to an individual who has felt lost and isolated. It can show the world how "manly" and forceful a person with private doubts really is. It can arrest attention and arouse public concern, and bring to the knowledge of the world a person—or his group— that has felt small and voiceless. The issue that was first the *reason* for violence can soon be lost beneath the sound of shattering glass and the outraged voices of protest. It can be lost in the very intoxication of released fury.

All men murder in some way, all destroy. Some learn to turn the potential violence to useful ends; most try to deny it; a number fail to restrain it. It is the latter group that now is showing signs of growing, and the campus as well as the city is the battleground—and the site where fateful and irreversible decisions are being made in the name of lofty causes that deserve loftier means of protest.

We have reached the point of individual decision on violence by a series of steps. And one important step has been the exhaustion of our language to express protest. People have run out of words to assert the fury they feel. The impotence of words to express adequately the anger inside people has been accompanied by a rise in rhetoric—rhetoric that is too often a substitute for reason and reality. The rhetoric has not only strained both words and logic, it has given people an easy out by over-classifying humans and events. As the world becomes more confusing and complex, we try to keep it simple—and in order—by extending the classifications and labels. But we run grave risks in these symbolic extensions, for what we end up doing is labeling and stereotyping, forcing individuals into slots where they do not belong, pushing groups of human beings into pigeonholes they have no business sharing. We seize upon gross resemblances among people and events, and label them related when they really are not. It is easier to deal with the world this way. But we do this labeling for other reasons too. It serves our goal to brand people with a stigma of guilt by association, even when the association can be established only by the wildest stretch of logic. The number of people being branded guilty today and held personally responsible for what is wrong with the world is growing as never before. The branding has overtaken the university, both black and white, which is supposed to be the citadel of words used with care and reason.

More and more, our language is becoming an instrument to polarize people and situations. We have the whole country split into two camps, depending on whether they are black or white, over 25 or under 25. This binary method of grouping people does a disservice not only to individuals but also to the language. We simply are settling for stereotypes and labels when we should be seeking words that point up what is special and different about people and the complicated world we live in. But the rise of rhetoric today is forcing labels on people whether they want them or not, and this is an influence that the campus, both black and white, is going to have to contend with more and more. The group that masters the rhetoric is likely to have a distinct advantage as long as we let the language go loose and not require greater precision in the use of words.

None of all this can be translated directly into explaining the revolts that are taking place on black campuses, or any other. But these points must be kept in mind for trying to understand what makes young people today tick and what contributes to their sense of impatience, restlessness and to their demanding demeanor and dogmatic positions.[22]

On the question of campus riots, this much is clear: the traditional underlying causes found in community violence—such as problems of employment and housing—cannot account for college revolts. These problems are sociological and they are not the primary issue. The issue on campus is more psychological. The underlying forces behind college upheavals often spring more from inside the individual than from conditions outside. Riots anywhere, of course, involve psychological dynamics of the participants as well as the sociological conditions that are being protested against.[23] The campus is one kind of Negro community where the psychological is in clear focus.

What can be done about violence on the campus? More understanding is needed of the deep sources feeding the unrest, but at the same time immediate action must be taken to keep violence from breaking out. One part of the solution lies with black students themselves. As one black man, Carl Rowan, has concluded:

> It will take voices of black men who do not fear name-calling, because they harbor no doubts about their manhood, to convince these youngsters that the violent tactics they employ in the name of racial pride are really manifestations of self-hatred, and that the sheepish way they follow the loudest demagogue is not manhood but the 'boy' quality that they have been taught to despise.[24]

As for what university administrations can do *now* about trying to prevent campus violence, I would suggest three recommendations: One has to do with helping more *non*-disadvantaged Negroes enter black colleges. These are young people from families making $10,000 or so a year. It is the first time in the experience of the father and mother—or their forebears—to have money to buy a new car, a new house, new furniture, a new hi-fi and all the other material comforts offered in American society. But after all these purchases, which keep being repeated, there is no money for college for the kids. And at many black universities, the kids do not qualify for grants or scholarships because they do not come from low-income families. Where the kids end up are at

big, white, prestigious universities that are champing des-
perately to raise their quota of black students. *There* the non-
disadvantaged Negro student can gain financial assistance,
as well as admission. But on white campuses they can have
no effect on what happens on black campuses. If they were
admitted to black colleges, they would be the young people
most likely to stand up and oppose the nihilism of black nationalists—they would know from first-hand experience that
opportunity is opening up for Negroes and the society does
not have to be destroyed in the process. So what I am saying
here is that an important buffer group is often missing on
Negro campuses and its absence is being felt. What com-
pounds this problem is that on the white campus, the much-
sought black student often finds himself in a superheated
atmosphere of "excellence," as well as permissiveness. The
emphasis on excellence comes from the increasing demand for
higher and higher scholastic qualifications on the part of
entering students. These qualifications are usually modified
in the search for black students. The Negro student may be
perfectly qualified to do good work, but pitched into a school
that demands excellence, he naturally will seek some haven
of security from the pressure put on him. The haven often
takes the form of what Columnist John P. Roche has called an
"island of black security." The relatively few black students
band together and, with support from faculty and white students, they demand separatism—separate eating facilities,
separate living quarters and a separate department of black
studies. This department is to be run by the students. With a
free hand, they can set standards to take the pressure off
that they feel from the super-competitiveness of the white
institution. I am not saying this is a pattern that holds true
for all black students in all white universities—just places
that have exceptionally high standards and at the same time
a great social concern to "help black people." What they end
up doing is hurting black people, black young people who
would make good leaders on Negro campuses.

The problem generated among black students at predominantly white universities is intensified when the young
Negro is from a disadvantaged background and is even less
prepared to cope with the pressure put on him. Black students
from poverty families, as well as ones from *non*-disadvantaged
backgrounds, gain admission to big, white universities, and
the result can be not only turbulence on the campus but a

disservice to the Negro students. I agree with Dr. Sawyer, president of Texas Southern University, when he says: "We have developed skill for handling deprived youngsters that does not exist on other campuses." The "other campuses" are large white ones, where administration and faculty have no experience and little aptitude for helping disadvantaged students. Much more benefit would come from giving greater support to Negro colleges to help them do a better job of working with such students than is to be gained by raising the quota of black faces on white campuses. With the sort of support that Dr. Sawyer sees as necessary for Negro colleges, black students *can* be adequately prepared for the world beyond the campus and *can* find a place in the mainstream after graduation.

None of this should be interpreted as meaning that all black students should go to Negro schools and that white universities should stay lily white. Black students should go where they have an opportunity to achieve and to gain a sense of competence, not a sense of superheated pressure and a fawning-over by hovering whites. There are small and moderate-sized white colleges, as well as Negro schools, where black students can gain this sense of competence. The Negro schools are better equipped to work with the most ill-prepared, but there are many black students who are quite capable of doing fine work at white colleges that do not emphasize a standard of "excellence" based on scores made on college entrance board examinations, scholastic aptitude tests and the dean's honor roll. Part of a sense of competency comes from developing relationships with other students, white and black, which permit young people to get to know each other as worthwhile individuals. Too often, in pressurized white college environments, the black person ends up being an object of curiosity or is taken on as a "project" by white students and faculty members who act as if they are pursuing some mission of mercy. As I say, my belief is that they only hurt, not help, the black student.

One other point that should not be misunderstood: I am not saying there is no merit to black studies departments, regardless of whether they are at white or Negro schools. It *is* important to promote group pride and identity, and studying the origin, the history and culture of black people is needed. But there is no reason to insist that because people have certain characteristics in common—whether its color, creed or national origin—they must separate themselves from the rest of the society. They can have their group identity and be part of the society also. This is the very nature of a pluralistic society, which is what has evolved in America. Belonging to a group offers protection against isolation, which is a growing problem not only in society as a whole but, undoubtedly, also on the college campus.

My second recommendation for reducing unrest and preventing campus violence applies to both black and white colleges. The psychological forces that feed violence often stem from feelings of isolation. This applies to the community as well as to the campus. It applies to the individual as well as to the group. By isolation I mean having no niche, no place where a person has close contact with others, no place where he can talk and feel accepted. Colleges have mushroomed to such size that to the entering student they represent the psychological counterpart of a move to New York by a person without friends or knowledge of the city. Even universities that do not have 20,000, 30,000, 40,000 enrollment, have become infected with a kind of impersonality and anonymity. I think schools must take on the responsibility of helping the student find a niche, and by "helping," I don't mean force him into some niche. I mean spell out to him the various niches that exist and see which fits him. It might be a niche built around students majoring in the same general field. It might be one centered on people interested in music or in student organizations or in operation of the student center. It might well be a group interested in service off campus. My own bias is toward a niche—a whole series of them—that is built around a place where a group of students can have their own hall or house to eat together, exchange ideas, hold their own seminars, bring in their own lecturers and sponsor their own activities on or off campus. I would have in that kind of niche one or more calm, reasonable, intelligent faculty members and competent adults who would have the courage to enter into the give-and-take and present their own experience and views on the world, as well as to listen to the young people. I recognize that a number of universities have something similar to this kind of niche, but I have the feeling that somehow students who want in do not always get in and some of those in do not really want to stay. In any event, my theory is that when a university fails to work with each student and counsel with him to make sure the right niche is found, then the young people will build their own. And the kind they build may well be dedicated to destruction of the very institution that activates their sense of isolation and powerlessness.

My third recommendation on steps to prevent campus violence would be to make use of student governments in adopting rules against violence and explaining them to each person who applies for admission to the college or university. These rules would be agreed upon in advance by the school's trustees, the administration, the teachers and the students, as represented by their student government. I am aware that student governments at some colleges have hardly been more than attractions for publicity-minded students, but at many others they have functioned with responsibility and respect. The student government required under this recommendation would have to be the latter type, complete with legislative, executive and judicial branches. I am confident that at most colleges, such student governments would join in endorsing a rule saying that violence will not be permitted as a method of protest and anyone who keeps others from going to class or entering a building on the campus will be suspended or expelled. So, assuming that it is agreed in advance that violence is outlawed, I would then leave it up to the students to see that the rule is widely understood. A student representative would sit down with each applicant and explain what is allowed and what is not at the school. The student would explain the rule prohibiting violence and make plain what the consequences are for breaking it. If there are any questions on the part of the applicant, a representative of the administration or faculty would be present to help clarify the rules against violence. But it would be the responsibility of the student government to judge offenders, under a procedure agreed upon in advance by trustees, administration, faculty and students.

In cases where young people have constituted courts and juries for judging their peers, the evidence is conclusive that offenders do not get off lightly. I am confident that where student governments were given genuine authority for adjudication, they would exercise it with responsibility. The vast majority of students, regardless of color, are against violence, but they have no mechanism for unified action. They should be given one.

Clearly, if student governments are going to be made a viable part of the rule making and enforcing machinery on college campuses, students are going to have to have a greater voice in decisions of the institutions—decisions that pertain not only to prohibiting violence but other policies that affect their lives. I think students *should* participate, along with trustees, administrators and faculty, in certain decision-making. I do *not* think the college or university can be turned over to students to run or that they can be given the decision to hire or fire faculty or administrators. If a university represents a community of scholars, then this presupposes that the scholars meet certain standards, which are best judged by their peers. So I think it should be made plain to students that there are *some* decisions that they cannot participate in. But there are many others that they can, and should. Helping to adopt and explain the rule against violence is one of them.

One of the compelling reasons that students should participate with faculty and administration in decision-making is to give the young people greater opportunity to get to know and talk with adults on the campus. The more personal contact there can be between the students and the adults, the more the communications gap between the two is likely to be bridged. The degree to which the gap is bridged, of course, also depends on how many of the campus adults have firm convictions that they are willing to state to students without equivocation. I recognize that colleges are overcrowded and, at many, there are not enough adults (with or without convictions) to have individual conversations and visits with every student. But this lack of personal contact is one of the *underlying,* as well as immediate, problems. It is up to the schools to correct it if some degree of prompt progress is to be made on curbing unrest.

None of the three recommendations I have offered here is proposed as any panacea—only a first step toward positive action in preventing the problem of campus violence. Just as unrest in the community can result from lack of communication, so can unrest on the campus. There are, of course, varying degrees of unrest both places. In the next chapter, we will examine some of the levels of unrest in various cities, as well as within different parts of Houston. We will also see what effect certain action had on violence in the city.

WHAT SHOULD WE BELIEVE?
POINTS TO CONSIDER—IV

A. Let's recognize that campus unrest is fed by many of the same psychological *forces that play a part in community violence—a need to be assertive after centuries of passivity, a need for acknowledgement as a black person with pride, a need to feel competent in an increasingly complex and demanding world, a need to establish some group refuge where there is security and acceptance.*

B. Let's also recognize that in the search for satisfaction of these needs there may be expressions of hyper-aggressiveness, black superiority, strong antagonism toward the white world and a retreat to an all-black separatism.

C. Let's quit pushing the black student into the pressurized environments of large, white universities where he becomes the object of "charity" on the part of white students and faculty members seeking a catharsis for guilt on the race question.

D. Let's recognize that Negro colleges and universities have an expertise for helping ill-prepared high school students to catch up and gain some sense of competency. Let's give the colleges the substantial support they need to do a better job.

E. Let's face the fact that among the psychological factors that play a part in violence is a very simple one called "kicks" and that students, regardless of their color, can easily raise issues and demands as a means to get their kicks.

F. Let's also face the fact that once anger and rage are released in the fight for an issue, legitimate or not, these powerful emotions can become paramount and, under such conditions, students cannot permit demands to be satisfied because they will lose their reason for rage.

G. Let's recognize that a feeling of closeness, cohesion and identity is important to students and that the powerful emotions of anger and rage can furnish the means to satisfy this feeling.

H. Let's not forget, however, that the growing impersonality and anonymity of colleges have militated against students gaining a feeling of closeness, cohesion and identity and that it is the responsibility of the institutions to help the student find a niche that will reduce the isolation he can so easily feel.

I. Let's also not forget that students should *participate in decisions that affect their lives at college and that even though they cannot be handed the whole institution to run, they should share in many of the policies that heretofore boards, committees, the administration and the professoriat have made alone. Acting responsibly often is a function of being responsible for something on which to act.*

J. Let's give students more opportunity to have one-to-one relationships with reasonable adults on campus and have a free exchange of ideas and emotions on an individual, *as opposed to group, basis. It is in the relationship of just two people that a person often finds himself and his ability to cope effectively with the world.*

K. Let's not double-talk to students. On the question of violence, let's spell it out in advance that any behavior that abridges the rights of others to attend class or carry out the functions of the institution will never be countenanced.

L. Let's not overlook the influence that a number of developments in the last 20 years have had on young people, regardless of color. These forces have contributed to the impatience, the unrest and the demands by students on both black and white campuses. To counter the developments, we must find ways to personalize a society that is growing increasingly complex and anonymous, we must point up the need for people to understand their own potential for violence, we must try to bring order to the chaotic array of images that television often leaves with the young, and we must try to restore some precision in the use of words and not let rhetoric drown out reason.

CHAPTER 5

DEGREES OF UNREST AND EFFECTS OF ACTION

When a city is faced with heightened tension or a community crisis, it is important to know if steps being taken to reduce unrest or preserve peace are having the desired effect. Making surveys to determine the degrees of underlying unrest is clearly useful. Long-term programs can be formulated on the basis of what people say their most pressing problems are. But often, short-term steps also must be taken to head off violence or keep it from spreading, and some systematic measure of the effect is needed.

In this chapter, we will examine the reaction of the black community in Houston to steps taken to reduce mounting tension. We will also look at the various degrees of unrest that were found in Houston as compared with other cities.

The root causes of social unrest have already been mentioned—problems such as employment, housing and education. We also saw how the degrees of unrest vary according to certain "sead" factors—the spotlight of attention given to violence and threats of violence, the expectations of people in the community, their attitudes toward existing conditions, the dispersion of the ghetto.

When violence breaks out, it is useful to see what the people themselves say about what caused it. It helps to know if they think so-called root causes are responsible or if more immediate influences played the biggest role. As I indicated in the Introduction, Houston was at the brink of a community riot when a service station operator shot a Negro man in August 1967 and, in response, people in the neighborhood (mostly youths) burned the station to the ground, looted two stores and set a supermarket down the street ablaze. During the next 36 hours there were 20 firebombings of white-owned establishments in Negro neighborhoods. To see what people in the black community felt about all this, a random-sample survey was promptly conducted. One question asked was this:

The burning of 20 buildings continued for three nights when Molotov cocktails or firebombs were thrown at buildings. Do you think the people who did this were protesting against bad living conditions in the city, or about lack of job opportunities, or about broken promises by the city, or about "police brutality," or were they just vandals who were trying to stir up trouble and start a riot?

Here were the answers we received: 22.5 percent of the people said the firebombings represented a protest against lack of job opportunities; 21.5 percent said "police brutality" was being protested (although police were not involved in this incident); 18.4 percent said bad living conditions; 8.5 percent said broken promises of the city. The largest number said none of these things was responsible—29 percent replied that the outbreak was due to "Vandals who were trying to stir up trouble and start a riot."

Various authorities have repeatedly stated that *all* community violence represents a revolt against the conditions imposed upon Negroes by white racism and oppression. The Houston findings would suggest that such a generalization may be overextended. This is not to say that root causes have no part. It is only a reminder that the people themselves recognize that other influences can be immediately significant in outbreaks of violence.

After the firebombings spread from the Sunnyside area where they began on the night of August 16, 1967, we were faced with the problem of how to stop them. As has been pointed out, the Negro community of Houston is widely dispersed. The firebombers were using a hit-and-run technique of driving into a neighborhood, throwing a Molotov cocktail at a store, and speeding away. I suggested to the mayor and police chief that we organize a "block watcher" corps of community people to stay on the lookout for any sign of the highly mobile firebombers. They agreed, and some 200 volunteers— many from the Harris County Community Action Association as well as from neighborhood groups—were organized into a team of "block watchers." Once they took their posts and the word spread that they were throughout the Negro community, the firebombings ceased. Ten people, most of them youths, were later charged with arson in the outbreak.

In a survey done in the community to determine the reaction to the block watcher program, most people gave it their approval. They also approved of the tactics that police adopted in greatly increasing the number of patrol cars in the most heavily-populated Negro area, the Third Ward. It was impossible, with a shortage of police and a spread-out Negro community, to step up patrols in all areas, but where there were no officers, there were block watchers.

By getting feedback from the community on steps taken to prevent the spread of violence or to restore peace, city officials have objective measures for determining whether tactics truly help or hurt. They can also assess the effects of programs that are designed to get at some of the root causes of unrest. For instance, it has already been noted that a Job Fair for disadvantaged youths was held for the first time in the hot summer of 1967. Some 1,300 young people from 16 to 22 years old, mostly Negroes, were hired on the spot by companies that were asked to set up interview desks at the downtown coliseum. To determine what the black community thought about the Job Fair and to see what effects it seemed to have on racial tension, interviewers were sent into representative black neighborhoods and asked this question:

> What effect do you think the summer Job Fair for disadvantaged youths had on racial tension in Houston?

There were five options presented to each person from which he could choose one or more answers. The responses were: 45 percent of the people had a favorable reaction to the fair (24 percent said it reduced racial tension; 21 percent said it "showed that employers in Houston and the mayor's office were trying to indicate that they do care about the welfare of Negroes"); 30 percent had a neutral response (they said the Job Fair had no effect on community tension); 15 percent had an unfavorable reaction (they said it "increased racial tension because not all the people who applied got jobs"), and 10 percent said they did not know that there was a fair held.

Employment for disadvantaged young people is just one factor, of course, that influences the degree of unrest that a city may have. To chart the tensions in a community, a number of other concerns must be considered, including attitudes toward the use of violence to advance the Negro's cause, attitudes toward the rate of integration, and toward religion—religion being one internal control that people use for curbing their potential for violence. As has been mentioned, by using such measures, we were able to put together a running "temperature chart" of tensions in the city for more than a year.

This chart was based on a composite of attitudes that members of the Negro community expressed toward concerns that contribute to tension in the city. The most volatile of these concerns is police relations. Figure 8 shows the relatively stable "temperature" that prevailed for police-community relations through January 1967. As will be noted, the majority of black people had moderate attitudes toward police, responding that some officers were okay and others were not. The top line on the chart indicates this prevailing response. The solid black line in the middle represents the attitudes of Negroes who had definitely negative feelings toward police —considering them "abusive." The smallest percent—repre-

Figure 8

SUBJECT S'ATTITUDE TOWARD THE HOUSTON POLICE TREATMENT OF THE NEGRO

1967 - 68

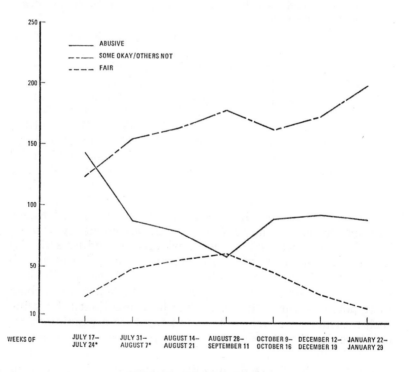

| WEEKS OF | JULY 17– JULY 24* | JULY 31– AUGUST 7* | AUGUST 14– AUGUST 21 | AUGUST 28– SEPTEMBER 11 | OCTOBER 9– OCTOBER 16 | DECEMBER 12– DECEMBER 19 | JANUARY 22– JANUARY 29 |

*Adjusted to conform with figures based on <u>300</u> interviews

sented by the dotted line at the bottom—gave the police a definitely positive rating, considering them "fair" in their relations with black people. As we saw in "The 'Sead' Factors of Unrest" and as will be noted in the chapter on "The Blue Minority," the prevailing moderate attitude changed sharply after violence occurred at Texas Southern University. In fact,

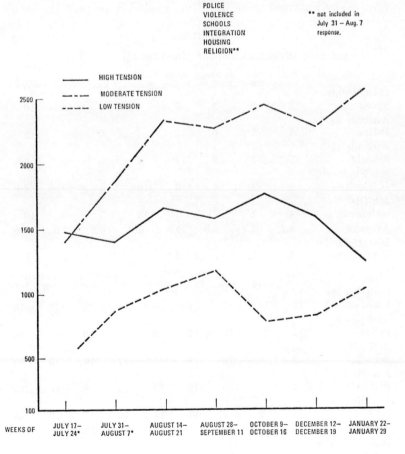

Figure 9

COMMUNITY TENSION SCALE

1967 - 68

based on combined responses in seven categories:

JOBS
POLICE
VIOLENCE
SCHOOLS
INTEGRATION
HOUSING
RELIGION**

** not included in
July 31 – Aug. 7
response.

HIGH TENSION
MODERATE TENSION
LOW TENSION

| WEEKS OF | JULY 17–
JULY 24* | JULY 31–
AUGUST 7* | AUGUST 14–
AUGUST 21 | AUGUST 28–
SEPTEMBER 11 | OCTOBER 9–
OCTOBER 16 | DECEMBER 12–
DECEMBER 19 | JANUARY 22–
JANUARY 29 |

*Adjusted to conform with figures based on 300 interviews

starting in February, activities by dissidents began to increase, and police were brought closer to outright confrontation. There were marches downtown, charges brought by university authorities for individual violence on campus, and a massive sit-in outside the courthouse.

In the community, tension was also plotted on attitudes toward six concerns in addition to police: jobs, use of violence to advance the Negro's cause, schools, integration, housing and religion. A number of questions were asked regarding each concern. Responses were recorded on the basis of whether people gave a negative, moderate or positive opinion on the subject. By adding up all the responses in each category—how many answers were negative, moderate or positive on all

TABLE 1

Index of Dissatisfaction for Minority Areas in Houston

	3rd Ward	5th Ward	Kashmere Gardens	Acres Homes	Almeda	Hts.	2nd Ward	Settegast
Civil Rights Speed	2	9	3	5	1	4	14	16
Attitude to Police	1	7	6	3	4	8	4	2
Attitude to Schools	7	4	8	12	1	8	2	5
Job Finding Difficulty	2	1	6	6	10	6	10	6
Job Dissatisfaction	4	1	2	2	13	5	5	10
Average	3.2	4.4	5.0	5.6	5.8	6.2	7.0	7.8
Dissatisfaction Total Rank	1	2	3	4	5	6	7	8

	4th Ward	1st Ward	West End	Clinton Park	Pleasantville	Sunnyside	Riverside	Foster Place	Harrisburg
Civil Rights Speed	12	11	7	7	10	14	13	17	18
Attitude to Police	13	14	15	17	18	11	10	12	16
Attitude to Schools	3	6	16	14	11	17	10	15	18
Job Finding Difficulty	2	2	5	13	12	16	18	16	15
Job Dissatisfaction	10	9	7	14	14	10	17	17	14
Average	8.0	8.4	10.0	13.0	13.0	13.6	13.6	15.4	16.2
Dissatisfaction Total Rank	9	10	11	12	12	14	14	16	17

the questions pertaining to jobs, police, violence, schools, integration, housing and religion—an overall tension scale was constructed, as shown in Figure 9. Again, it can be seen that up until February 1967, the overall tension level was moderate.

In addition to plotting the amount of tension existing in the whole community and toward each issue or concern, it was possible also to chart how much dissatisfaction existed in minority areas of Houston, as discussed in greater detail in the author's June 1968 report on *Detection of Potential Community Violence*.[1] Each area was ranked according to the amount of dissatisfaction expressed in regard to five concerns: the civil rights movement, police, schools, finding employment, and kind of work done. Table 1 presents the findings.* Figure 1 in Chapter 1 shows the location of the areas named.

It will be noted that the Third Ward ranked first in level of dissatisfaction. Although no community-wide riot occurred in Houston during the period the surveys were made and the chart of dissatisfaction was applicable, there was one near outbreak in the Third Ward in July 1967. This was described in the Introduction. Several windows were knocked out in white-owned stores and two Molotov cocktails were tossed in the street, but non-violent militants moved into the roving band of demonstrators and persuaded them to disperse. On other occasions, bricks were thrown at white people driving cars through Texas Southern University, which is in the Third Ward. All during the spring of 1967, there were demonstrations and marches at Texas Southern University. Although this activity did not involve the Third Ward as a community, a number of students who participated lived in the area and were included in the survey that ranked the area first in level of dissatisfaction.

One failing of the chart was the low level of dissatisfaction assigned to the Sunnyside area. It was in this area that a series of firebombings started in August 1967. But during the three nights that they occurred, stores hit were mostly in the Third Ward.

The Fifth Ward came up as second in the level of dissatis-

---

*I am indebted to Douglass Price-Williams of Rice University for analyzing interview data and designing the index of dissatisfaction by geographical area. Appendix D presents the method by which the analysis was computed.

faction. After the TSU incident, the Student Nonviolent Coordinating Committee—which had led the demonstrations and marches at TSU—moved to the Fifth Ward and held a number of rallies during the summer. Although no riot broke out in the area, attempts were made to stir the people to action. People did have grievances in that part of the city but they did not respond to highly vocal demonstrations. Black Power advocates distributed circulars door-to-door to residents in "the Bottom." A copy of one message is shown in Figure 10. The reaction was not what was sought. One homeowner in the area began sitting on his front porch with a shotgun across his lap, threatening to shoot anyone with Molotov cocktails. Neighborhood people organized a block-watch team to "cool" any efforts of riot-prone demonstrators. No efforts developed.

FIGURE 10

CIRCULAR DISTRIBUTED IN HOUSTON

ARE YOU READY

If Not let's get ready, just like Newark, just like Detroit. . . . What are we as concerned Negroes going to do about our present situation in Houston. Are you ready landlords, storekeepers, pawnshops, brokers, to meet across the conference table or would you rather the streets.

BROTHERS AND SISTERS
GET YOUR HEARTS RIGHT. ARE YOU READY TO USE
YOUR RIGHT ARM, LEFT ARM, MOLOTOV COCKTAILS,
CHILLI-BRICKS, MACHINE GUNS, SHOTGUNS,
OR ANY KIND OF GUN.

If not, you had better prepare yourself baby, because we are next, our day is coming.

FIGHT FOR YOUR RIGHTS
ARE YOU READY   ARE YOU READY   ARE YOU READY
WE BUILT AMERICA UP; WE WILL BURN IT DOWN.
GET READY   GET READY   GET READY
BLACK POWER
ARE YOU READY? GET READY!
ARE YOU READY? GET READY!

Now that we have taken a brief look at how tensions varied in the different sections of the Negro community in Houston, let's turn to some comparisons with other cities. In cooperation with William McCord, then of Rice, and Douglass Price-Williams, chairman of psychology at Rice, we arranged for 613 interviews to be conducted in Watts and Oakland, California. In Oakland, a formal questionnaire was employed instead of the "natural dialogue" technique, which was used in Watts and Houston. Findings will also be presented here from cities such as New York, Chicago, Atlanta and Birmingham. These surveys were made by John F. Kraft[2]; Gary Marx[3] and Brink and Harris.[4]

First, how do Negroes from different parts of the country feel about the speed of integration? As indicated below, the most dissatisfied appear to be people in New York and the most satisfied the members of the Negro community in Birmingham. The tabulation by city is as follows:

	New York (N=190) %	Chicago (N=133) %	Atlanta (N=192) %	Birmingham (N=200) %	Houston (N=2025) %
Too slow	51	38	31	24	39
Too fast	2	3	2	1	2
About Right	39	55	63	72	58
Don't Know	8	4	4	4	1

On the question of integration of schools, black people in both Houston and Birmingham expressed not as high interest, but nevertheless opinion was decidedly in favor of Negroes attending school with whites. When Negroes were asked whether they would prefer their children to attend an integrated school, 96 percent in the New York survey said yes, 93 percent in Chicago, 84 percent in Atlanta, 79 percent in Birmingham and 75 percent in Houston.

The subject of riots is one that finds few significant differences among cities. When asked about the value of riots in promoting the Negro cause, black people in New York were surprisingly the most condemning. Fifty-seven percent said that "no good can ever come from riots." Those who took the same position in other cities were: Houston—41 percent; Chicago—38 percent; Birmingham and Atlanta—26 percent.

As we have already seen, opinions toward police seem to change dramatically after violence occurs. Chapter 1 presents such changes after the Texas Southern University disturbance. Before the violence, opinion toward police was surpris-

ingly favorable. The same can be said of opinions in other
cities, as indicated by the question and responses below:

How would you say that the police treat Negroes—very well, fairly
well, fairly badly or very badly?

	Houston	New York	Chicago	Atlanta	Birmingham
	%	%	%	%	%
Very Well	5	9	11	13	5
Fairly Well	47	47	53	40	26
Fairly Badly	26	16	11	21	18
Very Badly	11	18	12	18	42
Don't Know	11	10	13	8	9

A number of disorders have since occurred in the four
cities besides Houston, and the level of dissatisfaction toward
police has undoubtedly increased. As has been mentioned and
will be discussed in some detail later, after the hostility increased in Houston in the summer of 1967, a program was
launched to bring policemen and members of the Negro community together in small-group sessions so that they could
get to understand each other better.[5] This pilot program has
received nationwide attention from the news media and police
departments as a means of reducing prejudices on both sides.

Since the "natural dialogue" technique was used in both
Watts and Houston and the same questions were asked of
ghetto dwellers in both places, it was possible to determine
which city was the more militant. Particular attention was
given to young men who were under 30, had attended high
school for at least a short period and were unskilled. This is
the group that seems most involved in riots. They were leading
participants in the Watts riot as well as the one two years
later in Detroit. The comparison by city was made on several
questions pertaining to unrest. In each case, the results presented here are for the under-30 matched group of young men,
not for the entire sample in Watts and Houston. There were
36 in this category in Watts and 141 in Houston.

The Results:	Watts	Houston
	%	%
In what situation is violence justified for Negro rights?		
Always opposed	19.4	25.5
If attacked	38.9	60.3
Gain attention	8.4	9.9
Only way to accomplish desired result	33.3	4.3

	Watts %	Houston %
What do you think of Black Power?		
Against it	5.6	41.8
In favor	77.8	34.8
Never heard of it	16.6	22.0
No answer		1.4

	Watts %	Houston %
What do you think of police treatment of Negroes?		
Fair	2.8	13.5
Some O.K., Others Not	44.4	55.3
Abusive	50.0	30.5
No answer	2.8	.7

Surprisingly, when men over 30 were compared with those under 30, no sharp differences of opinion emerged. This was true of both cities. In Watts, where a total of 426 "natural dialogue" interviews were conducted, 60 percent of the older men favored Black Power and 17 percent were "always opposed to violence." In Houston, the older men expressed even greater militancy than the younger on two questions. Forty percent regarded police as abusive and 45 percent favored Black Power.

The Watts riot showed, however, that a number of people can express militant views without acting upon them. The younger people led the action in Watts while the older gave support from the sidelines. Thus, the fact that the older group gave stronger opinions on several questions in the surveys made in Watts and Houston does not mean they are the most likely to participate in disturbances.

In the chapter on "The 'Sead' Factors of Unrest," it was emphasized that expectations play a major role in shaping the attitudes and opinions of ghetto dwellers. It was suggested that the expectations level of Houston people was lower than that in California. Many of the Negroes in California went there with high expectations. They were disappointed by what they found. They became frustrated and angry. And their strong feelings showed up in comparison of opinions between California cities and Houston.

Oakland results were gathered by a formal questionnaire administered to 187 ghetto dwellers. The same questionnaire was given to 572 black people in Houston. The following questions and results indicate the greater militancy in Oakland:

Q. Do you think the riots in Watts and other cities have helped or hurt?*

	Oakland %	Houston %
Helped	50.8	32.3
Hurt	26.7	41.1
No Effect	11.8	3.2
Both helped and hurt	2.7	11.2
No answer & don't know	8.0	12.2

Q. In what situations, if any, do you think violence on the part of Negroes is justified?

	Oakland %	Houston %
Self Defense	43.8	24.5
Never	20.3	45.6
Other reasons	13.4	1.6
No answer or opinion	22.5	28.3

It is likely that as the level of expectations rises in Houston, the degree of dissatisfaction and unrest will more closely approach that in California cities.

Because the surveys in Houston included such a large number of interviews, it was possible to make useful comparisons between sub-groups in the overall sample. Taking results from 2,026 "natural dialogue" interviews, a determination was made of the relationship of such factors as age, sex, education, occupation and religiosity to the opinions expressed by a person. Through this sort of analysis, a focus was drawn on which people were expressing the most concern and indicating the most unrest. Some findings:

On Black Power

Surprisingly, women expressed greater sympathy than men for Black Power. Older people of both sexes disapproved of it. There were no clearcut findings on the influence of education and occupation. Generally, high school graduates expressed greater approval than either persons with less or those with more education.

---

*John Howard was in charge of interviewing in Watts and Oakland.

On justification for violence

Men expressed more inclination than women to use violence in gaining Negro goals. Younger members of the white-collar class were more likely to sanction violence than the unemployed. However, when white-collar workers of all ages were considered, they expressed greater disapproval of violence than did all age groups in the unemployed. The effect of expectations and frustrations on attitude was found when a group was considered that was made up of college educated men who had been forced to accept unskilled jobs. They expressed strong sanction of violence. The same was not found among women in this category. The women perhaps did not expect so much from their college education.

On participation in civil rights

Women expressed almost no affiliation with civil rights activities or movements. Men claimed active involvement. Young men in particular said they were involved. One contradictory finding emerged when the opinions of young people were analyzed regarding satisfaction with schools, with police, housing and jobs. They expressed greater tolerance toward conditions than did older people. At the same time, they more often approved of Black Power, of the use of violence and they claimed greater participation in civil rights movements.

On police

It would seem that the amount of contact a person has with police would bear directly on his opinion of them. This was not confirmed, however, when the opinion of women was compared with that of men. Although the men undoubtedly had greater contact, the women expressed greater hostility.

The most significant shift in opinion toward police occurred among men who had graduated from college. They moved from a position of expressing the least antipathy (before the TSU disturbance) to the most (after TSU).

Black and white views

The degree of unrest that exists in Houston or any other city relates not only to concerns involving police, civil rights, violence, Black Power and riots, but also to the more personal equation of how blacks and whites regard each other. Since direct contact between the two is still limited, whatever opinions each has toward the other are largely based on second-hand knowledge. Negroes are still convinced that white people regard them as inferior. As long as this opinion is held, Negroes are naturally going to feel resentment toward whites. Many white people undoubtedly continue to give Negroes the impression they are inferior, and this contributes to a sub-surface friction between the races.

In Houston our Negro interview teams asked 572 members of the black community this question: "What do you think the average white person thinks about Negroes?" A total of 48.6 percent said they believed whites thought blacks were "ignorant and inferior"; 9.3 percent said white people believed Negroes were "bad in general" or "crazy"; 4.4 percent felt whites regarded them as highly aggressive, and 1.4 percent said whites looked upon Negroes as being both good and bad. There were 26.6 percent who had no opinion or gave no answer. Only 9.7 percent said white people have a favorable opinion of Negroes.

When an analysis was made by occupation of what Negroes think white people think of them, the results showed that the unemployed and unskilled worker was most likely to think that whites considered them "ignorant and inferior." It is from this group that riot participants are drawn, and there seems to be little doubt that they are motivated, at least in part, by a hostility toward "Whitey," as indicated by the following:

Q. What do you think the average white person thinks about Negroes?

	Unemployed (N=42) %	Unskilled Blue Collar (N=352) %	Skilled Blue Collar (N=107) %	White Collar (N=32) %
Ignorant and inferior	61	50	37	31
Aggressive against whites	0	2	9	9
Bad in general/crazy	9	11	12	10
Good in general	2	11	9	9
Mixed (good and bad)	0	2	2	7
No answer	26	24	30	34

An analysis was also made by age and sex. It was found that more younger Negroes think white people have a particularly unfavorable opinion of them. Again, as long as such a view is held, it can only feed the hostilities of Negroes. And with younger black people more inclined to take part in violence, it seems particularly important that the idea that they are regarded as "ignorant and inferior" be dispelled. The results by age and sex were: Fifty-three percent of those under 30 said the average person thought Negroes were "ignorant and inferior," as compared with 42 percent over 30. There was little difference in opinion among males and females. Forty-seven percent of the men believed whites considered Negroes "ignorant and inferior," compared with 48 percent of the women.

Although Negroes may have limited contact with white people, they nevertheless get mad at them. In a survey made among 895 members of the black community in Houston, 53.3 percent said white people made them mad either "often" or "sometimes;" 33.7 percent said "seldom," and 13 percent said "never." These figures probably represent conservative responses, since many Negroes are not willing to admit anger—even when asked by another black person.

There is not likely to be a day when human beings, regardless of color, will keep from getting mad at each other. But with more direct contact between whites and blacks, there ought to be less inter-racial anger as greater understanding develops.

The focal point now of so much misunderstanding and anger lies in the relations between police and ghetto dwellers. The police are a minority group themselves, subject to many of the same problems as other minorities. In the next chapter we will take a closer look at the troubled relations that can exist between Negroes and police and examine the embattled position in which law enforcement officers often find themselves.

WHAT SHOULD WE BELIEVE?

POINTS TO CONSIDER—V

A. Let's recognize that community people have a good grasp of what goes on in their neighborhood and when violence breaks out, they will often place blame where it belongs, even when their own kids may be responsible for it.

B. Let's not assume that police are considered such a natural "enemy" to neighborhood people that they do not want them in their area. People want protection and they rely on police to give it to them, even though they may have doubts toward police in general. In times of potential violence, it is not correct to assume that increased patrols will automatically heighten the tension. The patrols may be regarded as helping to prevent the spread of any violence, such as sporadic fire-bombing.

C. Let's recognize that many community people are willing to participate in efforts to prevent their neighborhoods from being burned down. They will join block-watcher groups to guard against firebombings, if they are approached with the facts and are asked to volunteer.

D. Let's recognize that when highly-vocal dissidents denounce efforts such as Job Fairs for disadvantaged youths because jobs were not found for all applicants they are not expressing the sentiments of community people. The people themselves usually consider such projects worthwhile.

E. Let's also recognize that separatists loudly denounce integration, but that surveys in cities across the nation show that the people want it.

F. Let's consider what Negroes believe white people think of them. Better relations in this country are going to come very slowly if white people continue to give the impression that black people are inferior. Many white people are not doing this, but Negroes believe they are. Their belief, rather than the fact, is what we must address ourselves to. For a white person to go overboard to "prove" that he does not believe black people are inferior is not going to help. What will help is for white people to treat Negroes with the same dignity that any human being deserves. Nothing more and nothing less.

CHAPTER 6

THE BLUE MINORITY

This is the way it used to be between police and Negroes—
and still is, in the minds of an undetermined number of
black people:

"You're a smart nigger. Take off your hat."

Abner Calder, 28, reached up to take off his hat.*

"Leave your hat on, nigger."

Now it was the second policeman talking. He said leave
the hat on. His partner said take it off.

"I can't do both," Calder said.

"Don't get smart, smart nigger," the first policeman said.

Each time he heard the word "nigger," Calder felt a
surge of anger. It wasn't that the insult was new to him. He
had just been away from it awhile—but not so long that he
did not remember that he was expected to keep his place. His
place was pretty much decided at birth. He was born in a
small Texas town, graduated from the "colored" high school
there; finished two years at a Negro college, and served in the
U. S. Army in Korea. Now he was back home, a veteran, but
he knew that to white policemen, he was still a "nigger."

To the two policemen who had put him in their patrol
car, he was a "smart nigger." This they agreed on. What they
went to great pains to disagree overtly about was whether he
should or should not remove his hat while in their patrol car.
There was also the problem with his hands. He was told by the
officer who insisted he remove his hat that he should keep his
hands between his knees. He knew the two white men were
baiting him, but he kept from saying what he wanted to say,
which was: "Look, you bastards, you're determined to make
me act the part you have cut out for me. You're determined
I'm going to prove to you that I am a 'smart nigger' by sass-
ing you or 'failing to obey an officer.' I'll rot in hell before
I give you the satisfaction."

So Abner Calder, a tall, well-built Negro citizen of the

---

*"Calder" is a pseudonym.

177

United States, dropped his eyes, kept his hands between his knees and vowed that he would not lose his temper. Ten years later, when he recounted this episode as his introduction to life in the urban South, he found reason to be grateful for the fact that there were two policemen baiting him that spring afternoon instead of one.

"I knew then, as I know now, that I would never let any one man, white or black, armed or unarmed, treat me like that. It was just a question of two against one that kept me from doing something that day I felt very much like doing— and that was beating hell out of someone for calling me a 'smart nigger'."

At one time in his life Abner Calder would have accepted the "nigger" label as a role from which he could not expect to escape. His father had lived with it. His mother had. So before he entered the Army to fight in Korea, he had no reason to believe that he would not have to live with it also.

But the Army did something to Calder. He found in the push on Pusan that the blood of the Negro was the same color as the blood of the white man. He found that the color of a soldier's skin could hardly be distinguished in the cold mud of a battlefield where race was as irrelevant as the price of eggs in China. If Calder had not found affirmation in his own human value, completely apart from the question of color, he might have gone on accepting the faceless image that his father and mother had learned to live with all their lives. But Calder found affirmation if for no other reason than that the Army let him know that he had intelligence, leadership potential and the ability to become a platoon sergeant. In Korea, when he earned his three battle stars, no one cared what color was beneath the mud, and he almost forgot that back home he could ever be considered a "smart nigger" by people whose flag he was fighting under.

But "smart nigger" he was, because after working all day in a hot dry cleaning plant, he boarded a bus in the late afternoon and dared to take the only vacant seat, which happened to be beside a white man.

It did not even occur to him that when the driver made motions toward the back of the bus through the big mirror in front, he was being summoned to account for "breaking the law." And it did not occur to him that when the bus stopped beside a patrol car at a red light that the two policemen who got out were boarding the bus to remove one Abner Calder,

28-year-old-man, U. S. Army veteran. But now he knew, as he was riding to jail, with one officer telling him to take his hat off and the other one saying to keep it on, that he had not escaped the role of "nigger."

Ten years later, Calder was manager of a five-chair barber shop in a small Negro shopping center. It was next door to a grocery store where a Negro was shot to death as the aftermath of being accused of shoplifting. Calder watched the white police who gathered at the scene after the shooting—after one of their fellow officers, also white, fired three bullets from a .45 revolver into the chest, arm and aorta of the Negro accused by the white store owner of shoplifting. Calder had never even talked with a white policeman after his own brush with the law, after spending two hours in city jail 10 years ago while his wife was contacted and came to bail him out on a $25 disorderly conduct charge.

But standing at the barber shop window, Calder remembered his role as a "smart nigger," and when he saw the buttons being passed out, he went outside and took one. It read: "I believe in human dignity." He pinned it on his white barber's jacket in front of a white officer who looked at Calder as if he wanted to say "smart nigger" but decided not to. Ten years had changed some things.

Like Abner Calder, many black people live with vivid memories of an encounter with police. Many say they do not have to remember back very far to re-live their own experience of insult and indignity. Many relate episodes of far more than verbal abuse. But there is little doubt that things have changed and that the "old days" of police routinely calling every black person a "nigger" and beating up on those who said anything back are largely gone.

However, the anger and hostility, long suppressed by the black person, are not gone. And neither, of course, is every instance of abuse, injustice or brutality. Paradoxically, though, the accusations of brutality have increased during the very period when metropolitan police forces have undergone the greatest change. The experience of the New York Police Department is an example. As one observer said:

> The New York City force is more humane; it observes the civil rights of Negroes more carefully than ever before. Its public relations program is concentrated on projecting a spirit of friendliness and decency, but that does not seem to have helped. In

the past few years, New York's policemen have been subjected
to unparalleled physical and verbal attack, especially from members of minority groups.[1]

The answer to this puzzle lies in two primary points:
(1) Not all abuse and brutality have been eliminated; what
does remain is given much more vocal attention than such
treatment 10 years ago when Negroes feared to speak out, and
news media did not spotlight the "brutality" issue; (2) Police
are a constant reminder of a white society that is being increasingly identified by militants as oppressive and racist.
Police have become a whipping boy for the sins of the white
world, as perceived by the militants. Launching bigger and
better community relations programs with minority groups
will help. But it will not be the total answer. Arthur Neider-
hoffer, a former officer who has studied the sociology of
police, believes that "as long as the Negroes comprise an
alienated ghetto society, the police will symbolize to them
all that is detestable in an oppressive white social system."[2]
"Alienated" and "oppressive white social system" have now
become such codewords that they contribute more to rhetoric
than reason. But it is true that police represent the indignity
and inhumanity that many Negroes feel they have suffered
at the hands of whites. In pinning on a button reading, "I
believe in human dignity," Calder said he was acting for all
Negroes who want white society to know that they not only
believe in human dignity, but that they demand the dignity
of black people as humans be recognized. Since police are the
most habitual white visitors in the ghetto, they are a logical
choice to carry the message—and bear the brunt of the rage
behind it.

"Their very presence is an insult," Negro author James
Baldwin says, "and it would be even if they spent their entire
day feeding gumdrops to children. They represent the force of
the white world, and that world's criminal profit and ease, to
keep the black man corralled up here, in his place."[3] The
policeman, Baldwin adds, is "like an occupying soldier in a
bitterly hostile country . . ." where he faces "people who would
gladly see him dead."

The feeling of being in "enemy" country cannot help but
affect police attitudes. "The ghetto beat can toughen up a
policeman so that he compensates for fear by looking tougher
and assuming a swagger and developing a chip on the shoul-

der," says Lieutenant William Osterloh, director of community relations for the San Francisco Police Department.[4]

Through the cries of brutality and the bitter accusations and condemnation, police have been hearing—and openly receiving—the rage that was for so long bottled up. As previously mentioned, 1,400 policemen in Houston have had a six-weeks course of meeting in small groups with members of the non-white community.* They heard complaint after complaint of police abuse, of police calling people "niggers" and grown men "boys." To help them understand the rage that came mostly from the younger black participants, the police were given copies of a paper by Dr. Alvin F. Poussaint on "A Negro Psychiatrist Explains the Negro Psyche." In it, Dr. Poussaint tells of the passivity and non-assertiveness that he believes white society has required of the Negro. He tells of the self-hate the Negro has experienced from feeling powerless to speak up and assert. And he tells of his own self-hate in the face of an encounter with a policeman:

> . . . as I was leaving my office in Jackson, Miss., with my Negro secretary, a white policeman yelled, 'Hey, boy! Come here!' Somewhat bothered, I retorted: 'I'm no boy!' He then rushed at me, inflamed, and stood towering over me, snorting, 'What d'ja say, boy?' Quickly he frisked me and demanded, 'What's your name, boy?' Frightened, I replied, 'Dr. Poussaint. I'm a physician.' He angrily chuckled and hissed, 'What's your first name, boy?' When I hesitated he assumed a threatening stance and clenched his fists. As my heart palpitated, I muttered in profound humiliation, 'Alvin.' He continued his psychological brutality, bellowing, 'Alvin, the next time I call you, you come right away, you hear? You hear?' I hesitated. 'You hear me, boy?' My voice trembling with helplessness, but following my instincts of self-preservation, I murmured, 'Yes, sir.' Now fully satisfied that I had performed and acquiesced to my 'boy status,' he dismissed me with, 'Now, boy, go on and get out of here or next time we'll take you for a ride down to the station house.'[5]

Dr. Poussaint says this is the way the white world—through its police arm—has stripped the Negro of his manhood and castrated him. "The self-hate that I felt at that time was generated by the fact that I and my people were completely helpless and powerless to destroy that white bigot and all that he represented. Suppose I had decided, as a man

---

*At the behest of the mayor's office, Houston business and professional men—led by Attorney Gail Whitcomb—organized a group called Community Effort, Inc. to raise more than $100,000 and make the program possible.

should, to be forceful? What crippling price would I have paid
for a few moments of assertive manhood? What was I to do
with my rage?"[6]

In many ways, verbal abuse can be worse than physical
aggression, and this is why Negroes are now so quick to cry
"brutality" when they interpret the words of a policeman to
be demeaning. Dr. Melvin Sikes, a Negro psychologist who
worked with Police Chief Herman Short in directing the community relations course in Houston, says: "It is logical and
reasonable that a people struggling for identity, acceptance
as persons, and dignity and worth as human beings would react with rage against the verbal abuse that has done more to
de-humanize and demoralize them than has the physical abuse
of the years."[7] Dr. Sikes believes a man can fight honorably
against physical aggression, and avoid the self-hate that
comes from taking verbal abuse. "What defense has one
against verbal brutality? How does one retaliate? All becomes
empty and foolish, yet this weapon of the oppressor is the
most devastating."[8]

What to do with the rage? In Houston, some of it was
siphoned off in the program that put police face-to-face with
black people in small groups. The groups were under the guidance of trained psychologists, who used psychodrama and role
reversal techniques to let both the police and the community
people know what it feels like to be in the other's shoes. The
problems of being a member of the blue minority were understood, probably for the first time, by members of the black
community, as were the problems of the Negroes by the police.

Based on material brought out in the group sessions, Figure 11 presents the image police had of community people,
both black and white. Figure 12 presents the image that
black community people had of themselves and what they
believed the police thought of them. One purpose of the community relations program was to try to reconcile the differences that the two groups had toward each other, particularly
when the views were not based on fact.

The face-to-face sessions did seem to bring positive results. Complaints against police, as received by both the National Association for the Advancement of Colored People in
Houston and the mayor's office, dropped sharply after the
intensive community relations program got underway. A
questionnaire was distributed to each policeman who participated and to each community person, to be filled out anony-

mously. In brief, the community gave the program an extremely high rating, with 93 percent evaluating it as being either "good" or "excellent." As for the police, their response was less enthusiastic, but 85 percent gave it a "good" or "excellent" rating.*

FIGURE 11

POLICE IMAGE OF COMMUNITY*

We see the community as a heterogeneous group and on the basis of our experience as police officers, we have something to say about different groups; that is, the Negro groups, the Latin Americans, and the white groups. We will discuss each of these groups separately, but the focus here is on Negroes and whites.

A. General Statements
  1. We see the Negro group as being apathetic.
  2. We see them divided among themselves.
  3. We feel that there is a lack of pride.
  4. We see them as being easily influenced.
  5. We see them as a troubled spot because of the above statements.
  6. Additional comments on specific elements of the community:
     a. The Negro, criminal group that we come in contact with:
        (1) They are rebellious and violent and have little regard for life and property.
        (2) Non-cooperative.
     b. The younger element of the Negro groups:
        (1) We see them as potentially good citizens if led in right direction.
        (2) We would like to see them take pride in their community and express same.
     c. The older group of Negroes:
        (1) We feel like this group has lost the respect of the younger generation.
B. General Statements (about the white community)
  1. The upper-class whites tend to look down upon the police and to see themselves as better.
  2. They are very self-centered.
  3. They tend to see the police as being intruders.
  4. They have false pride.

*Compiled by Don Wallace, Ph. D., group leader.

*See Appendix E for details of results as evaluated by a questionnaire formulated by Sidney Cleveland, Ph. D.

FIGURE 12
COMMUNITY IMAGE*

OF THEMSELVES	BY THE POLICE
1. We see ourselves as human beings and not animals	1. (no comparable view of community by the police on the first three points.)
2. We want law enforcement officers to know that we can show respect and proper cooperation.	2. ....
3. We see ourselves as stereotyped by policemen.	3. ....
4. We show lack of cooperation because of intimidation.	4. We recognize that there is a lack of cooperation between the Negro race and the police department.
5. We don't get equal justice under the law.	5. We see them demanding jobs they are not qualified for because they are members of the Negro race, political pressure, etc.
6. Our chances to be heard are not equal.	6. ....
7. We see ourselves as responsible citizens dedicated to the American cause.	7. We see them as a political structure demanding and receiving excessive tax funds out of proportion to their number in the general population.

*In this example, the focus is restricted to the Negro community. Information was compiled by Dr. Wallace.

Even with these promising results, there can be no claim that hostility is no longer present between police and ghetto dwellers. On a deep and unconscious level, there is probably still much rage, and in other cities it has found expression in riots. In many cases, the riots were preceded by an incident between police and Negroes. The question was not just what the police may have done to incite anger but also what ghetto dwellers thought the police did. As we indicated in Chapter 1, perception can be influenced by attitudes of hostility. In Watts, the crowd thought the police manhandled a pregnant woman. But the "maternity dress" of the woman turned out to be a barber's frock. In Grand Rapids, Michigan, one of

hundreds of cities that had racial explosions in 1967, these
were the facts, as reported by the National Advisory Commission on Civil Disorders:

> . . . police attempted to apprehend a Negro driving an allegedly
> stolen car. A crowd of 30 to 40 Negro spectators gathered. The
> suspect had one arm in a cast, and some of the younger Negroes
> in the crowd intervened because they thought the police were
> handling him too roughly.[9]

Some observers believe that the hair-trigger tendency of
militants to cry, "Police brutality!" is keeping some officers
from acting when the facts of the case warrant action. There
are reports in some cities of police hesitating when there
should be no hesitation. A policeman in Detroit tells of what
happened in that city:

> It was an Attempted Robbery in progress. . . . So we got over
> there real fast. . . . Got over there and the guys were fighting
> in the middle of the grass of one of the houses. Jumped out of
> there. Got the guy—he had attacked an old man. They were two
> colored people. This old man backed off so we could deal with
> this guy. Well, we were wrestling all over that ground with him.
> After a little while we got him cuffed. We had five thousand
> people out there, screaming 'Police brutality!' and rocking our
> scout car. Wouldn't let us leave with this guy. And this man,
> this colored man who was standing there, he couldn't do a thing,
> the colored man who was being attacked. They didn't care about
> him. In a colored neighborhood.
> Well, a lot of police officers, they'd just—it might not be evident,
> they might not say, 'Well, next time, I'm going to slow down and
> I'm not going to go over there very fast. Maybe the guy'll run
> away and I won't have to take this abuse.' But in the back of
> his mind he realizes this, whether conscious or otherwise, and the
> next time, if he's a little ways away and there's a red light, well,
> he'll stop for it! And he'll know that he's stopping for it because
> he doesn't want to go there. . . .[10]

Some police, then, are increasingly self-conscious about
the black hostility directed toward them. Many will defy it,
some may even challenge and invite it. But whatever they do,
the hostility is too often still there and must be dealt with.

It would be wrong, however, as the National Advisory
Commission agreed, "to define the problem solely as hostility
to police. In many ways, the policeman only symbolizes much
deeper problems."[11]

As we have seen, the deeper problems go back to all of
white society's treatment of Negroes. After the assassination
of Martin Luther King in April 1968, it did not take a police

incident to touch off riots in Washington, D. C., and nearly 200 other cities and towns. The rage welled up without police precipitation. It would be an oversimplification to say that all of the 233 disorders that occurred were a direct result of anger over King's assassination. Many began with youths seeing an opportunity to play "king-for-a-day," and an opportunity to loot and burn with a rather safe degree of impunity. But once the rioting began, whatever its trigger, rage was released.

The police are the people who most have to live with the rage, regardless of what touches it off. And their problem becomes a vicious circle. Rage leads to riot, riot leads to police intervention, police intervention leads to rage. Because of "the fears and perils the policemen are subjected to while pursuing their duties in the Negro community," Arnold Rose thinks that when the police do intervene, they do so with a vengeance.[12] And the vengeance only leads to more rage and the rage to more disorder.

After police intervened at Texas Southern University in Houston, hostility toward police shot up in the remotest sections of the Negro community, as we saw in the chapter on "The 'Sead' Factors of Unrest." People began seeing police abuse in incidents that they previously had considered innocent. People began remembering cases of police abuse that they had not remembered before. There has now been enough violence across the country to sensitize the perceptions of vast numbers of community people toward police abuse. This is not to say that actual abuse, particularly verbal, does not occur. It simply means that police are often caught in a cycle of greater intervention, which leads to greater hostility, which leads to more accusation of abuse.[13] The human dignity that undoubtedly was withheld from black people for so long is now being fiercely cultivated and jealously guarded by them. Nearly all are beginning to wear (symbolically) the kind of button Abner Calder pinned on: "I believe in human dignity."

Not only police, but all of white society, must read the words closely if we are to break the vicious circle. The black community must also help. As Carl Rowan has pointed out, the community must recognize that human dignity is an individual matter and not all the preaching in the world about black culture and black pride can bestow dignity on a whole group automatically. As for the police, they are in a position of having to treat people with dignity who denounce them with bitter criticism. They must bear disrespect without overreacting. On this point, the President's Commission on Law Enforcement and Administration of Justice noted:

> Quite evidently, it is not easy for a man who was brought up to obey the law and to respect law enforcement officers to maintain his poise and equanimity when he is denounced, sneered at, or threatened. However, policemen must do just that if police-citizen relationships on the street are to become person-to-person encounters rather than the black-versus-white, oppressed-versus-oppressor confrontations they too often are.[14]

Police are being called on to play a more and more exacting role in our society. They feel they are doing so without being properly appreciated or rewarded. Many, in short, feel besieged and faced with the frustrations of their own minority group status.

An Embattled Institution

Miami Beach Police Chief Rocky Pomerance put it this way: "A policeman these days has to be part priest, part psychologist, part social worker, part karate expert—and he has to be able to make a decision in a few seconds that will stand up before complex legal scrutiny clear up to the U. S. Supreme Court."[15] Police today feel they are at war not only with crime but also the courts, politicians, civil rights leaders—and sociologists who tell them they must be more understanding of people who break laws. In the ghetto, as we have seen, they face their toughest assignment. The National Advisory Commission on Civil Disorders observed:

> . . . police responsibilities in the ghetto are even greater than elsewhere in the community since the other institutions of social control have so little authority: The schools, because so many are segregated, old and inferior; religion, which has become irrelevant to those who have lost faith as they lost hope; career aspirations, which for many young Negroes are totally lacking; the family, because its bonds are so often snapped. It is the policeman who must deal with the consequences of this institutional vacuum and is then resented for the presence and the measures this effort demands.[16]

The frustrations experienced in the face of heavier and heavier responsibility are increasing at such a rate that a blue minority rebellion is now brewing in some of the cities where conditions are particularly bad. Just as with any minority, there is a limit to the dissatisfactions that police will accept,

and when that limit is reached, it is then a short step to
"revolt." Rebellion has already been seen in the form of police
"slowdowns." In New York, in October 1968, "20 percent of
the force took sick leave each day and officers on duty refused
to write parking tickets" for six days.[17]

People want all things of police, but they seldom consider
that the law enforcement officer is no more a super human
being than they are. The police are trained to do tough jobs
and to do them objectively. But they are still influenced by
the people they must deal with everyday and by the risks
they run in performing their duty. Former Los Angeles Police
Chief Thomas Reddin said:

> The young policeman deals with filth, the dregs of humanity on
> a minute to minute basis. It's not hard for him to reach a point
> where he says that people are no damn good, so to hell with
> people.[18]

Joseph LeFevour, president of the Chicago Lodge of the
Fraternal Order of Police, suggests that the public ought to
see what police have to put up with in the daily course of their
duty. He says:

> Policemen have a tendency to become calloused. But if people saw
> the dirt, the filth, the muck that the police deal with from sunset
> to sun-up, they'd have a different view of the policeman's work.[19]

Undeniably, many of the people the police deal with are
black. The policeman does not stop to consider the frustration-aggression hypothesis that may be involved in a Negro's
breaking the law. This is not the policeman's job. He simply
sees that a crime has been committed and a person with dark
skin did it. He will usually deny, though, that he has any racial
prejudice. Those who admit any will usually say they do not
let it affect their behavior in line of duty. As one Detroit
police officer put it:

> . . . we're not prejudiced . . . we do have certain conclusions,
> but they're based on fact, and they're not conclusions singling out
> any race . . . even though police officers will say, as a general
> statement, 'I don't like coloreds' or 'I don't trust coloreds'—be-
> cause they happen to work in a colored area. Most police offi-
> cers . . . are actually anti-crime.[20]

Although many officers deny that prejudice affects
them, most do admit that the danger involved in being an
officer is something that sticks in their mind. One told me:
"Every day when I leave home, I can't help wondering if this

will be the last time." There were 20,523 officers assaulted,
6,836 injured and 53 killed during 1965.[21] It has been reported
that in 1967, one out of every eight officers was assaulted.[22]
The danger is even greater now with the increase in civil disorders. For instance, three policemen were killed at one time
in Cleveland in the riot that broke out there in late July 1968.
But the biggest risk still comes from the day-to-day handling
of offenders. Commenting on the 1965 figures, the President's
Commission on Law Enforcement and Administration of
Justice said:

> Many of the serious injuries and deaths were inflicted by felons
> or other persons attempting to escape and therefore had little, if
> anything, to do with problems of police-community relations.
> However, many of the minor assaults (and some of the more
> serious ones as well) resulted, at least partially, from general
> hostility toward the police.[23]

This focusing of "general hostility" on police, coupled
with an increasing feeling on the part of law enforcement
officers that they inevitably end up in a damned-if-they-do
and damned-if-they-don't position, may result in what other
groups have traditionally done when mistreated: They organize. Police have long had their law enforcement associations,
of course, and they can be quite powerful as a lobby, but the
type of organizing I am referring to here is unionizing on a
national basis. One organizing attempt that has been launched
is the establishment of a coast-to-coast group called The National Federation of Police Officers. If police do go the union
route (and I am not advocating it) the result could well be
what Labor Columnist Victor Riesel has predicted: "Soon,"
he says, "it will become an unfair labor practice to bite or
scratch a cop, hurl rocks, beer cans or invectives at him or
tear down the picket signs he plans to wave on high."[24]

I do not know how "soon" soon is, but I do know it is time
to examine closely the embattled position police are occupying
in many American cities, and the sources of frustration that
affect many officers.

The average policeman sees himself as a protector of people. He is in the community to help. It is baffling and crushing to him to be faced with the fact that many people believe
his intention is to hurt and scare. Most black people do not see
the policeman as a protector, and their now-open criticism
only adds to his feeling that he is unappreciated and abused.
In Houston, the police-community relations course helped per-

suade some ghetto dwellers that officers are sincere in their wanting to protect people, not hurt them.

What the public, both black and white, often overlooks is that police themselves qualify as members of a minority group, and behave accordingly. Dr. Sikes calls them "the blue race." Michael J. Murphy, former police commissioner of New York City, said that "the police officer belongs to a highly visible minority group and is also subject to sterotyping and mass attack. Yet he, like every member of every minority, is entitled to be judged as an individual and on the basis of his individual acts, not as a group."[25] Not only do many officers believe, as members of other minorities do, that they are disliked and taken advantage of, many also feel discriminated against. I sat in on a session where police officers were describing what their family life is like. One policeman said that he cannot drink a beer on his back yard patio for fear his neighbors will see him and gossip. Another said that other children would not play with his children because they were "a cop's kids." A third complained that "people don't invite you over for a friendly game of cards once they learn you are a police officer." Another contended that he had to act as a model for his block because he was a policeman. "I don't dare put a garbage can out on the curb for pickup without the lid being tightly on it."

Police are called on to do all sorts of things, off duty as well as on. One case I know of involved a woman who could not get a check cashed at the hotel where she was staying. She called a friend in the same city and asked for help. The friend knew that a policeman lived in the same apartment building. She got the officer to go to the hotel and tell the clerk it was all right to cash the woman's check.

When off-duty, police generally stay to themselves. "We maintain a distance from other people," as one said. Their social circle is often made up of other policeman. As with other minority groups, much contact with people "outside" is formal and in line of duty. Police admit to a suspiciousness about people. "We're trained to be suspicious. We couldn't do our job if we weren't."

James Q. Wilson, the Harvard University political scientist who wrote *Varieties of Police Behavior,* believes it is part of the informal "police code" that people are not to be trusted, and help should not be expected from the public. Wilson says the code teaches policemen to "show physical courage; always be ready to take charge of a situation; never duck responsibility for your acts; don't trust civilians; never expect help from the community."[26] Because there *is* distrust of "civilians" and because there *is* the conviction that officers must retain a posture of strength, authority, and "being right," police often appear defensive. They are slow to admit error. They are taught to be authoritarian, to take command. Many fear that admitting an error will reduce their effectiveness as a person in charge of the situation. The defensiveness is also a natural consequence of feeling unappreciated. "People have already found enough wrong with police without our admitting faults and mistakes ourselves," one officer told me.

Many of the community relations sessions with police in Houston dwelt on this point of not admitting error. Community people would keep pressing the officers on whether a policeman could have been wrong in a certain situation. Often, officers would dismiss reports by community people of police abuse, contending that what the people saw or heard was not factual, not first-hand. The people would press back with, "Isn't it possible that it could have happened that way and the officer was wrong?" Finally, there would usually be an admission that "just like in any organization, there are some bad apples" or "police are only human, they can make mistakes too." The latter reply would be the one the people were wanting. They wanted to hear the policeman admit their fallibility.

Another feature to the blue minority is the effect that the death of an officer in line of duty has on bringing fierce unity to the police. Black militants are not alone in saying that a blow struck at one black person is felt by all. The police react the same way toward their own. John Hersey, author of *The Algiers Motel Incident,* feels that the fatal shooting of the three Negro youths at the motel during the Detroit riot of 1967 grew in part out of the emotion surrounding the shotgun death earlier of a policeman named Jerome Olshove. Said one Detroit officer: " . . . after Olshove died . . . everything just went loose. The police officers weren't taking anything from anyone."[27] This does not mean that police blatantly take the law in their own hands if one of their kind is killed. It does mean that the death of one officer reminds others of their own vincibility and imbues them with an implacable determination to put an end to whatever violence was responsible for the death of a fellow policeman. In such a situation, however, they must be on guard against letting their emotions overcome the public trust they bear as enforcers of the law, and to exercise all caution against becoming judge, jury and executioner.

If police feel that people in general do not understand them and that their dedication to service largely goes unrewarded, they are particularly certain that people in the ghetto do not understand them or their role. The police find it hard to understand that anyone could believe that they are in the community to hurt, not help. It pains them to think that there is so little appreciation of the good that a policeman stands for. It is also irritating to them to know that many unflattering theories are advanced as to why people become law-enforcement officers—theories such as "they have a need to brutalize and bully other people." The police feel they join the force out of a sense of public dedication and service. Dr. Morton Bard, who originated the Family Crisis Intervention Unit in the New York Police Department, says the policeman "is somebody who wants to help. I suspect very strongly that a significantly large percentage—not all—of them who seek to become cops do so out of a wish to help."[28]

But officers know they are often not accepted in that light, and this adds to their suspicion of the world. Members of both "the blue race" and the black minority often seem convinced that everyone is against them. Both minorities need to be brought into closer contact with the public on a person-to-person basis. Patrolman Alphonso Deal, a Negro policeman in Philadelphia, says: " . . . we've got to do more to build bridges—to help the people see the policeman as a human being."[29] Sociologist Jerome Skolnick has raised the question of whether it is really necessary for patrolmen to wear uniforms. "Wouldn't a badge or an armband do nearly as well under some circumstances, yet symbolize a closeness to the citizenry?"[30] Answered a police officer: "That kind of idea is a good example of the misunderstanding so many ivory-tower experts have of us and our role. We have to listen to that kind of stuff nearly every day now."

The police role at present is schizophrenic, but through no fault of the police themselves. Few people, black or white, realize that many police spend much of their time trying to restore peace among small groups of people, such as members of families, friends or acquaintances. In such a role, as Wilson has pointed out, police are not law-enforcement officers, they are public peace managers.[31] The disputes they arbitrate often involve arrests only if a participant swears out a formal complaint. In most cases, such a complaint is not sworn out and the policeman is left on his own to restore order the best he can, with no clear-cut rules of law to enforce or act upon. When the patrolman is not acting as a peace manager, he is often performing—or being asked to perform—some service for an individual citizen. He is taking somebody to a hospital, or trying to get a stalled car started. In any case, he is *not* spending most of his time doing what the public thinks he does—that is, chasing robbers, rapists, burglars or thieves.

This fact has enormous implications in the relations between police and ghetto dwellers. Undeniably, black people need police to catch robbers, rapists, burglars and thieves because Negroes are the biggest victims of them. But they also have an enormous need for police to be peace managers and service dispensers. The problem is that the two roles require quite different methods and types of policemen. To catch criminals, the most advanced means of technology need to be employed; police must be highly mobile, having the latest in electronic gear, go to the air in helicopters, if necessary, to flush out and capture a suspect in flight. But to intervene in family fights or even barroom brawls between friends, such technology is as out of place as a computer at a corner grocery checkout stand. And the man to restore peace and help people with their stalled cars and runaway kids is not the same as the one required to bring a high degree of analytical thinking and deduction to solving a murder mystery or a string of rape cases. The policeman who manages the peace and dispenses service needs the manner of a kind but firm dutch-uncle, with an almost unlimited capacity for being called on to do an incredible variety of things. He needs to know the neighborhood in which he works, and often he needs to be on foot, not in a car.

The peace-management role not only is one that calls for different methods and men, it is also one that needs acknowledgement by the public. No one pins medals on police for breaking up a fight between friends, or stopping a wife from bludgeoning a drunk and abusive husband with a baseball bat. But such is a policeman's role, along with catching crooks and reversing the rising tide of "crime on the street."

As has already been suggested, the public wants police to be all things to all people. They cannot be. If their role is to be a dutch-uncle arbitrator of neighborhood trouble, then the public should acknowledge that this is what they want of their police. If the police role is to be crime detector and crook catcher, then the public should recognize this role requires other methods and men. Clearly, the public wants both. But to saddle police with both roles and recognize only one of them, can only result in confusion, controversy, misunderstanding, frustration and bitterness. And, this is particularly true in regard to relations between police and minority-group people.

None of this should be interpreted as meaning the schizophrenic role of police is the one and only reason that relations between them and black people have been so volatile. It isn't. But it certainly adds to the schism between the blue minority and the black one. The schism is as wide as it is because it also encompasses all the other points that have been mentioned in this chapter. Although a start has been made on bettering relations, the schism will not be bridged any sooner than that which exists between all of white society and black people.

The blue minority wants law and order to reign. They want respect. But so does the black minority. They want human dignity. To the degree that black people get respect from the white world in general, and not just police in particular, the gulf separating all of us will narrow. To the degree that black people recognize that dignity comes from within, as well as from sources outside, the gulf will continue to narrow. It will narrow even more as the public, both black and white, makes up its mind as to what the *primary* role of police should be and then develops whatever other means are necessary to take care of the additional functions that are now expected of the policeman.

This chapter has been concerned with the police arm of that ubiquitous body called "The Establishment." The amount of violence and unrest that a city experiences is not just a function of police relations with the ghetto. It is also related to how responsive the whole Establishment is to the needs of Negroes and how willing black people are to accept the responsiveness in good faith and make use of it. Black nationalists across the land have contended that only violence will wake "The Establishment" up. They ignore the non-violent means of dealing with the "power structure." In the next chapter, some of the alternatives to violence will be explored.

WHAT SHOULD WE BELIEVE?

POINTS TO CONSIDER—VI

A. Let's take cognizance of the fact that historically the Negro male has had to play a passive role in American society and that he sees the police officer as the symbol of white authority that has kept him from asserting himself as a man.

B. Let's accept that there is much unvented rage from the passivity and that a high degree of hostility is likely to be felt toward police. The challenge is to find constructive avenues for release of the rage, avenues that do not lead to violence or clashes with police.

C. Let's understand that police deal daily with people who commit violence, show little regard for the lives or property of others and often give officers a hard time when arrested. Let's recognize that it is an exceptional human being who can keep from letting his view of humanity be affected by this kind of job. But let's also recognize that police do learn to keep their opinion of people from affecting their conduct, which should at all times be fair.

D. Let's realize that black people, having been subjected to indignities at the hands of white people for many years, are understandably going to be sensitive to police as a symbol of white authority. For many Negroes, the policeman is the white person he sees most in his neighborhood and he may well believe he is there to hurt, not help.

E. Let's face up to the fact that as institutions such as the family and school have abrogated responsibilities of social control, the police have ended up with having to act as father, teacher, big brother, social worker, judge and many other things to black and white kids alike. One misstep and they are pounced on with cries of brutality.

F. Let's also recognize that the embattled position that many police feel they are in could lead to national unionizing and strikes. Most police feel a dedication to public service, but the damned-if-they-do, damned-if-they-don't position they are now in is having an effect on that dedication.

H. Let's not sink into pessimism about relations between police and black people, as if the problem is insuperable. The more that each can have the opportunity to get to know the other as an individual, rather than someone wearing a blue uniform or having a dark skin, the more optimistic we can be about improved relations.

I. But let's not also delude ourselves into thinking the problem is just between police and black people. All of American society is involved in the question. The police role is widely misunderstood, principally from the standpoint of people failing to recognize that police spend much of their time answering calls to settle disputes and problems between a small group of people, often a family, friends or acquaintances, and not in pursuing robbers, rapists, burglars and thieves. The latter is the role the public thinks the police has, but the former is what much of the force is involved in—offering service, and arbitrating personal conflicts. Until the public makes up its mind that this is the sort of duty it has given police and should recognize them for it, then policemen are likely to feel alienated and just as misunderstood as any other minority group. What all this adds up to is that both police and black people have legitimate reasons to feel that neither understands the other, but in both cases the misunderstanding extends to the white society which is badly misinformed about both minorities.

CHAPTER 7

BARGAINING WITH *THE POWER STRUCTURE*

In a large city in a fast-growing area of this country, there is a mayor's office, there is a city council, there is a school board, there is a county government, there is a regional council, there are any number of state and federal offices, there are huge corporations and countless smaller businesses, there is a chamber of commerce, there are large newspapers and major television stations, there are strong labor unions, there are important universities and colleges, there are big churches and denominational offices.

In each of these institutions—the political, the economic, the mass media, the educational, the religious—there are leaders who wonder where all the power is that they are supposed to have. Why is this? They belong to the "power structure," to "the Establishment." How could they see themselves as without power?

Power is the ability to get something done. The mayor cannot get a housing code passed, city councilmen cannot get water lines extended or streets paved, one school board member cannot get free breakfasts for children from low-income families, another says he cannot get anyone to understand the financial plight of the school district, a federal worker cannot get authorization for a secretary so that he can do the work in the community he is assigned to do, a state employment official feels frustrated in trying to participate in 16 local job programs for minority group people, a corporation vice president feels he has no experience or expertise in the urban problems being pressed on business to solve, chamber of commerce chairmen keep wondering how they can implement action on community problems once they identify them, newspaper and television executives worry about not reaching the minority groups in the city and telling their stories, university administrators are faced with demands by—and in behalf of—black students who want action now, church leaders feel they do not know how to get actively involved in problems that goad their conscience.

A common denominator to the "powerful" feeling "power-less" is a sense that when they try to solve social problems, they are in an area where no one has answers and, as one said, "it's like trying to find a handle on a big rubber ball." So, individually there are doubts of power among members of "the power structure." But more important, there is no single structure in which they operate. "The power structure" is a misleading myth. It is misleading and a myth not only because the powerful wonder where all the power went, but also because there is no concerted pool of power that can be simply and efficiently tapped for action. A structure is something organized. In this large city, there is no organized unit or arrangement where people from government, business, the mass media, labor, the academy and religion get together to control the destiny of the community. There is not even a disorganized unit, or a hidden "interlocking" complex that links all the people of power together so they still end up controlling the city. In fact, members of this non-existent single power structure disagree as much or more as they agree. And the disagreements are aired publicly by the media, as they should be.

Yet this combination of institutions is "the power structure," "the Establishment," which supposedly controls the city. It doesn't. The city is too diffuse, power is too diffuse for such control. There is no monolithic source of power that permits urban America to be so simply divided up between people who belong to "the Establishment" and those who do not. But if the idea of a single power structure is a myth, if it is something that merely serves to give the angry a catch-all label for their hostility, then where does a person turn for action on community problems? There is no central source.

Community problems concern employment, education, housing, health, police relations, crime and delinquency, family instability, welfare, consumer purchasing. They also concern streets, drainage, traffic signals, lots overgrown with weeds and rats in houses. City Hall has responsibility for city services, and these include police, health, streets, water, sewerage and garbage disposal, but what about all the rest?

The man in the slums needs a decent job, a good education for his children, decent housing—and most of all, some sense of hope for the future and competence to cope with the present. Where is "the" power structure to which he can turn for help on the cycle of problems he faces—problems that interlock and confront him from all directions? There is no single institution. This city government does not run the schools. It has no housing department. It does not dispense welfare. It is not the anti-poverty agency for the area. It does not control jobs in industry. It cannot pave streets without property owners along the streets sharing in the costs. It cannot even participate in the cost-sharing unless the public votes bond issues for street paving, or sanitary sewers or water lines—so many of the basic services that are inadequate or completely absent in low-income areas.

But the fact that there is no single power structure to address for a bigger piece of an affluent society does not mean there is nowhere for a man in need to turn. There is simply no one institution that has been developed for mounting a sustained attack on social problems. In the turmoil of the cities, the blame has been laid on "the" power structure and "the" Establishment, as if a tight little group of men in a back room had kept the city under their thumbs. There may be cities like this, but not the one discussed here.

What a mayor's office in such a city can do—and what it has tried to do—is to serve as a catalyst and a pivot point for mobilizing resources. The mayor's office cannot vote bonds for streets, it cannot build houses, it cannot find everyone a job, but it can stimulate and coordinate and initiate. It can work with people and try to mobilize the resources that have the power and experience to help with problems. It can listen to community people and try to give them a sense that the city *does* care, and that someone *will* work with them on problems.

The process involves bargaining. It is working with people, listening to them, explaining what the city establishment can and cannot do, explaining why, and arriving at some compromise between what is needed and what can be provided. It is also trying to find other resources to help meet needs. It is a coming to terms, but with the recognition that not everything is likely to be done that is needed.

Bargaining is non-violent. Would violence bring greater results? Has it so far in the cities of America? Violence will not create an all-serving institution to solve the problems of slums. Institutions develop out of consensus among people, not conflict. Institutions, such as City Halls, are trying to change to get more needs met, but violence does not build a solid basis for change. What is needed now is to bring institutions and resources together to work with community people on their problems, and to give people an opportunity to share the power of the society in which they live.

Some persons contend there is no such thing as sharing power. To them, power is like a physical commodity that comes in limited amounts. They feel there is a small circle of people who hold it in a city and that only conflict and violence will break their hold and make power available to a greater number.

In this chapter we will take a look at such theories. We will also want to see where the idea came from that only conflict can bring power to those who do not have it. We will examine other alternatives, and what community people in an urban area have done through neighborhood associations and bargaining with *one* so-called power structure—the city establishment or City Hall. But first, let's explore some of the ideas on power being hoarded and conflict being necessary to get some of it.

Marx and the Second Law of Thermodynamics

> Most intellectuals after the French Revolution [1789-1799] were concerned with the problems of either conflict or consensus. Revolutionaries were naturally primarily concerned with furthering conflict, conservatives with maintaining social stability. . . . But few men were concerned with analyzing the conditions under which conflict and consensus were in balance.[1]

Seymour Lipset makes this observation in introducing the historical figures concerned with conflict and consensus. Karl Marx had a simple position on these two issues. Every society, he felt, except a communistic one would necessarily be characterized by constant conflict. In a communist society, with no "antagonism" between man and man or man and nature, there would be no conflict and no need for consensus.[2]

Along came Max Weber [1864-1920], who was studying at the University of Heidelberg when Marx died in 1883, and decided that the whole question of power, conflict and consensus was quite a bit more complicated. In an essay published posthumously in the early 1920's, Weber put forth some rather unorthodox ideas suggesting that economic position, social status and power could be—and often are—three separate "dimensions."[3] Weber did not rule out that power could involve conflict. In fact, in *Basic Concepts in Sociology*, he defined power as "the opportunity existing within a social relationship which permits one to carry out one's own will even against resistance and regardless of the basis on which this opportunity rests."[4]

But, more importantly, what Weber did was to recognize that power is not so simple a concept that it can be characterized as solely involving conflict or consensus or any other single factor, for that matter.

The simplistic school that envisions power as necessarily involving conflict has been joined from time to time by those who introduce physical scarcity into the question. For instance, as we noted, there is the idea that there is just so much power to go around and those who have it are not going to give it up voluntarily or out of the kindness of their hearts. Robert Lynd is one advocate of this "scarcity theory."[5] The origins of his theory apparently go back to the study of "Middletown," in which much was made of the power of the economic and occupational elite in a Midwestern industrial city of about 38,000 population in the 1920's.[6]

Lynd did not get into physics, much less the Second Law of Thermodynamics, with his scarcity theory of power, but other social scientists have. For example, there is the concept of "social entropy," which holds that there is social decline and diminution of power simply because a limited quantity of power exists and it is not so much being given up as simply being "given off." All of this is derived from the Second Law of Thermodynamics, which conceived that the energy of the universe is fixed and limited and is being expended into the heating of empty space. "Social entropy" ties directly into the idea that there is just so much power available and those who have it are going to hang on to it just as long as the social equivalent of the Second Law of Thermodynamics will permit.

More recently, and with greater militancy, James Forman of the Student Nonviolent Coordinating Committee took up a brand of physics and power by emphasizing that two objects or forces cannot occupy the same space at the same time.[7] By this he means that white power and Black Power are going to compete for the same "space" and that "something's got to give."

Lipset holds that the concern with conflict as the one and only way of dealing with "the power structure" really comes from emphasis on "social composition" as the main determinant of who the decision-makers are. If the conflict theory is accepted, then the conclusion that follows is this:

> The only way in which fundamental changes in power can be made in a society is by changing the incumbents of power positions, usually defined as positions in the economy or government. In this sense, the social-composition approach is closely linked to the scarcity view of power, since as one group gains, another loses.[8]

However, Lipset points out, the scarcity theory of power and its close association with the "composition" of the power elite—which does not want to give any up—is far from being the only view of how social power works and how anyone gets in on it. Just as conflict-confrontation is an oversimplified, reductionistic theory on obtaining power, so is the "composition" theme in terms of what is really important in understanding power.

An alternate approach is to focus on "access" to power rather than "composition." The "access" approach seems more compatible with understanding power in the complex urban society. The "composition" theory appeals to those who believe in "power-elites" and in "Middletowns," where the social background and economic position of the "decision-makers" are likely to determine who holds power and who is going to get any benefit from it. Lipset says, "if one knows the salient group affiliations of decision-makers, one knows who will benefit from their decisions." On the other hand, Lipset notes:

> The access approach assumes . . . that the decisions of men in power, like those of men in any other role, are determined by a complex analytic calculus of the consequences of decisions. To the extent that the predictable reaction of any group or individual to a decision will affect the results of that decision, the group or individual has access to the decision-making process.[9]

Lipset illustrates his point by citing the power of the working classes in Britain and the United States to participate in decision-making processes. He says:

> . . . the members of the Establishment have continued to supply a considerable number of the key decision-makers, yet the middle classes and later the working classes sharply increased their influence on major societal decisions. In the United States, similarly, the power of organized labor and of the working class in general is considerably greater than it was thirty years ago, and many times greater than the increase in the number of labor leaders or others of working-class origin in actual positions of power.[10]

So what all this means is that you don't have to be in the "social register" or know someone who is to have access to power today—to affect policies and decisions. But just how does a person go about getting this access? Alex de Tocqueville offered the basis for one approach. He emphasized the value of "voluntary associations."

The Theory of Voluntary Associations

Tocqueville did not suggest that if people would only organize themselves into private associations, harmony would reign throughout society because they could bargain successfully for everything they wanted. But he did recognize that consensus as well as cleavage could co-exist as paths to power.[11] Tocqueville was primarily concerned with electoral power, but this does not keep us from applying his ideas on voluntary associations to bargaining with "the Establishment" in terms other than votes.

After his study of American society in the 19th century, Tocqueville decided that the way to keep power from being concentrated in a central structure or establishment was to involve people in local self-government and voluntary associations. He believed that those belonging to one association would have consensus internally but conflict externally with other groups. And in the process, he felt that the most competent of the voluntary associations would emerge with power that would detract from any concentration in a central source, such as government.

As for defining a voluntary association, Arnold Rose says it is "simply a public with a more permanent relationship among its members and a more formal structure than would be found among just a bunch of citizens at large."[12]

By organizing into a voluntary association, a group is in much better position to bargain with power structures and obtain desired action. Weber felt one key to action was finding allies among the bureaucrats who make up power structures. Unlike Marx, he did not believe capitalism was doomed and existing institutions would be destroyed. He saw a modification of society through bureaucracy.[13] This does not mean that Weber favored bureaucratic authority. In fact, he felt that the socialism resulting from extended bureaucracy would bring a world "filled with nothing but those little cogs, little men clinging to little jobs and striving toward bigger ones. . . . The great question is . . . what can we oppose to this machinery in order to keep a portion of mankind free from this parcelling-out of the soul, from the supreme mastery of the bureaucratic way of life?"[14] This question remains unanswered. There is no doubt that society has become so complicated it has given rise to complex bureaucratic organization in economic, political, educational and too many other institutions. But the question here is: How can people get a response from bureaucracy without waiting for some vast overhaul to take place that will presumably simplify life for everyone? Contact—communications—with the bureaucracy is a first step. By contacting the appropriate agency and making the needs of a neighborhood or a group known, the machinery is stimulated for getting action. The contact may be initiated by the agency itself in an attempt to establish better communications. But in any case, if a voluntary association exists, the bargaining process is accelerated. Action may not always be the end result, for reasons we have already mentioned—namely, lack of money in the case of City Halls or city establishments. But this does not negate the value of voluntary associations.

Rose sees voluntary associations as being particularly useful for additional reasons. He views them as having functions important to society as well as to individual members. Among the useful functions: (1) "The power-distributing function" (parallels what Tocqueville said)—this prevents a concentration of strength and spreads it out among many citizens. "Pressure groups and lobbies are prime examples of voluntary associations functioning to distribute power"; (2) "The orienting function"—this helps participants become aware of social, political and economic processes in society; (3) "The social change function"—voluntary associations offer a powerful mechanism for social change; (4) "The social cohesion function"—many voluntary associations tie society together and minimize the disintegrating effects of conflict, and (5) "The function of personal identification"—the voluntary association often gives the individual a feeling of identity with some small group that he can comprehend and influence in major ways.[15]

So much for the theory of voluntary associations. Now let's see what attention they can get in urban life today.

The Influence of "Voluntary Associations"

This is different from any other city I know of. You deal directly with the grass roots here—the people in the neighborhoods.

There's a town hall type of organization in more areas than I can name, and I've been visited by and have talked before more of them than I can count.[16]

These are the words of a member of the City Hall establishment, W. G. Scheibe, director of parks and recreation in Houston. He came from Dallas, where he said that when community people wanted to bargain with City Hall for a service, they did it through some branch of the chamber of commerce or other powerful economic interest group that first passed on the merits of the case.

"I like it better this way. You get to talk with the people themselves and they don't hesitate to let you know what they think that their neighborhood needs," said the Houston park director. Scheibe has been instrumental in establishing 60 neighborhood councils to give community people a greater voice in the reaction needs and programs in their area.

In Houston, where Negro communities are scattered 25 to 30 miles apart (see Chapter 1), there are some 96 civic clubs and neighborhood associations. They are in 20 areas that are identified by neighborhood names—such as Acres Homes and Studewood on the north side; Sunnyside and Almeda Plaza on the south; Pleasantville and Clinton Park on the east, and Carverdale and Blossom Heights-Jeanetta on the west. Each of these areas has at least one neighborhood association. Many have several. In the section that constituted one of the worst concentrated slums in the city—the area that was known as the Bottom—there is the People's Civic Club.

Many members in these voluntary associations look upon City Hall as the single, central power structure in Houston. It is *one* of the power structures, as we have seen, but not the only one. And its ability to respond to the needs of people is dependent on both the funds that the total public gives it and on the bureaucracy that operates it.

What follows are examples of the kinds of bargaining that have taken place with the city establishment, as represented by the mayor's office, and some results obtained:

1. There were approximately 2,500 minority-group people who visited the mayor himself in 1966-67. Some went to the mayor's office individually, others appeared in small, "private-citizen" groups, and there were those who represented delegations. In the majority of instances, the people were bargaining on behalf of some voluntary neighborhood association.

2. The action sought by the visitors concerned complaints ranging from improper water drainage and the need for better streets to more police protection. The mayor called an assistant or the appropriate department head to take action. He explained to many of the people the need for the public to pass bond issues so that the city will have funds to help pave more streets and improve services.

3. A series of question-and-answer sessions between the mayor and members of neighborhood groups were held in six major minority-group areas. Approximately 300 to 350 people attended each meeting. Discussion centered on a host of community problems, many of them touching on police relations and the need for more recreational sites.*

4. Staff members of the mayor's office maintained a "complaint desk" at each meeting, where individual problems could be presented. Action taken on requests from residents is illustrated by the following: Street repairs—79; improved water drainage—47; park improvements and weed cutting—29; additional traffic signals—26; more adequate police patrols—16; improved water pressure—13; improved sanitary conditions and waste removal—7; removal of safety hazards —5; and clarification of sewer and building permits—4.

5. In 1967-68, after mayor's aides met in the community with neighborhood people, special clean-up drives were conducted in minority group areas with door-to-door visits made to urge residents to collect litter and place it in front of their dwellings for pickup.

6. In 1968-69, in cooperation with neighborhood people and their voluntary associations, "Operation Uplift" was launched in an area known as Blossom Heights-Jeanetta. Weeds were cut, drainage ditches cleaned, streets topped, traffic signs installed, health service improved, a rat eradication program was conducted, street lights were put up, some houses were repaired with the cooperation of volunteers. All this activity was conducted out of a Neighborhood City Hall stationed in the area. A mayor's aide worked with the neighborhood people and associations on their needs to help them upgrade the area. The Harris County Community Action Association, which had other programs in the area, assisted.

---

*The "Meet-the-Mayor" programs were in cooperation with the Houston Council on Human Relations, with George Lloyd and Ken Rachal taking active parts in the project.

7. Also in cooperation with various neighborhood groups and residents, community aides working out of the mayor's office went into low-income areas to trace the ownership of abandoned, dilapidated houses that were health and fire hazards. Scores of the houses were torn down.

8. Most notable of the bargaining efforts to work with neighborhood people to upgrade a given area was "Project Partner," begun in early 1967. The People's Civic Club in the Bottom wrote a letter requesting that improvements be made at a park nearby. The Bottom had no park of its own. Without knowledge of this request, I made a visit to the Bottom one Saturday. What I saw were dusty streets, lined on each side by shotgun houses in varying stages of dilapidation. The mayor was receptive to a recommendation that the area be improved through a partnership between City Hall and the people there. A branch of the mayor's office would be opened in the neighborhood and a mayor's aide assigned there. I visited with leaders of the People's Civic Club and discussed the proposal with them. They were equally receptive to the idea. The process then began of interviewing the aide to work in the area. The people from the civic club participated in the process. Ernest Carswell was named as the aide, and "Project Partner" got underway. It included the tutoring of some 300 children, the building of four vest-pocket parks, paving of 12 streets, installation of street lights and stop signs, establishment of a health center and opening of a recreation center, which featured free movies, sewing classes, an auto club, drama classes, athletics. There were clean-up drives and distribution of free garbage containers. Success of the project was made possible not only through the cooperation of residents living in the area but also through the assistance of people, both black and white, from outside the neighborhood and from church contributions. In 1969, a $58,000 community center was erected for the Bottom. A substantial portion of the funds collected for building it was raised by a long-time, noted lawyer who had been district attorney in 1917, when Houston had a race riot. He had grown up in the Fifth Ward, just north of the Bottom.

After "Project Partner" began to produce results, people living in the area renamed it Swiney Addition, as earlier noted. They no longer felt they were "on the bottom," so they wanted another name for their area.

"Project Partner" and each of the examples included here involved bargaining with a number of neighborhood groups in

the sense of finding out their needs and acting upon those that
could be met. Action by the mayor's office is just one example
of results of bargaining with the city establishment. Voluntary
associations make appearances every week before city council
and representatives visit with individual councilmen, as well
as the mayor, bringing statements of their needs. Department
heads or their deputies meet with neighborhood groups, trying
to work out ways to satisfy needs. The bargaining is not always successful, but numerous efforts are made to arrive at
some agreement.

To simplify the process of addressing the city power structure, a central service center operates to receive complaints
from all citizens, regardless of whether they belong to any
neighborhood association or not. Some 2,600 calls from addresses in the Negro community were processed and acted on
during a 12-month period in 1968-69. These concerned drainage problems, rats, litter, and lots overgrown with weeds.
Almost as many calls were for area-wide upgrading and rehabilitation, requiring major capital improvements. The city's
inability to act on these area-wide problems points up the
need for greater financial resources on the local level. As we
will see, the job of removing urban blight depends not only on
responsiveness from "the Establishment," and the participation of community people in decisions affecting their lives, but
also on money—money that cities do not have.

For the problems on which one city tries to act, a booklet
on city services has been printed to inform neighborhood people in Houston of what steps must be taken. Mayor's aides in
the community distribute copies of the booklet in working with
community people on their problems and priming the machinery for action. As explained on the opening page of *You
and Your City Services:*

> Houston is a sprawling city over 450 square miles—about 6 square
> miles smaller than Los Angeles. It has grown rapidly and there
> are people inside the City limits who do not have services. . . .
> A city, in many ways, is a partnership between its people and
> their local government. Since such a partnership requires action
> and responsibility on the part of both the people and their gov-
> ernment, to obtain needed services often means that steps must
> be taken by individual citizens as well as the government that
> tries to serve them. It also means that money must be available
> for the services to be provided.[17]

Although the city establishment is constantly playing
"catch up" by reason of the number of service requests it re-

ceives, the implication should not be left that it responds to existing needs only after people point them out. A number of the programs listed in Chapter 9 represent action, not reaction. The establishing of a branch of the mayor's office in one of the worst slums was an example of initiative. The stationing of a mobile Neighborhood City Hall in minority group areas represented an attack on problems, not a response. The development of a six-man human relations division in the mayor's office was an example of initiative. The assignment by the mayor's office of four aides to work in the community on neighborhood problems was a "reaching out," not a "sitting back." The setting up of a center to help promote economic development of minority group neighborhoods was action, not reaction. The sponsorship of annual Job Fairs for Disadvantaged Youth represents initiative.* These examples provide no complete accounting, but they serve to illustrate the point that a mayor's office does not just sit there and wait for community people to bring problems to it, or for voluntary associations to show up to bargain for their solution.

On the other hand, the implication should not be left that City Hall is on top of all problems in minority group neighborhoods, or in any other area, for that matter. There are just not enough people or money to take care of all the problems in a fast-growing urban center, regardless of whether the decision to act upon them comes from "power structure" initiative or through bargaining with neighborhood groups. As has been noted, bargaining, even when it is successful, usually represents a compromise between what a given neighborhood group wants and what is possible to provide. Mayor Welch has a stock answer to the question of what the most pressing problems are in a city such as Houston. They are three, he says: "Money, finances and revenue."

One reason that Houston, as well as other cities across the nation, face financial problems is that a disproportionate amount of the tax dollar goes to the federal government instead of staying in the local community. Councilman Homer Ford, whose district includes the Third Ward, points out that

---

*Fred Wiener, long-time executive director of the Vocational Guidance Service who died in 1969, originated the Job Fair concept in Houston. The mayor's office is prime sponsor of the Job Fair, in cooperation with some 500 volunteers and representatives of about 20 organizations, including Vocational Guidance.

the federal government gets 64 cents of every tax dollar, while
local governments receive 17 cents. And with this 17 cents,
local governments are supposed to provide adequate streets,
sewers, storm drains, fire and police protection, health service,
libraries, as well as schools and a host of other services.

Cities not only fail to get enough money back from Washington to apply on city services, they are also faced with increasing resistance from local voters to pass new bond issues.
It cannot be emphasized too strongly that blighted neighborhoods are in bad need of even some of the most basic services—
such as extension of water lines and sanitary sewers—and
bond money is needed to help provide the facilities.

But even with limited "money, finances and revenue,"
cities still must decide what allocation they will make of the
funds they do have. In Houston, a greater allocation of bond
dollars has been going to neighborhoods in greatest need. In
the last five years, Negro neighborhoods have received more
benefits than ever before—more street topping, more health
centers and fire stations, more paving and sanitary sewers,
and more storm sewers. Figure 13 on Page 211 presents the
million-dollar increases in black neighborhoods. The extension
of full service to all minority group areas still falls short, however.

This "reaching out" with bond money to previously neglected areas has been followed by other stepped-up efforts of
City Hall to employ more minority group people, again within
budgetary limitations. In the last five years, there has been
an increase in employment of both Mexican-American and
Negro employees. Figure 14 on Page 212 shows the rise in employment of Negroes classified above the semi-skilled level.

Although City Hall must be responsive to the needs presented to it by neighborhood groups and individual citizens,
the mayor is aware that increasing bureaucracy, as well as
limited money, brings increasing risk of no action, or little
action, being taken when quick and full action are indeed possible and should result. Keeping the structure responsive is a
problem the mayor recognizes as just as important as the
pressing need for more funds. And responsiveness, of course,
is a function of how much the people in any power structure
want to act on problems.

There is no doubt that in many cases, the people that the
city establishment bargains with represent community people
with middle-class values who are seeking benefits for their

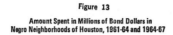

Figure 13

Amount Spent in Millions of Bond Dollars in
Negro Neighborhoods of Houston, 1961-64 and 1964-67

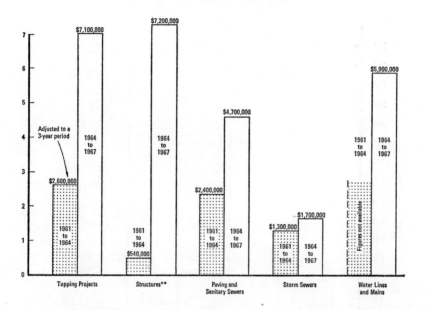

* Source: <u>A Report on Minority Group Problems and Progress,</u> Louie Welch, Mayor of Houston, 1968, p. 13.
** Includes fire stations, health centers, parks, miscellaneous buildings, etc.

neighborhoods but without really involving many others who
live there. The "many others" are those who show little inclination for meetings or little overt interest in their community.
Too often, their community is made up of houses owned by absentee landlords and businesses operated by "outsiders" who
make money there but leave the area at night to live in some
comfortable neighborhood across town.

Even where the mayor's office has exerted special effort
to seek involvement by people in their area, the results have
often been the same: the residents who end up participating
are only a fraction of those in the area and in some cases may
not even live in the neighborhood. But apathy, of course, is not
confined to low-income areas. Civic associations in middle and
high-income areas also often end up being run by only a rela-

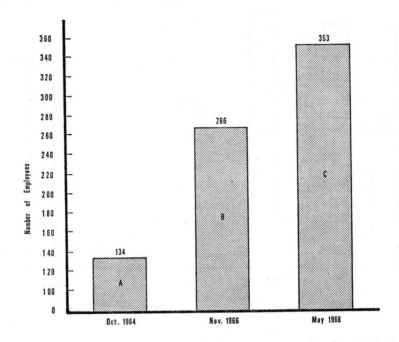

Figure 14

Increase   in   Negro   Employees   of   City   Government
Classified   above   Semi-skilled   Level**

A.   3.8 % of total city employees.

B.   7.2 % of total city employees.

C.   8.5 % of total city employees.

*Source: A Report on Minority Group Problems and Progress, Louie Welch, Mayor of Houston, 1968, p. 13.
   **Of all employees working for the city, more than 20% are Negroes.

tively few people, who have the most interest in the neighborhood and take the time to work on improving it.

Even in the Bottom, now Swiney Addition, where special
effort has been made to involve a large percent of the neighborhood, many people remain apart from the activity going on
there. But there should be no sense of hopelessness on this
point or any conclusion that only violence can move the im-

movable and instill in them a sense of power. The children in
the Bottom are not defeated. They have dreams. In tutoring
classes, they drew pictures of big houses and cars that they
wish for their futures. They saw some of the world outside of
the Bottom on chartered bus tours that took them to the
Manned Spacecraft Center, the Astrodome, Museum of Fine
Arts and other points of interest in the city. They did not show
hate for white people. They were spontaneous and friendly
toward white students who came to tutor them. They may
change. But if they continue to have access to those who can
work with them on their dreams, they may see that violence
is not necessary and that a sense of power and being somebody
can come from other means.

It cannot come from staying in the Bottom and not helping to improve it. The young must be shown that they do have
a future, and that power structures do care. They must be
shown that there is access to "the Establishment" and bargaining is possible. But this requires knowing what "the Establishment" is and defining it. Let's look now at how it is perceived by both theorists and community people, and why it is
more an abstraction than a reality when considered in the
singular.

Studies of Power and "The Power Structure"

Arnold Rose, in his book, *The Power Structure*, says that
"there is an elusiveness about power that endows it with an
almost ghostly quality. . . . We 'know' what it is, yet we encounter endless difficulty trying to define it. . . ."[18] Rose follows with a 10-page discussion on the definition of power.
Floyd Hunter comes to the point faster. Basing his definition
on the study of the power structure in a southern city, he de-
fines power as "the ability of men to command the services of
other men."[19] In his 1953 book on *Community Power Structure,* Hunter describes the "community leadership" in "Regional City" (later identified as Atlanta).[20] The "leadership"
consisted of a small group who made community decisions in
their own interests. Studies such as by Hunter, have been described as being based on a "reputational method" of determining the power structure. The "reputational method" is
"naive," in the opinion of such authorities as Scott Greer, professor of social and political science at Northwestern University. Greer says that when "careful scholars investigate the

way key decisions come about in the metropolis, they find neither the dominance of business interests nor the simple order assumed in the myth." As to where the "myth" was born and how it continues to persist, Greer notes:

> There always have been many Americans who prefer to believe that power in the local community is tightly organized in the hands of a few persons who represent "the interests." Perhaps this is a rural survival, for in the small town there is some evidence of consistent domination by those who control land credit, and wealth. Such an image can be easily transplanted to the city, where the mass media emphasize a few large-scale images connected with the polity, ignoring the supporting organizations and their dependence upon the citizens. The average urbanite, viewing these affairs from a great social distance, can easily believe that a small circle of the powerful exists and runs the city.[21]

Among those who continue to perpetuate the myth are not only Floyd Hunter but also C. Wright Mills, who was a professor of sociology at Columbia University. In insisting that a "power elite" runs every city, Mills manages to live in the days when social status and membership in "gentlemen's clubs" automatically put a person in the center of decision-making. That day is dead as far as metropolitan areas are concerned. If there are exceptions to this, as perhaps in Atlanta and Dallas, they are few.

Fred Powledge, former reporter for *The New York Times*, also pursues the "myth." He says that in power structures in the South, small groups of men are in control. These men may be "druggists, morticians, or schoolteachers," but more likely they will be bankers, attorneys, county judges, and the owners of the largest local industry.[22]

Carol Estes Thometz's study of Dallas is along similar lines. She found the Dallas Citizens Council to be the power structure of the city. The council's membership is limited to men with power in large business concerns.

> This body has the power to make or break any idea or proposal that certain groups may come up with. It is such a powerful group that nothing can succeed without its support.[23]

There are signs that this tight network of control is loosening. The broad-based participation that was sought in a project called "Goals for Dallas" indicates that attempts to communicate with an increasing number of citizens is a growing characteristic of whatever monolithic power structure still exists in Dallas.

Powledge contends that it is due largely to the power structures of the South, and the white South's hunger for economic progress, that the southern civil rights movement achieved its level of success. Because the power structures wanted to bring in new industry to the South—but "the South" is never really defined—they allowed "token" integration. Powledge says they believed that no decent northern industry would want to move into a southern city where there was racial strife. "As power structure after power structure reacted to the racial crisis, it became part of the movement's strategy to point out that the peaceful solution of the problem was an economic necessity."[24] Powledge says that the power structures of the South had enough influence to be able to manipulate and propagandize the public into doing what they thought was best. Unfortunately, Powledge wrote at a time prior to the biggest riots and racial strife this nation has ever seen—all occurring in sections outside the South. If his thesis on location of industry were followed, industry should have made a mass exodus from such cities as Detroit and Newark.

Arnold Rose, in his book, takes a position different from Powledge and Hunter with their "reputational" theory. Rose concludes that as a city grows from a self-contained entity to one that is more interrelated with the national economy, its power base "changes from a monolithic one dominated by persons possessing great economic power to a bifurcated structure" of the economic and public leaders. He sees a separation between the economically powerful, the political leaders, and those influential in civic associations. Dominance in a city by the economic-elite may be characteristic of the older, smaller towns and cities, such as "Middletown"—and perhaps of a few larger ones—but there is no such simplicity and concentrated control in most urban centers today. Even in Atlanta, the "newer pattern of separation between economic dominants, political leaders and civic association influentials" now seems to hold true.[25]

What Rose says about power structures seems to be characteristic of cities such as Houston, and most other modern cities which have escaped, or grown out of, the stratified structure that places wide power in a tight little circle of men.

But regardless of whether it is Rose, Greer, Hunter, Powledge or Mrs. Thometz who dissect "the Establishment," equally important is what community people think about who controls the city in which they live.

What The People Think It Is

When Rose surveyed a group of people in Minnesota to ask who the unnamed power source of the community might be, he found many refused to answer. Those who did respond gave such answers as "the politicians" or "government officials." The second most frequent choice was a reference to a "power elite" or hidden economic leaders.[26]

In Houston, a random-sample survey was conducted in March 1967 in which 299 community members were asked if they knew who the most influential people in the city were. There were 56.7 percent who answered "yes" and 43.3 percent who said "no." Of those who said "yes," the following is a list of "types" named as the most influential, together with the percent of "votes" they received in the survey.

"Most Influential"	%
Politicians (mayor, city council members, etc.)	39
Professional people (physicians, lawyers, teachers)	23
Wealthy businessmen	20
The wealthy in general	12
Owners of communications media	2
White people in general	2
School board members	1
Jews	.5
Social workers	.5

In another random sample survey in Houston in July 1967, 333 community people answered a question about who they thought made up "the power structure" in the city. Thirty-one percent believed it to be composed of "people with the most money in business and industry"; 16 percent thought it was "city officials"; 12 percent "civil rights leaders here" and 18 percent said they had no idea what the power structure might be.

In another study, those who are usually considered part of "the power structure" of a city were questioned as to what they thought it was in Houston. Al Henry, a Negro administrative assistant to the mayor, said there were various interest groups in Houston to be considered when thinking of a power structure. He also said that "certainly those persons whose economic interests are directly affected take a more active role in politics," but he could find no central establishment. Robert Y. Eckels, a leader of the conservative faction and president of the board of education of the Houston Independent School District, named the mayor's office, school board (which is separate from city government), county commissioner's court, and the chamber of commerce as examples of a power structure, but said that no single overriding group had developed in Houston. A liberal member of the board of education, Mrs. Gertrude Barnstone, said that "if there is a power structure in Houston, it is one based on economics."

Henry, Eckels, and Mrs. Barnstone stated their views at a VISTA conference (Volunteers in Service to America is an anti-poverty agency).[27] The consensus of the VISTA delegates present was that "the power structure" was the moneyed class in Houston or in any other community.

Similar views were expressed in interviews with members of the Student Nonviolent Coordinating Committee in February 1967. The common ingredient in the definitions of the power structure as supplied by SNCC members were the words "money," "economics" and "capital." The power structure was seen as being dominated by the white man, or simply "the man." The common solution given on what must be done about "the Establishment" was to shake it up and change it until it distributes more of the white man's money among black people.

A popular view, then, of "the power structure" focuses on economics. Such a position usually leads to the conclusion that there is a single power structure, made up of people with money. In smaller cities, this may be true. It is not true in a more open, industrialized urban area such as Houston.

"It" Is Plural

Ten men, all economically influential, sat down in one of Houston's plushest restaurants in the spring of 1967 and set about drawing up a list of people who might popularly be considered as part of "the power structure."

Within 15 minutes, the effort became hopeless. Said one: "There isn't any such thing in this town as a single power structure—or even a network of power structures that is based on the same factor, such as money. We have just proved this by not being able to name people that the majority of us know, much less agree upon."

These were white men. They were, for the most part, rich. But even the rich do not know the rich. Nor did these particular men know many people with power from sources other than money—power from political office, power from the mass media, power from educational and religious institutions, and labor unions. Later, a portion of the same group had occasion to do research on the local foundations that exist in Houston. The names of many of the philanthropic groups surprised them because so few had even heard of the foundations, although all had sizeable funds.

Mayor Louie Welch was asked what he considered "the" power structure to be. He had not been present at the meeting of the ten men at the restaurant. He answered:

> Houston, as I suspect is the case with many new and large cities, has no single power structure. It is true that there are some outstanding, wealthy or influential families whose names endure—the Jesse Joneses, the William Hobbys, Ima Hogg, the Cullens, the M. D. Andersons, the Scanlans, the Espersons. . . .
> But economics don't dominate the so-called Establishment. There is an educational power structure in Houston, a religious one, a labor power structure, and of course, a political one, and they don't interlink.

The executive vice president of the Houston Chamber of Commerce, Marvin Hurley, says in his book *Decisive Years for Houston* that he is reluctant to apply the expression "power structure" to Houston.

> I prefer to think in terms of 'community leadership structure'. . . . When I came to Houston, this leadership structure was somewhat rigid. For example, there were members of the Chamber of Commerce board of directors who had held that responsibility for more than 20 years. Today our leadership structure is more flexible, with individuals moving in and out of the top leadership group with a high degree of mobility. It is a highly democratic leadership. . . .[28]

Hurley names several factors that have contributed to the democratic and flexible qualities of Houston's "leadership structure." One of the chief factors is the rapid change which has been accepted as a fact of life in Houston.[29]

Hurley further feels Houston leadership structure is basically confined to those who take an active role in community affairs and decision-making processes. "Holding a position with great potential for power has not automatically enrolled a person in the community leadership structure of Houston. An active engagement in community affairs has been almost universally a prerequisite for recognition as a community leader."[30] The concept of the community leadership structure, says Hurley, is much broader than the political and governmental power structures, which "involve but one area of leadership relations in the community."[31]

Regardless of whether the term "power structure" or "community leadership structure" is used, there are various techniques for those who consider themselves outside the structure to address those inside. All involve some form of communications, and the form preferred by someone like Whitney Young is "negotiation."

Young, executive director of the National Urban League, has long recognized that in dealing with the economic power structure, there must be more than protest and picketing. "You can holler, protest, march, picket and demonstrate," he said, "but somebody must be able to sit in on the strategy conferences and plot a course."[32]

Young's course is to get more and better jobs for black people. He has been described as having instant access to almost any corporate board room in the United States. "Without retreating one iota from his own ideals or minimizing his demands, Young manages to communicate with America's top executives on their own level—and most important—bring them over to his side."[33]

That's one method of addressing the power structure—communicating and bargaining. But there is also conflict-confrontation, and we have yet to examine it in action. Agitation that results from it can occur not only at City Hall but, as we will see, right in neighborhoods where other methods are preferred.

Professional Protesting

Saul Alinsky was trained as a sociologist and a criminologist, but he has been described as "a specialist in creating mass organizations on a democratic basis in order that the so-called 'little man' can gather in his hands the power he needs to make and shape his life."[34] Alinsky is the founder of Industrial Areas Foundation (IAF), a non-profit institution which has organized a number of "power" groups around the country. It has a staff of "professional agitators" (their term) who enter the "unquiet" poverty area by invitation of the residents and help them to organize for the things they want. Methods usually include protest and confrontation with the power structures. The Woodlawn Organization (TWO) in Chicago and FIGHT of Rochester have been cited as two of Alinsky's more successful examples of organizing the poor so they could bring pressure to bear in ways that would accomplish their goals.

There are four steps to Alinsky's method of building an organization: (1) Organizers from the IAF filter through the neighborhood, asking questions and listening to discover the residents' grievances; (2) At the same time, the organizers try to spot the individuals and the groups on which the people seem to lean for advice or help—the "indigenous" leaders; (3) The organizers get these leaders together, discuss the problems and "frustrations" of the people in the neighborhood, and suggest ways in which power might be used to ease or solve them; and (4) A demonstration or series of demonstrations are put on to show how power can be used. These may take a variety of forms: rent strikes against landlords, a boycott of stores, etc. "What is crucial is that meetings and talk, the bedrock on which middle-class organizations founder, are avoided; the emphasis is on action, and on action that can lead to visible results."[35]

Alinsky has often been described as a radical because of his methods. He sends in outside agitators who get the neighborhood "riled up" enough over an issue to organize themselves and defy the power structure. His purpose is to obtain results through conflict. Alinsky was employed for a while as a consultant and lecturer at the Community Action Training Center at Syracuse University. Part of an Office of Economic Opportunity grant to the center was to be spent on training the poor to organize.[36]

Though Charles Silberman is impressed with some of the results of Alinsky's methods, he concedes that there are other approaches to solving slum problems. Militancy, he says, can become an end of its own and power can be used or misused. Even Alinsky admits the dangers, Silberman says. "'Anything that is worthwhile', he [Alinsky] argues, 'carries a calculated risk; and we can be sure that any time we solve one problem we are creating new ones in the process'."[37]

Alinsky's organizers dramatize the strength of concerted action. The Office of Economic Opportunity, as originally conceived, borrowed Alinsky techniques to use in creating "gut issues." As this plan operated, organizers would ferret out an emotional event on which to fix community attention. For example, they might choose the eviction of a tenant by deputy constables to raise the issue of "police brutality." This occurred in a case in Houston in 1966, resulting in a mass protest at City Hall and a "demand" to see the mayor. The mayor appeared before the group, but he could only ex-

plain that deputy constables are accountable to the county
government, not to city officials. They were confronting the
wrong power structure. The group reboarded their buses and
went to the county courthouse, to seek officials who had jur-
isdiction over constables. At the heart of this approach is a
dramatic situation.

> This situation becomes the 'Gut Issue' around which the com-
> munity organizer rallies the people to initiate action. The per-
> sons who displayed interest in this 'Gut Issue' are brought to-
> gether to work on its solution. Leadership is then developed in
> this group as they work together.[38]

Participation of the poor requires initiative, cooperation,
and leadership from the poor. "Arousing" the poor is an in-
novation that can, and has been, abused in community organization, as Alinsky himself has noted. One of the problems
created can be an internal power struggle within the neighborhood which has been picked for "gut issue" action. Organizers have not always been invited into areas where they
have sought to work. Many neighborhoods already have their
own organizations and when outside organizers come in, conflict is almost inevitable.

In 1967, when the community action association was
using the "gut issue" approach of Saul Alinsky, organizers
were sent into areas where they met strong resistance. One of
these areas in Houston was Settegast, where already established civic association leadership put such heat on the community action association that the organizers were trans-
ferred elsewhere. Since 1967, the community action program
has used a different approach in working with neighborhood
people, more in line with what they themselves have expressed as their own preference. In a survey conducted in the
summer of 1967, community people were asked which method
they preferred for a neighborhood: (1) have organizers sent
in to "talk people into organizing"; (2) "let the people decide" how to organize and on what issue, or (3) "stir people
up to get them to organize."

The replies were: 49.2 percent said "let the people decide"; 35.9 percent said "talk people into organizing"; 7.7
percent said "don't know," and 7.2 percent said "stir people
up." The "stir people up" method has been succeeded by less
abrasive methods in the anti-poverty program. Coordination
and bargaining have become more the style. Daniel P. Moynihan notes that coordination with local government and city

resources was the original intent of the community action program, which he helped to draft.[39]

The question that remains, however, is whether local governments have the resources and support necessary to help community people bring substantial changes in their lives. The lack of funds on the local level cannot be overstated. Too many blighted areas are continuing to deteriorate as a result of the inability of local governments to check decay through adequate capital improvements: streets, water lines, storm drains, sanitary sewers. As pointed out in the report, *One Year Later,* "The nation has not made available—to the cities or the blacks themselves—the resources to improve these neighborhoods enough to make a significant change in their residents' lives."[40]

But violence is not the answer. Violence will not remove blight; it will only contribute to it. People not only need help from local governments to upgrade the physical environment of blighted areas. They also need greater opportunity to enter the economic mainstream, which we will examine next.

WHAT SHOULD WE BELIEVE?

POINTS TO CONSIDER—VII

A. Let's stop dealing in all the catchy codewords that imply there is some omnipotent source of power in the city that can solve all the problems of people if it just had the will.

B. Let's recognize that although City Halls may have been long overdue in acting upon problems of the ghetto dweller, many are trying to be much more responsive within the limits of the power and funds they have.

C. Let's acknowledge that in most cities, funds are limited in comparison with the problems to be overcome. Let's also recognize that until local governments get a greater share of the tax dollar, the funds to attack the problems will continue to be limited.

D. Let's get away from the small-town idea that the city is run by a small clique of men who sit in seats of power because they are rich or are listed in the "social register." In most rapidly-growing urban centers of this country, neither money 'nor social position bestows such power on people that they influence every decision of importance in a community. This is not to say there are no power structures, but the structures are multiple and, in most cities, they do not interlock.

E. Let's recognize that power structures not only do not interlock, they often may be at odds with each other.

F. Let's not underestimate the power of people in a neighborhood getting together and making their needs known. Whether action results is not likely to be a function of what "connections" the group has at City Hall. Action is most likely to depend on whether there is money available to provide whatever service is being sought.

G. Let's not discount bargaining, negotiation and consensus as useful means for getting action on problems. Conflict and confrontation may satisfy needs to release long pent-up anger but in cases where City Hall has demonstrated it cares about the problems of community people, it should be given a chance to act without being shouted at and presented with ultimatums.

H. Let's face up to the fact that bureaucratic organization has overtaken the operation of just about every large political, economic, educational and religious institution in this country, and that the larger the bureaucracy, the more risk there is that it will fail to be responsive to the needs of people.

I. Let's try to figure out ways to put the levers of control closer to the hands of people and reverse the tide of growing bureaucracy.

CHAPTER 8

A WAY TO THE MAINSTREAM

He was 17, black, and a "picture reader." But he was tired of handouts and slums. He said:

> Man, help me be square. I can't make it like this. I don't like a lot of things they do, but I got no choice. I want out of the slums. I want out of handouts. Man, help me be a man.[1]

This was a young man on the bottom talking. A Negro on the top had this to say:

> This country has no use for a man or woman who doesn't produce. . . . I tell them that white people don't have as much bias against Negroes as they think. . . . I tell them they have to learn and produce.[2]

Certainly, white people do not have as much bias against Negroes who are millionaires, as they do against the man on the bottom. If money talks in this country, it should not to the extent that a man is automatically branded as useless if he does not produce. It takes opportunity to "learn and produce," and many black people have not had it. A fraction have overcome the lack of opportunity and have learned and produced—and made money—anyway. But they are the exceptions. The young man on bottom has not had opportunity. The challenge is to provide it to him and millions like him.

What is done with the opportunity, once it is truly provided, is up to the individual. The young man said his goal was to "be square." He meant he wanted out of slums. The goal of most Negroes is to be part of the mainstream of America, and by mainstream I mean the place where opportunity exists for fuller participation in the fruits and decisions of this society.

Despite what the highly-vocal black separatists say, the evidence is quite conclusive that the goal of the mass majority of Negroes *is* to enter deeper into the mainstream of American society. Even at the height of tensions in the summer of 1967 in Houston, Negroes were saying (as borne out by surveys) that they did *not* want to have their children in all-black schools, that they did *not* want a separate state for black people. What they said they wanted was a choice—a choice to have their children go to whatever school they thought best, a choice to live where they believe they would be happiest.

A choice comes from, first, having opportunity, and, second, making use of opportunity. It comes from living in decent housing, going to decent schools, having decent health, and being free enough from the defeating (and often crushing) effects of slums to possess the motivation to develop whatever potential an individual has. Once that opportunity and freedom are real and truly do exist, the conditions for a choice have been met, and the person then must decide what his goal is.

If the goal of the Negro is to be part of the mainstream of American society, as I believe it is, some people have the idea that the only door is through the middle-class, through being like white, middle-class people. They think that true participation in the decision-making process comes only from middle-class status. The black militant objects strenuously to the idea that a Negro must be molded into the image of white middle-class America before he can share in the fruits of society.

I think the hang-up here is over the term "middle-class." If by middle-class we mean that a person must take on the manner of white suburbia, with cook-outs on the patio and two martinis before dinner, then why should it be insisted that people adopt these tribal rites before they can live in a decent house and have a taste of prosperity?

S. M. Miller, New York University sociologist, agrees that "we have become caught in the trap that any kind of improvement necessarily implies a middle-class style of life and that the poor are dying for it or are repressing their desire for it." He makes this additional point:

> It is possible to have a better standard of living without having other stylistic accoutrements of it. To a large extent we are not primarily trying to change a style of life but trying to change the possibilities of life. The goal is to make it possible for people to make their own decisions. The goal is to maximize opportunities and not to insist on a thin roster of choice. The professional's aim is to increase the opportunities of individuals, not to make their choices.[3]

But what the professional must guard against is looking at all ghetto dwellers as though their lives were nothing but pathology and despair. He must guard against looking at black people as if they were all the same and not individuals who have varying capacities to cope with hardship.[4] Slums *can* be crushing and being black *has* meant unconscionable hardship for many people. But they are not all cripples. Robert Coles discovered this in his work among the poorest sharecroppers of the South.[5] Ralph Ellison finds it necessary to remind sociologists that Negroes have developed a life style that many do not want to lose by white people trying to take black people out of their "wretched lives." He notes:

> . . . we have certain choices, we have various social structurings which determine to a great extent how we act and what we desire. This is what we live. When we try to articulate it, when we try to define it, all we have is sociology. And sociology is loaded. The concepts which are brought to bear are usually based on those of white, middle-class, Protestant values and life style.[6]

Both Coles and Ellison recognize that there can be much strength in the life style of the black man. Ellison adds that it is also not impossible to find love of the land, the very land where life may have been hardest and cruelest. It is not "an utterly outrageous idea," he says, that a Negro could love the South. So in considering "a better life" for poor people, particularly the black who are poor, there are many subtleties and nuances that can be easily overlooked. The challenge is to cultivate the strengths of the poor, not obliterate them, as opportunities are opened for people to enter the mainstream. Frank Reissman has commented on some of the "traditions" that have helped the poor to survive, and these, too, must be preserved.

> . . . the poor have developed their own informal systems and traditions in order to cope and survive. Store-front churches, cellar clubs, hometown clubs, the extended family, the use of the street as a playground, the block party, the mutual assistance of siblings . . . are just a few of these forms of adaptation. . . . Only through the utilization of these traditions can the poor be genuinely brought into the mainstream of our society and, not incidentally, can our society benefit enormously from incorporation of some of these traditions. . . .[7]

Black people, then, and any other minority, should be able to maintain life styles of their own without apology. If they have more "soul" than white people, more tone to their way of life, then that is to their advantage. They can hardly be expected to develop a pride and identity if the dominant society insists they submerge themselves in white America. America, it must be remembered, is *not* a melting pot, but a pluralistic society in which people of different backgrounds and religions *are* part of the mainstream, and *do* preserve group identities. As for "middle-class," if that means work and money, then it is not a sinister status that anyone should be ashamed of. Black people want work and money. They want the same material comforts that white America has had almost as a monopoly. In this sense, there is abundant proof that a vast majority of black people in the United States want to be "square" and "middle-class."

The most important lesson learned by Willis Wardell, the 17-year-old Negro who said "help me be square," was that "to enter 'the good life' you have to have certain skills, abilities and behavior."[8] The skills and abilities do not come easy to someone who has been trapped in a ghetto where the problem is not only no money but also sickness and crimes and broken homes and little education and even less motivation. All the problems of ghetto life must be attacked. But the money and work problem is basic, and it goes back to "skills, abilities and behavior." The behavior part of this triad simply means to show up every day at work, get along with people on the job and to perform.

Education has been hailed as "the answer" to "the Negro problem." It instills in people the "skills, abilities and behavior" that Wardell recognized as essential. But conventional education is too slow for giving preparation and skills to Negroes now. And it is often too inaccessible. What better system is there? Or, at least, what supplement can be offered to the present school system? One that has been proposed is called "neighborhood linear learning." It would be for both children and adults.

Under this process, much of the current educational system would be restructured for ghetto dwellers. Neighborhood linear learning would be akin to what has been called the "linear community approach" to education.[9] The neighborhood linear learning system would be a "saturation" approach to education and training. It would place great emphasis on taking training and education to "the doorstep" in Negro neighborhoods and instilling motivation in children before they ever get near the traditional school age.

The learning system would be so decentralized and accessible to neighborhoods there would be no transportation problems. Mobile units would be used to take learning to the doorsteps for people of all ages. There would be some people who would not be motivated enough to take advantage of the system, no matter how much it saturated a neighborhood. But the system would make a point of reaching out to children at an early age so that motivation would be acquired despite an unfavorable home environment. There would be enough teacher-counselors to work closely with children and instill early motivation because much of the actual teaching and training process would be electronic. The teacher would be free from the chore of repeating herself, or himself, to class after class, year after year. The chief job of the teacher would be to show personal interest in each child, to work with him on problems he cannot solve by himself in school and to counsel him on those outside of school.

The electronic gear in the neighborhood "doorstep" mobile units would be hooked up to a central "brain bank" where information on a wide range of subjects and skills would be stored. Children would be taught how to use the gear so that they could make a daily practice of going into one of the units and being taught by "machine learning." Teachers would be on hand to give individual counseling and to keep order, although the units would be small enough to accommodate only a few students at a time.

In addition to the mobile units for individual learning, there would be "home centers" that would be conveniently located in neighborhoods for providing additional guidance and "social development" and to train tutor-advisors, as in the approach proposed by Cyril Sargent and Judith Ruchkin. There would also be "special learning centers." These would train staff, develop learning sequences and provide public information. Just as much opportunity would be provided to adults, as to children, under neighborhood linear learning. They would have centers for enhancing any skills they already had or for acquiring new ones. The centers would permit a person stepping into them to plug into the central brain bank for as much or as little time as he had.

In any event, learning would be concrete rather than conceptual and would be tailored to individual needs. Surveys could be made among young people in the community to determine what occupations they would like to enter, and tests would be given to see how close to their aspirations their innate abilities might permit them to come.

As can be seen by Table 2, the specified aspirations in one sampling we made in Houston were not unrealistic. Those who simply said they would like to be "a millionaire" would have to be reminded that an exceedingly high income is not as important to most people as occupational satisfaction.

TABLE 2

WHAT NEGROES ARE BY OCCUPATION AND WHAT
THEY SAY THEY WANT TO BE*
(N=600)
Present Occupation

	%
Common Laborer	32
Domestic/Housewife	17
Skilled Laborer/Postman	16
Unemployed	15
Clerical/Sales	9
Professional/Musician/Preacher	4
Construction Laborer	4
Own Business	2
Student	1

Desired Occupation

	%
Professional	32
Skilled Worker	22
Secretary/Clerical/Sales	11
Teacher	7
Government Official	7
Engineer/Scientist	6
Actress/Model/Musician/Writer	5
"Millionaire"	5
Housewife	4
Farmer/Rancher	1

As for the children, the saturated neighborhood learning system would not require choosing an occupation before there is any realistic prospect of knowing what they want to be. Analysis of the demands of business and industry would be published in the neighborhood to provide information on where the greatest opportunities exist. Counselors would offer guidance on careers.

Neighborhood "doorstep" education would also include subjects on black history. There would be nothing in the system to prevent ghetto dwellers from getting a thorough exposure to the contributions of black people in history and

*Based on a random-sample survey taken in eight Negro areas of Houston in the spring and summer of 1967.

the evolution of African culture. Although the system would
provide an accelerated means to acquire skills, it would also
offer college preparatory courses and encourage young people
with the aptitude to gain higher education.

One of the greatest services of the neighborhood linear
learning system would be to permit ambitious adults to obtain better jobs by upgrading their skills. Charles Silberman
believes that automation has not eliminated "entry jobs"
that permit a rise up the ladder.[10] As for whether sufficient
adults would have the ambition to attend learning centers,
the community would be so saturated with an atmosphere of
upward mobility that incentive would be stimulated.

But could the nation afford such a saturation program?
A better question might be: Can it afford not to try drastic
innovations in education?

Even an accelerated, super-saturated system of education, however, would not alone be enough. As we mentioned,
it would have to be supplemented on the home front by programs attacking ill health, bad housing, the problem of absentee parents and crime in the streets. The Model Cities
program would seem a natural supplement to the door-step
approach in education. But, regardless of whether this system or some other were tried in education, the key to entering
the mainstream will lie in large part with industry. Industry
must not only open up jobs but also see that people stay on
jobs, and have a future on jobs.

Why should private companies be obligated to do this?
"They're doing it," Leo Beebe said, "because they've decided
they're guilty—or the system's guilty—of holding part of our
population down, of not giving them the chance to get in the
mainstream of American life."[11] Beebe was a vice president
of Ford Motor Company when he was asked, in 1968, to become the executive vice chairman of the National Alliance of
Businessmen, which set a three-year goal of putting 500,000
(now 614,000) hard-core unemployed to work.* Beebe's philosophy toward the hard-core unemployed applies to all un-
trained and unskilled minority group people.

Industry is now offering not only jobs and training but
also personal attention. Beebe observed: "Helping one of the
hard-core people can get you into the whole human spectrum.
That's why job coaching, counseling or the buddy system—

---

*Executive vice chairman for 1969 is Paul W. Kayser of Pepsico.

whichever works best—can be a very special thing."[12] Providing this sort of personal attention cannot be regarded as encouraging dependency or coddling. It is the experience of offering hope and a future. These are people, as Beebe found out, who are "physically, mentally and emotionally impoverished."[13] Virgil E. Boyd, president of Chrysler Corporation, told of his experience in putting the hard-core unemployed to work.

> . . . some of these people signed on for job training—with an 'X' of course—but failed to show up. And many of those who did report were very late. As we registered those who did report, we found that many of them had no social security number, had never been counted in a census, or registered to vote, or belong to any organization of any kind. In most of the accepted senses, they really didn't even exist.[14]

They were, indeed, invisible. And for the tough job of making them visible for the first time in their lives, extraordinary measures must be used. Industry must spend time with ghetto people on such fundamentals as showing up for work, coming back from lunch. As one observer said:

> Ghetto life prepares its young residents for survival. It doesn't prepare them for normal work. They have been trained in a society that told them, "Work hard and you may become a janitor." Now it demands, "Why can't you do white-collar work?"[15]

There are many who have lived so long without a future that they cannot see the point of taking a dead-end job. The urgency for extraordinary measures by industry are emphasized by the forces that crush hope out of so many in the slum. One analysis of the pressing problem put it this way:

> There is no time. Forces at work in the slums are destroying the pride and humanity of the people who live there. The psychologically unemployables are being created in great numbers and this is irreversible. Many of the hard-core unemployed in the ghetto over 35 may as well be written off. They have become outcasts and the enemies of society, and this is not strange.[16]

But there are many who are still salvageable, if just given a chance. Shown some personal attention and with a "role model" of someone from the same background who "made it," many will develop motivation and competence. Shown a job with a future, many will work hard for advancement.

Richard Alston, 21, is a case in point.[17] He was a hard-core kid. He killed a man at 16 with a knife. He served a prison term for manslaughter. Upon release, he heard of the

Opportunities Industrialization Center in Roxbury, Mass., his home town. He signed up and learned to be a machine operator. He said: "I've seen the streets and I've seen the night life. But OIC opened my eyes. They make me leave my dope at the door, my wine and knives and guns outside. They opened up a whole new world." Alston was another ghetto dweller who became "square" and got a glimpse of mainstream prosperity. Industry must accept such people, people with prison records, people with no work histories, and more and more businesses are in fact doing so.

Jobs are a key to building pride. Ownership of a home is also. Both give the ghetto dweller some stake in society. Willis Wardell, the young man who asked the Job Corps to make him "square" left training with such a stake. He said: "A teacher once told me I would end up in jail. She is wrong. I know how to run a 101 card sorter. I know how to get along. You guys made me square and it's O.K. with me."[18]

In some ghettos, the word seems to be gradually spreading that society is opening up, that there is reason to hope. The commitment to spend extraordinary time and effort on the problem is only beginning, however. It will require much hard work and patience—this time on the part of the white world.

The "Whole Human"

The problem of poverty is so multiple and pervasive that, ultimately, the country must face up to a program based on the "whole human." It must ultimately stop offering piecemeal solutions to unsegmented, human problems. It must stop trying to solve education over there, employment over here, health somewhere else. A person who is caught in poverty or confined by the invisible walls of the ghetto cannot segment himself. He cannot set aside one portion of his being and try to fill it with education, while another portion is empty from poor housing. He cannot let one space be for love and care and ignore it if it stays void. He cannot say, "this part of me will be for health," and hope that it will always brim full. He cannot assign only one segment of his being to work and try to keep whole by having a job. People live lives on a total, unsegmented basis. Impoverishment of any part affects the whole. A man does not live his life piecemeal, particularly the poor and the black man. Even when given every chance on a

job, he cannot ignore the pressing concerns in other quarters
of his life:

> He may be worried whether his wife and children are well.
> He may have to stay home or leave work to take care of them.
> There may be no day care available for his children. He may
> be concerned because his youngsters are failing in school. Perhaps
> the school is failing his youngsters. Perhaps his teenagers are
> getting in trouble.
>
> His flat may be unheated because the furnace is broken. His
> apartment house may be infested with rats. His landlord may be
> raising the rent or threatening eviction. His food prices are ris-
> ing. His wife may not know how to run the house economically.
> He may be threatened with having his new wages garnisheed.
> He may even live in danger of being arrested on doubtful pretexts
> and booked on charges that look bad to his employer even though
> no conviction results.
>
> He may be so distracted by a variety of problems that he cannot
> work. He may quit his job. He may give up. He may drop out,
> the way he has dropped out of other jobs, out of school, out of
> society.[19]

There is an interrelatedness to the problems of a slum
that cannot be ignored. The "integration" in the life of many
ghetto dwellers is not a concern to mix with white people or
send their children to white schools. Their kind of "integration" applies to how much one problem combines with another. Kenneth Clark has taken recognition of this point
repeatedly.

> . . . the problem is so great that unless we attack all at the
> same time, the work we do on any one is bound to fail. Jobs
> for parents affect education of children. So does housing. And
> jobs affect housing and housing affects jobs. And education
> affects jobs and housing. And the quality of family life affects
> all and in turn is affected by all.[20]

And as added by James Farmer: "If it is futile to work
on one part of the problem and not at the same time work on
all others; it is just as unproductive to work on any part just
a portion of the way."[21]

The "whole human" approach would concentrate on the
whole man: his health, his family, his housing, his education,
his employment. Because his employment is so central to his
life, because the mainstream in American society starts with
the economic, because a job is where a man spends so much
of his time, the "whole human" solution must revolve around
employment. A job is the nub of a man's very identity and

must furnish the framework for bringing into his life co-
herence and meaning.

> In America what you do is what you are: to do nothing is to
> be nothing; to do little is to be little. The equations are implaca-
> ble and blunt, and ruthlessly public.[22]

So that a man *can* be something and not nothing, he
must do a job and for him to do a job he cannot be sick or
have rats biting his babies at home or live in a house without
plumbing or running water. He lives his life as a whole and
no part of it can be futile and hopeless. Accelerated, doorstep education and intensified programs in training and employment are *partial* measures. The ultimate solution to giving people a true opportunity to make of themselves what
their potential permits, to have a sense of being somebody
instead of nothing and to gain a stake in society, will be to
find ways for attacking *all* the problems of the quagmire—
and doing it in a manner that elicits participation by the
people themselves. There are already programs designed with
this philosophy. Some, such as the War on Poverty, have
failed to meet the unfortunately high expectations they
raised. Others, such as the Model Cities program, have yet to
show what they can do.

Meanwhile, there have been other possibilities suggested.
One suggestion has been to call on American industry not
only to provide jobs but also housing and other needs of the
hard-core unemployed. Large corporations in the United
States have been approached by the federal government to
set up subsidiary companies that would offer housing for
low-income people. The program would be designed to take
the efforts that industry is now making in getting jobs for
the hard-core unemployed and extend them to the housing
field. After housing, it is a short step to health, education,
transportation and related concerns.

In discussing the degree of responsibility that industry
has in social problems, Robert Austin makes this point in a
Harvard Business Review article:[23] Industry has unwittingly
generated enormous social changes—as well as problems—in
this country through the tremendous technological advances
it has produced. The simple illustration, he says, of Henry
Ford's introduction of assembly-line techniques for mass pro-

duction of inexpensive cars should be sufficient to point up
the social consequences of technological power. Austin notes:

> The face of America has changed radically since the days of the
> Model T. There is change in our farm community, in the urban-
> ization of society, in our educational methods and location of
> schools. . . . All these things grew out of Henry Ford's one,
> simple decision.[24]

It is questionable whether that "one, simple decision"
was truly responsible for *all* those social changes, but it did
lead to many. And business today is creating other changes
with technological advances. Some of the social changes constitute social problems. Automation has brought a demand
for higher skills and training. Black people, and others who
historically have had less education and training, may be
given all the "equal opportunity" in the world to fill the good-
paying jobs of automated industry, but if they have insuffi-
cient skills and training, the opportunity is meaningless.

It would be ridiculous to attribute all the social ills of the
day to technological changes produced by the corporate technique and innovative genius of business. But it would be
equally naive to believe that industry has had no effect on
the existence and extent of the social problems. The question
is: Does industry have a responsibility to help solve them?
In his *Harvard Business Review* article, Austin thinks it does,
and I am inclined to agree.

It is not only the right thing for business to be involved,
it is also to the self-interest of business. Dr. Charles F. Jones,
president of Humble Oil & Refining Company, points up his
position in these words:

> The fundamental reason for business involvement in the so-
> called 'social marketplace' must rest on the fact that it is the right
> thing to do. Like those in any other line of endeavor, we have a
> duality of purpose: we are both businessmen and citizens.[25]

M. A. Wright, board chairman of Humble and former
president of the United States Chamber of Commerce, en-
larges on the inter-relationship between businessman and
citizen by noting that "business can only be profitable if
society is healthy, and society can be healthy only if it has a
sound and progressive economic base."[26]

The self-interest of business in helping solve social problems touches on some very concrete economic issues. As Wright has said:

> . . . the inner city today represents a by-passed island that has not developed economically. It represents an untouched source of manpower, a pent-up market. The people who live there can be creators of income, producers, and consumers. They could be paying taxes rather than receiving tax revenue. . . . If the average family income for non-whites was raised to the average for whites, total personal income in the United States would be higher by about $15 billion. Such an increase in earnings would benefit not only those directly involved but would improve the whole economic structure.[27]

The question, then, is no longer whether industry is going to be involved in social problems—or why it should be. The question now is: How much? How far does the responsibility go and how much help must industry give?

Any answer to such a question must take into consideration the fact that industry does not have the expertise to work on the whole spectrum of social ills. Even if it did, there would be great waste if resources outside of industry were not used. It seems to me that one of the biggest problems today is not the lack of resources but the efficient use of them. The problem is one of connecting, interfacing, coordinating, getting the know-how people together, bringing neighborhood residents in for their contribution and participation. The resources lie in industry, in government, in voluntary organizations, in the neighborhoods and a whole host of other places. I think we should work on bringing all these resources together before saying we ought to turn the whole job over to the private sector.

But there should be no underestimating of the extent to which some companies are already committed to attacking social problems in this country. There already *are* companies that have set up housing development corporations for low-income families. There already *are* companies that have established plants or financed business enterprises in the ghetto, staffed and managed by Negroes. There already *are* companies offering classroom education in their plants. There already *are* companies that are going into day-care services for employees to reduce absenteeism. So it may not be far-fetched to forecast that industry *will* end up leading the attack on social ills of this country. In reality, the attack will probably be broader based, with emphasis on the people themselves sharing in the solution of the problems.

One proposal to bring people closer to controlling their own futures lies in community development corporations. These would be made up of neighborhood residents who would buy stock in them at a very nominal price. The corporations would be run by people in the neighborhood and might be multi-purpose: They might set up business and industry to offer sources of employment to residents, they might run schools, build houses, operate a security unit. Under this theory, for every service they offered a given neighborhood, the local government would refund to the corporations whatever cost it would require for the city itself to offer the service. Already, of course, there are many neighborhoods in many cities that form clubs or associations that contract for their own garbage collection or private police. The community development corporations would be a modification of this practice for lower-income areas.

The objective would be to give greater power and a bigger voice to neighborhood people—people who have been cut off too long from power, from the opportunity to develop themselves, and from the right to participate in a meaningful way in decisions that affect their lives. The intent is good. But I do not know if the community development corporation is feasible. What I do know is that a city is by nature organic, and that no part of it can be totally removed from the whole— and survive—any more than a man's kidney can be taken from his body and be expected to exist on its own. This point has also been made by Washington officials such as Ralph Taylor, former assistant secretary of the Department of Housing and Urban Development.[28]

Much of what has been discussed here falls under the heading of that new codeword "decentralization"—decentralization to neighborhood government. The theory, as I say, sounds appealing and probably looked that way when the Ocean Hill-Brownsville school plan went into effect as part of the decentralization experiment in New York. What happened in that case, of course, was a massive upheaval in 1968 that involved teachers being fired by the neighborhood governing body, followed by a strike of teachers all over the city, and a shutting down of schools.

What also seemed to happen was a memory lapse on the part of the decentralization supporters as to what the purpose of a school is. As John Everett noted at the time, it is not to give adults the unlimited right to sound off in strident voices or to demonstrate their control over the school; it is to educate children.[29] But children have a hard time getting educated, at least in the usual sense, when the school is closed down.

There is no reason that such a fiasco must occur in every experiment with neighborhood government. There is no reason that some practical system cannot be developed so that people, poor people, can have greater say-so about how their neighborhood is run and by whom. There is no reason that contracts cannot be worked out with local governments on letting neighborhoods set up their own garbage service, their own street cleaning, their own day care centers, rat control—and maybe even schools. There is no reason, provided careful thought and attention are given to decentralization, and the organic concept of a city is kept in mind. A number of preliminary steps are necessary. Decentralization requires a community to figure out just where it starts and stops and who is going to speak for it. A neighborhood, just as city government, must have some system of leadership. And once leaders are picked, they must be given an opportunity to exercise authority. If they are elected and their decisions are contrary to what is wanted by a certain segment of the neighborhood, is their authority to be subverted and flouted? If so, as Daniel P. Moynihan has recognized, "this quickly enough becomes government . . . by a process of private nullification. . . ."[30] It certainly would not be democratic neighborhood government.

But to the extent that a neighborhood *can* define itself and *can* set up a system of effective leadership, decentralization may offer promise. If a neighborhood did provide itself with certain services and saved local government money in the process, some return of taxes to citizens in the neighborhood would be expected under the decentralization plan.

Fine and good. But the result would probably be something less than a "whole human" system. Decentralization to the neighborhood level might well leave out services pertaining to employment, hospitals, training centers, police—any number of things. And frankly I do not know if it will ever be feasible for one part of a city to set up a system whereby it can have direct control over all these services.

I do know that whatever is tried and considered will not happen tomorrow. And since this bald truth must be faced, it is necessary not only to examine what may be a solution in the future, but also what other doors are being opened to give hope and opportunity *here and now*. The here and now is what people live with in the slums; it is what people live with who have been excluded from the mainstream and have reacted violently, particularly in urban America.

The peace we seek in our cities will never be total. But the conditions that exist in slums and block opportunity for people are clearly breeding grounds for violence, and those conditions must be attacked here and now, even if the attack appears to be piecemeal or falls short of a "whole human" solution.

WHAT SHOULD WE BELIEVE?
POINTS TO CONSIDER—VIII

A. Let's don't assume that the majority of black people in this country want to set up a separate state or society. People who live in ghettos and slums want most a choice as to where their children go to school and what kind of neighborhood they live in. A choice requires opportunity to gain a stake and voice in society.

B. Let's recognize that poor people in this country do want to work and they will if they are provided an opportunity. Most of all, they need an opportunity to taste success instead of the failure they have known so much of their lives.

C. Let's face the fact that to overcome the conditions that contribute to a sense of failure, there must be someone present on the job who can be used as a model for success—someone who came from the same adverse conditions and knows what it means to fight for daily survival.

D. Let's recognize that some of the rules in this country actually work against poor people rather than for them. A man with 10 children who makes $6,000 a year is poor, but he is ineligible to enroll in a government training program because his income exceeds $4,500. Even with the motivation, then, such a person cannot upgrade his skills to pull himself and his family out of poverty.

E. Let's don't consider that "special favors" are being done for black people when industry pays extra attention to training them and helping them acquire skills. Many would have had the skills had they not been sent to schools that offered inferior education and given little chance to acquire on-the-job training.

F. Let's remember that despite the central role of a job in a person's life, the individual in poverty is subject to a set of interlocking conditions and all must be attacked if he is to have a true opportunity to gain self respect and pride. He cannot be expected to do well on a job if he lives in inferior housing, is burdened with sickness in the family, has rats biting his children, is worried about the schools that fail to give his kids a good education and has a high rate of crime and delinquency in his neighborhood. A frontal assault on all these problems must be made simultaneously, with the individual himself involved at the very center.

G. Let's don't assume that people who fail to achieve much formal education, or are products of poor schools, cannot be trained for good jobs. Many learn fast. It is a question of showing the person that he does not have to live a life of failure and can achieve competence and a sense of achievement.

H. Let's recognize that American industry is undergoing radical changes in taking on greater responsibility for social problems but there are many resources outside of industry that also are contributing. Government, in many instances, has been the stimulus for the attack on the problems, and is more and more entering into a partnership with the private sector to help solve them.

I. Let's make up our minds that there is a minimum level of decency below which no human being should live. The fact that a person can adapt to slums, and even say he does not mind living in them, is no reason to believe that this is the way human beings should live. People can adapt to all sorts of things—congestion, radiation, pollution, noise—but this does not mean they should.

J. Let's accept as a national goal the freeing of people from the conditions that contribute to their being down and out. Let's work on a "whole human" approach that will provide opportunity for people to have a choice as to what they make of their life.

K. Let's acknowledge the contributions already being made by American business in attacking social problems and build on the start that has been made.

CHAPTER 9

WHERE WE ARE HERE AND NOW

It has become fashionable among social critics to dismiss the work done on minority group problems by City Hall—any City Hall—as band-aid work, as putting patches on a problem of such size and depth that the treatment is about as effective as a bandage on a cerebral hemorrhage.

If we insist on using medical analogies, however, I think we must recognize that in order for the patient to survive long enough to get to the hospital for surgery, some emergency first-aid work in the field is first necessary. But I think that what is being done goes beyond first-aid. I think in many cities, Houston being one of them, serious efforts are being made to provide genuine opportunities for people to gain a bigger voice and a greater stake in their society.

A bigger voice and a greater stake are essential. This was brought home repeatedly in the more than 7,000 interviews conducted in the Negro community of Houston. It was confirmed by visits to the ghettos of Los Angeles and Oakland, after both those cities had experienced riots.

Violence is often spawned, as we have seen, in the lives of people who feel isolated, cut-off, with no sense of belonging to the society in which they live. No one wants to feel left out. Each person wants at least enough of a voice in his society to feel he has some say-so about decisions that are made which affect his life. No one wants to feel that nothing in the society belongs to him. I mean to him personally. I mean something as basic as a house.

But before taking a look at just where we are here and now, in terms of people gaining a bigger voice and a greater stake in society, let's review for a minute some of the findings from this book. Here is a brief summary:

1. When a violent disturbance occurs in a city, even when it is limited to the campus of a Negro university, the effects are felt throughout the black community off campus. In Houston, the effects carried to Negro neighborhoods 15 miles away and more.

2. A dominant feature to the effects is a sharp rise of tensions in the community, increasing the potential for more violence—violence that could constitute a community-wide riot rather than a campus upheaval.

3. Increased hostility is focused on the police. A greater percent of Negroes report being personally abused by police in after-violence surveys as compared with before-violence findings, as a change in their perception occurs.

4. To prevent the ignition of community-wide violence, several steps seem indicated: (a) Representatives of the mayor's office must be in touch with every situation that is potentially explosive and at every scene where trouble is developing. Rapport with non-violent militants and neighborhood people must be such that they are willing to go in and help tell crowds to "cool it." They did this three times in 1967-68 in Houston; (b) A police-community relations program, properly designed, serves to reduce hostility and brings better understanding between officers and minority group people. Such a program was organized in Houston and each officer met in small-group sessions with community people in the neighborhoods for six-week periods; (c) A "peacekeeper corps" should be organized and made up of community people and workers willing to help prevent outbreaks of violence in their neighborhoods during times of heightened tension. Such a group helped put a stop to a series of firebombings across the city in August 1967, and circulated throughout the Negro community for three nights following the assassination of Martin Luther King—a period when 233 riots and disorders occurred in more than 200 cities and towns in the nation. Scores of volunteers from the Harris County Community Action Association were helpful both in 1968 and 1967 in "peacekeeper" efforts.

5. Based on other surveys done in the Houston study, it became evident that there is misunderstanding about the so-called Establishment, principally in terms of people believing there is some monolithic power structure, made up of a select group of men which makes all the decisions for the city. This is not supported by the evidence which shows that there is no single power structure, that it is plural in nature and that among the "power establishments" that exist, there is often disagreement among them and within them. It was also found that bargaining with power structures is not only possible on the part of community people, but also encouraged.

6. An analysis of student unrest on Negro campuses shows much concern over questions of identity, guilt from leaving the ghetto, the quality and nature of the college education received, competition upon graduation in a work world made up predominantly of white people, and many other influences that are bearing on all young people today, regardless of color.

7. An examination of individual violence, in the form of crime in the ghetto, showed that many of the factors that go into shaping and making the "rebel without a cause" are also contributors to unrest in the Negro community.

8. The "sead" factors of unrest were presented to suggest that the spotlight that is turned on a community by the media has an influence on what people do, that the expectations of ghetto dwellers toward what they believe they should have in life, compared with what they do have, is a very important consideration, that their attitudes toward existing conditions have a strong bearing also, and that the community's dispersion is still another strong factor in terms of how much social unrest occurs.

9. In considering "A Way to the Mainstream" for ghetto dwellers who are pressing for a greater share in society, we looked at a system of neighborhood education and training that would saturate an area with the opportunity to acquire learning and skills, by both children and adults, through advanced technological techniques of teaching. We also examined the need for a "whole human" system that would attack all the major problems contributing to keeping people down and out. Also, a look was taken at the proposal for the private sector to take on greater roles and for neighborhood corporations to be developed.

This brings us to here and now—what is currently being done, what good it is doing, and why it is needed. As I see it, where we are here and now is at a point of trying to accelerate the rate of offering greater opportunity for people to gain a voice and a stake—people who have been cut-off from each for too long. The programs recommended for adoption in Houston, many based on the surveys that we did in the city, have been aimed at increasing this kind of opportunity. They represent *only a start,* but it has been gratifying that a number of these programs have been put into effect, thus demonstrating that surveys and studies *can* re-

sult in action and do not have to end up gathering dust on
a shelf.

The very act of asking people questions was a first step
toward opening up greater opportunity for them to have a
voice in their society. Many black people told our interviewers that they had never been asked their opinion before about
what problems and concerns they had. They were only too
glad to have a chance to voice grievances to someone who
would relay them to City Hall. But this was only a very
nominal first step. There was the need to provide people with
opportunity not only for (1) a bigger voice, but also (2) a
greater stake. There is still a long, long way to go, but here is
a brief rundown on City Hall activities and programs in each
category:

For A Bigger Voice

1. Neighborhood City Hall*—a mobile trailer was leased
by city council to operate out of minority-group neighborhoods to give people a chance to come and talk their problems
over with a representative of the mayor's office. This is face-
to-face communication with the city establishment, with City
Hall. The mayor's aide has the job of seeing to it that the
people's problems are acted on promptly.

2. Neighborhood branch of the mayor's office—quarters
were rented in the area of the city that was formerly called
the Bottom and that was considered the worst concentrated
slum in Houston. Out of the branch office, a mayor's aide,
Ernest Carswell, has worked with the people to upgrade the
area. The people formed a recreation center in a small building once used as a cafe, they established sewing classes, auto
repair instruction, tutoring classes. The city set up a health
center in the area, paved streets, installed lights and helped
organize athletic teams for youths. Downtown business and
professional men raised money to go with city funds for
erecting a community building in the area. The people decided they no longer were on the bottom and changed the
name of their area to Swiney Addition, named after the man
who first owned the land in that part of the city.

3. Communications with militants—the mayor's office
tries to maintain communications with militant groups to

---

*Two more Neighborhood City Halls have now been proposed.

encourage dialogue and to seek solution to problems through non-violent means.

4. City Hall Service Center—the mayor established a central service center at City Hall for all citizens to use in voicing complaints about city services or making requests.

5. Community aides—four representatives from the mayor's office work with people in the community on their problems. The aides meet with neighborhood groups and participate with the people in trying to work out solutions.

6. "You and Your City Services"—a booklet was printed giving specific details on the procedure for seeking action on needed city services, such as getting a street patched, a stop sign installed, or action on a number of other problems.

7. Communications with police—in the fall of 1967, a program was launched, as previously discussed, for face-to-face dialogue between community people and police. In addition, the police department has a community relations division that operates programs aimed at minority group people. One is an "observation corps," which give young black people an opportunity to work with line officers as observers. Another is a summer program for poverty youth that offers employment to young people as information aides, physical training assistants, supply assistants and similar jobs.*

8. Recreation councils—sixty of these have been organized in neighborhoods to give people a direct voice in recreation programs in their areas and in the operation of community buildings where citizens meet.

9. Summer youth program—in 1968, a total of 14,312 low-income young people participated in "Operation Glow"— a program they helped to design, under the leadership of Al Henry of the mayor's office and the Houston-Harris County Youth Opportunity Council. A 12-week project was set up offering ghetto youth opportunities to go camping, to make trips to cultural events, to participate in community service. Again, there was a voice by people—in this case, young people —in shaping programs of which they became a part.

10. Mayor's open door—any citizen can bystep all the other avenues listed here for a bigger voice and talk directly with the mayor. Those with urgent problems are given priority on the mayor's appointment book.

---

*At the suggestion of Rev. C. Anderson Davis and the NAACP, a citizens' committee for police also was formed.

11. Communications with city council—time is reserved
each week for citizens to appear individually, and in groups,
before city council to discuss any matter they wish. Each
councilman maintains an office at City Hall and meets with
a number of people there and in the community every week.

For a Greater Stake

1. Job Fair—Houston has been credited by Washington with leading the nation in holding an annual event to
obtain jobs for disadvantaged school youths, 16 to 22 years
old. Having a job is basic to a person feeling that he has
some stake in his society. It is felt that minority youths
should be given work experience early so that they can get
a taste of what it means to have such a stake. The young
people use the money they earn to buy clothes and to cover
expenses incidental to returning to school in the fall. As has
been mentioned, the first Job Fair was held in 1967, when
1,300 youths were hired. In 1968, some 4,500 got jobs, and
both employees and employers said they benefited from the
experience (see Appendix E for evaluation of results). The
Job Fair committee, led by the mayor's office and made up
of representatives from 20 organizations and agencies covering a broad spectrum of the city, takes "job orders" from
companies, which do on-the-spot hiring of youths at the downtown coliseum. Applicants are pre-registered at their schools.
The National Alliance of Businessmen, which is concerned
with both summer employment for disadvantaged youths and
permanent jobs for adults, pays personal visits to the largest
employers asking them to offer employment for the summer.
Not only are business and industry asked to give youths "a
stake" in the world of work, the Job Fair committee also
calls on churches, foundations, civic clubs and the public at
large to "sponsor" employment of youth by donating money.
The funds are used to pay for the employment of disadvantaged young people at non-profit agencies, which cannot afford to hire the youths themselves. The third Job Fair in
Houston was held in May 1969.

2. Business development in the ghetto—through an arm
of the mayor's office, a center with a six-man staff works
full time on getting businesses established that are owned
and operated by minority group people. Local banks provide
the financing and the Small Business Administration guar-

antees the loans. Groups of experienced businessmen make
up a managerial pool that is drawn upon to give guidance to
minority group people new in business. More than $700,000
in loans were made during the first eight months of the
center to help minority group people establish and expand
such enterprises as a clothing store, silk-screen processing
plant, laundry, a landscaping company, a motel, an appliance
store, a pharmacy, five small manufacturing companies, an
insurance agency, a machine shop, a car wash and a cafe.
The same center, called the Business Resource Development
Center, also works on getting major industries established
that provide opportunity for minority people to share in operation and ownership of them. The BRDC also is helping
set up a car-lease service that will help minority group people
have an automobile to travel to and from work.

    3. Housing—it has already been mentioned that owning
a house represents a stake, a very personal and meaningful
stake. Home ownership by minority group people in Houston
is stimulated through the Mayor's Citizens Advisory Committee on Housing and by the non-profit Houston Housing
Development Corporation, which it helped organize. Both

Figure 15

Houston Housing Development Corporation
Status of Projects and Target Dates
1969

PROJECT	PRELIMINARY DISCUSSIONS	INCORPORATION	PLANNING OF PROJECT	SUBMISSION TO FHA	INITIAL CLOSING	UNDER CONSTRUCTION	OPERATION
PLEASANT VILLAGE							
CARY-WAY TOWNHOUSES				4-1			
HOUSTON INTER-FAITH / TEXAS HOUSING / INDUSTRIES				3-15			
VOLUNTEERS OF AMERICA				3-1			
UCC FOUNDATION			3-1				
BRAZOS PRESBYTERY		5-10					
BAYTOWN INTER-FAITH				5-1			
HHDC LEASING						4-15	
221 (h) REHABILITATION				3-15			
SWINEY ADDITION				3-1			

groups are made up of representatives from Negro and Mexican-American neighborhoods, as well as leaders from business, industry and city government. Figures 15 and 16 present status reports on projects initiated or promoted by the Houston Housing Development Corporation (HHDC). Again, this program represents only a start on a basic problem affecting the poor.

4. Employment in city government—City Hall encouraged employment of minority group people in an attempt to help set the pace for the city as a whole. As seen in Chapter 7, the percent of Negro employees above the semi-skilled level has sharply increased since 1964. In 1969, the mayor's office had four minority group people among nine assistants and aides. The fire department had 56 Negroes, including five junior captains and four inspectors, out of a total of 1,530 men on the roster. The police department had 58 Negroes,

Figure 16

HHDC Projects: Analysis of Programs

1969

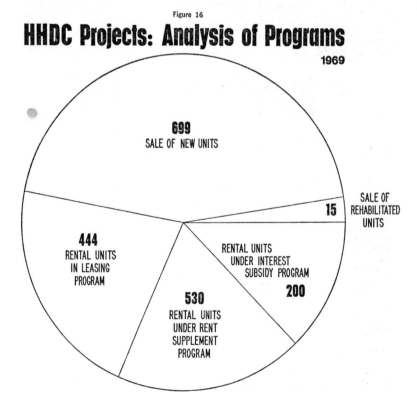

699
SALE OF NEW UNITS

15 SALE OF REHABILITATED UNITS

444
RENTAL UNITS IN LEASING PROGRAM

RENTAL UNITS UNDER INTEREST SUBSIDY PROGRAM

200

530
RENTAL UNITS UNDER RENT SUPPLEMENT PROGRAM

with 13 above the rank of patrolman, out of a total of 1,580
men and women.

Emphasis also needs to be placed now on opening up
more opportunities for Mexican-Americans. The fact that the
mayor has not had a Mexican-American on his immediate
staff with the title of administrative assistant has been of
increasing concern to Mexican-American groups, although a
Spanish-speaking aide was added to the mayor's human relations division in April 1969 to work on special assignment
out of the Neighborhood City Hall. More vocal Mexican-
Americans feel their minority group has been largely overlooked in the whole civil rights movement. Undoubtedly,
more needs to be done, particularly in terms of the Mexican-
Americans who cannot speak English well enough to have a
bigger voice and greater stake in the society.

5. Training for increased skills—the city has offered a
program for any employee wishing to learn to be a heavy
machine operator. Free classes were held on Saturdays. By
participating in this training, laborers—most of whom are
black—could increase their wages from $15 a day to $25.50.
Again, it is believed that greater skills, leading to increased
wages, mean a greater stake in society.

Neither this list, nor the one just preceding it, was meant
to be all-inclusive in terms of what one city is trying to do
by way of providing more opportunities for minority group
people. It leaves out the many efforts that are also being
made by agencies, organizations and individuals outside of
city government, such as the Harris County Community
Action Association. It has not mentioned, just as one example,
such projects as the one in Bordersville, an area of abject
poverty within city limits, where the Houston Jaycees have
taken an active role in working with the community people
to help them gain some of the bare essentials of 20th Century
urban living. The mayor's office worked with the Jaycees,
the Harris County Community Action Association and the
Bordersville people on this project. The project serves to illustrate how the office tries to coordinate efforts and cooperate with all people and groups genuinely interested in com-
batting problems of the disadvantaged. The mayor's office
not only tries to coordinate and cooperate but also initiate.

In doing so, it has actively solicited the assistance of
business and industry. As already indicated, the business
community has contributed support through providing per-

sonnel, office space and funds to help launch programs covering a wide-range of problems—from housing to police relations.

On both a local and national basis, the *here and now* is undoubtedly being improved through the efforts of American industry. In the last chapter, we touched on some of the programs that companies have launched, and the problems they face, in opening up job opportunities for the hard-core unemployed. More specifically, there should be recognition that industries are employing people who would never have been hired before. They are employing people with police records, with poor work records, with little or no formal education. And they are finding that many of these people can learn a job fast and become hard-working, competent employees. Many are taken who have self-doubts about whether they can learn any job. But with proper training, they *do* learn and they *do* acquire confidence. What is so often important in whether a poverty person learns and acquires confidence is the presence of someone like him who has made the grade. It is important that a "role model" in the form of a successful person, a person who came from the same background under the same tough conditions, is provided for the newcomer to work around and receive training from. Many companies have learned this lesson in training the hard-core unemployed, and more poverty people are working than ever before. The National Alliance of Businessmen, which set a goal of having 100,000 hard-core people on jobs by June 1969, already had 125,000 placed by the end of 1968.

Jobs are clearly important, just as improved housing, education and health are. But many black militants insist that none of these "essentials" touch on what they consider to be the basic problem. They insist that the only problem is really one of too little power. All else is simply a "symptom" of the problem. It is silly, they say, to work on problems of employment, housing, education and city services, since these are merely symptoms and "manifestations" of what is really wrong. If black people were not deprived of power, they say, there would be no sick society and hence no symptoms. So to talk of a bigger voice and a greater stake also is irrelevant, they believe. If black people had power in this country, they would have that voice and stake. But this line of thought raises the question of how a person gets power in this country. Black militants insist he should not have to get it, that power comes as a birthright. But there are degrees of power. A better education brings more power; a better job brings more power. Increased knowledge means increased power. There is no denying that regardless of how little education a person has or how little money he makes, he still should have the power to take part in the democratic process, to vote, to organize, to do whatever is necessary—short of violence—to participate more fully in decisions that affect his life, and to have a voice and a stake. This *is* his birthright. It is also his right to have the opportunity to develop his potential to the fullest. And in that development, he will gain greater power. Many people have not had the opportunity to develop themselves; the right has simply been something stated on a piece of paper. Now that the opportunity is becoming more real, there are some people who prefer to believe it is all a trick or a mirage.

There are those people and then there are others, the critics who simply dismiss every effort of City Hall as superficial bandaging of problems that really require extensive surgery. They too believe there must be a restructuring of society, a redistribution of power, but they seldom spell their program out in terms of just how people in slums are going to get a better education, better employment, better housing and more security from crime and delinquency.

The Model Cities program, I think, offers some promise for getting down to these practical matters. It does not deal in the rhetoric of "restructuring society" and "redistributing power." But if it works, it should help people gain more power in their lives and find a better place in the structure. Houston was one of 75 cities selected in 1968 for the Model Cities program. One reason I think the program offers real hope is that it is designed to focus a coordinated attack on all the major problems that contribute to keeping people in slums—problems of employment, education, housing, health, crime and delinquency. Another reason I think the program has promise is that it recognizes that people in slums are often caught in an interlocking set of conditions. They cannot afford better housing without a better job. They cannot get a better job without increased skills. They cannot get increased skills without a better education or without the energy and motivation to attend school or training classes at night. They cannot attend school or training classes at night if they do not have good health or if their energy and motiva-

tion are being drained off in daily battles at home, where
there is usually poor family stability, or out on the streets,
where there is usually a high rate of crime and delinquency.

To break the cycle of the slum ghetto dweller—one that
he is often caught in—all the major problems must be attacked simultaneously. And the attack must directly involve
the ghetto dweller himself and actively enlist his participation toward improving his own life.

No one can give another person a better life. But what
can be given is opportunity, and freedom to take advantage
of it—which means freedom from the conditions that keep so
many people down and out. I am convinced that what every
person really wants, if he truly has a choice, is an opportunity
to gain some sense of competence to cope with life. With
competence comes a sense of autonomy, of self-direction and
self-determination. And with these come self-respect and
human dignity. This is what a better life is all about. And
nobody can give it to anyone else. Nobody can give a person
a bigger voice and a greater stake. But if that person truly
has the opportunity to break out of the cycle in which he is
caught, and if he is shown what it means to develop the
potential he has, then he will achieve for himself that voice
and stake. He will gain competence and some sense of autonomy, self-direction and self-determination. And most of all,
he will have a feeling of self-respect and human dignity.

It is to this end that I think we need to dedicate ourselves. If we achieve it, we will have a society in which we
all can have increasing pride. And, I believe, we will have a
society in which there will be decreasing violence in the city.

WHAT SHOULD WE BELIEVE?

FINAL POINTS TO CONSIDER

*A. Let's resolve that the problem of race and the problem of
violence are going to be overcome. But let's not leave it to
others to do. Let's not leave it to City Hall, to Washington,
to everyone else but ourselves—because we all are involved.
B. Let's devote as much vigor to pitching in and helping do
the work that must be done as to standing off and criticizing
what others are doing. Just about every mayor's office, community council, church, service group and neighborhood association in most sections of the country today has some
kind of project that people can volunteer to work on and*

apply their time and effort in helping others achieve a better life. For those who don't have the time and effort to spend, they can reform their own pattern of belief and behavior to the extent that they drop the myth of superiority and inferiority being based on skin color.

C. Let's all resolve to address each other on the basis of individual merit and stop the stereotyping that has been going on for centuries. Let's don't permit the "black-white" rhetoric that is the fashion of the day to cause us to lose sight of the fact that there is no such thing as a monolithic black people any more than there is a monolithic white people.

D. Let's pay less attention to the codewords and epithets that generate publicity for prophets of doom and bearers of ultimatums, and more attention to the problems *that continue to exist and are going to be solved by work and determination, not rhetoric and threats.*

E. Let's recognize that if a human being is given a chance, starting early in life, to make use of his full capacities, he will choose to do so, for every human being wants to develop and to achieve. He will not always succeed, but in a just and fair society, he will succeed often enough to respect himself and have respect for others. He will know what human dignity is and he will recognize it as a universal spark waiting to be kindled in the lives of all human beings.

F. Let's prove that human beings are superior creatures not only in their ability to modify nature and to make life more comfortable but also in their ability to modify themselves to make life worth living. In both cases, let's resolve that the method to modify must not be violence, for if it is, man is not superior—he is less than other creatures that populate this planet.

APPENDIX A

Definitions and Terms

The following are terms and concepts considered significant by the author and are defined on the basis of his own point of view as reflected in this book.

BLACK COMMUNITY—a shorthand term that should not be interpreted as meaning that all people with dark skin think and act alike any more than all people with light skin do. The black community is not a monolithic group of people but is made up of individuals who share many of the same problems. One of the historic problems has been racial discrimination. As used in this book, the black community refers to both the geographical area where black people live in cities and to the characteristics they share in common. The fact that all do not think and act alike does not mean that there are no common concerns or a subculture of interests. To the degree that such concerns and interests are shared, there is a black community. The term "community people" or "neighborhood people," as used in this book, refers to members of the black community.

BLACK PEOPLE—a term preferred by those who put particular emphasis on promoting black pride and one that is used interchangeably in this book with the word Negroes. Militants insist that "Negroes" is a word imposed on black people by white people. Some militants use it with derision to refer to "Uncle Toms," or Negroes they label as having sold out to the white man. Some militants prefer the term "Afro-American" to refer to all black people. The author does not share this point of view, or the one that would delete the word "Negroes" from the dictionary.

BLACK POWER—see footnote at bottom of Page 15 in Chapter 1 for the context in which this term is used in the book.

COMMUNITY VIOLENCE—collective violence on the streets, loss of life or property in a given section of the city by group action. As used in this book, the term applies to group violence off campus, to violence that involves destruction of businesses and dwellings.

DISADVANTAGED—people who are at a disadvantage in competing for a decent standard of living because of not having had equal opportunity to gain a sound education or employment that permits a person to advance as far as his ability and ambition will carry him.

GHETTO—any place that people live because they do not have any other choice *and* because the conditions that provide them with opportunities for options are either missing or have appeared so recently that they still do not belong to the mainstream of this society. A ghetto is a place where there is, or has been, inferior schools and inadequate opportunity to gain some sense of coping with the world. The author does not consider all Negro neighborhoods ghettos, but the term is used in this book in a generic sense to refer to any area where people have not had equal opportunity to live under different conditions. By "equal opportunity" is meant not simply a law that permits a person to live where he can afford to, or one that prohibits discrimination in employment because of color. Equal opportunity means that a person has equal access to resources necessary for him to develop whatever potential he has. It also means he has equal opportunity to free himself from the conditions that keep that potential from ever coming to life.

HUMAN DIGNITY—a sense of self-respect that all human beings want. It most often comes from an individual gaining some competence to cope with the world around him without transgressing against others or excessively depending on them. If the world around him degrades him and devalues him because of his color or for some other irrational reason, it is acting against his right to dignity. Human dignity is not something each person must "earn," but it is something that an individual can sacrifice by how he treats his fellow man or acts toward himself. It is also something that can be deprived him by a society that refuses to let him grow and achieve with decency.

INDIVIDUAL—the "forgotten" representative of humankind, whose importance is frequently overshadowed by the emphasis on group and collective concerns. The individual is often regarded as being completely shaped and determined by the group to which he belongs or is assigned—and by conditions that have acted upon the group. He is increasingly viewed as having little responsibility for his own actions and no "self-thrust" to determine his own behavior. The individual often gets lost in the rhetoric that describes all people as alike by reason of color (black or white) or occupation (policeman, "member of the Establishment"). Recognition of individual differences is essential to breaking down stereotypes and to people addressing one another as human beings with special qualities and characteristics. Recognition of the individual is also essential to understanding that a sense of competence, which is so important to pride and dignity, more often comes from "within" than from "without"—that is, more from inside the individual than from the group outside to which he belongs.

POVERTY—a condition that robs people of human dignity. Not all poor people are without pride, but it is hard to be poor and cope with the surrounding world. A poor person often has only one source of pride: refusing to ask others for the help he needs. He is thus caught between losing his pride or failing to survive. In an affluent society, poverty is a set of interlocking conditions that explodes the myth that all a person needs is enough gumption and motivation to pull himself up by his bootstraps and get out. The poor person is caught in a cycle that drains the very motivation he needs to break out. The cycle is made up of a job that pays too little, of an education that is inferior, of housing that no one can respect, of poor health, chronic strife in the family, crime on the streets—and a future that often looks hopeless. There are those who break out despite the cycle, but they are the exceptions. Negroes are disproportionately represented among those caught in the cycle.

REASON—the use of the mind, as opposed to mouth or muscle, to arrive at understanding and an attempt to solve problems.

RHETORIC—language designed to put people down and simplify the world by stereotyping, labeling, branding, pigeonholing, and denying individual differences among people and events—people and events that may bear only gross resemblance to each other. Most rhetoric comes from loud or angry voices. In the case of white people, it often comes from those who engage in self-flagellation or other forms of masochism in hopes of achieving catharsis and relieving an overwhelming sense of guilt. It also comes from people, both black and white, who prefer to stand off and criticize rather than to move in closer and work on solutions to problems.

THE SYSTEM—a catchall term that capsulizes for critics all that is wrong with the country. For purveyors of rhetoric, it is usually called a "racist" system that is characterized by a power elite that has succeeded in setting up an interlocking complex with one single-minded goal: perpetuation of power. In reality, there *is* a system and it is made up of all the institutions—from the family to the largest economic or governmental structure—that operate in this country. Those who most vehemently oppose the system say it must be destroyed. Those who work within the system and want to improve it believe it can be fixed so that people who have been left out can be brought in. By "left out" is meant that they have not had equal opportunity to share in the benefits of the society or in the decisions that shape it. Negroes represent a disproportionate number of those who have been left out. "The Establishment" and "the power structure" are terms often used concomitantly with "The System." See the chapter on "Bargaining With 'The Power Structure'" for elaboration on these two terms.

APPENDIX B

Findings of Grand Jury in
Texas Southern University Disturbance

We, the Harris County Grand Jury, after due investigation find that our law enforcement officials acted with due restraint in bringing under control the disturbance at T.S.U. on the nights of May 16 and 17, 1967.

With numerous rumors of police brutality we find that the law enforcement officers acted in the best interests of the community.

We find that this trouble was caused or encouraged by a few agitators and trouble-makers. We feel that the vast majority of the students at T.S.U. are there for an education. The administrators of the school have done a good job taking into account the tools they have to work with. However we feel that a closer communication and support should come from the Board of Regents of T.S.U. especially in discipline of students and non-students that appear on the campus.

We hope the fair minded and responsible citizens will work together for the return of peace and harmony and strive for the goal "Love thy neighbor as thy self" in this community as well as the world.

Although the above represents an official statement of the grand jury on the Texas Southern University incident, the report seems to over-simplify the cause of the "trouble." It is suggested that a number of factors were involved, including some of those discussed in the chapter on "Psychology of Student Unrest."

APPENDIX C

What Community People Say About Life in Their Neighborhood: A Statistical Profile

I. Summary of Questionnaire Given to 34 Fourth Ward Residents in Houston*

   A. Facts and figures on people and their conditions
1. Total weekly income ....$70.50 (average)
2. Number in house ....Four (average)
3. Ages of neighborhood residents ....One to seventy-five
4. Own/rent ....3 own, 31 rent
5. Weekly payments ....$14.65 (average)
6. Number of rooms ....5 (average)
7. Own a car ....22 no, 12 yes
8. Who does not drive in household ....Wife and children (on the average)
9. How long has family lived here ....8 years (average)

   B. What people say about moving
1. What respondent likes best about house or apartment........Nothing 13, low rent 2, location 3, size 5, general conditions 9, everything 2
2. What respondent likes least about house or apartment........Size 14, nothing 3, satisfied 3, general conditions 11, no answer 3
3. Desire to move............................18 yes, 16 no
4. Willing to move to better housing ....24 yes, 1 maybe, 9 no
5. If not, why ....Ownership 1, likes neighborhood 6, hates to move 4, no answer 23
6. Improvement or repairs needed ....General repair 27, everything 4, more space 1, nothing 2
7. Would house be satisfactory if improvements were made....26 yes, 6 no, 2 no answer
8. If looking for house, what are first things respondent would look for ....Fenced yard and more space 31, location 3
9. Prefer to rent or own.................26 own, 6 rent, 2 no answers
10. Could make a down payment....19 no, 10 yes, 5 no answers
11. Possibility of someone in household helping with payment ....9 yes, 19 no, 6 no answer

---

*Taken from a survey made in 1967 by interviewers for the housing committee of the Houston Council on Human Relations.

12. Building skills ....Painting, carpentry, masonry, electrical, 17 had none at all

C. What people do at home and in neighborhood

   1. Spend time outdoors ....Seldom 7, often 12, some 13, no answer 2

   2. Thing respondent does outdoors ....Barbecue, sit on porch, play with children, work in yard

   3. Like to have porch ....33 yes, 1 no

   4. Ways respondent would use a porch ....Flowers, sit on, entertain, relaxation, play with children

   5. Choice of small porch or yard..Small yard 21, front porch 10, both 1, no answer 2

   6. What respondent does for fun, relaxation and entertainment ....Church, TV, f i s h i n g, visit friends, play cards and dominoes, drink beer, coffee . . .

   7. Do neighbors visit ....Some 16, seldom 12, often 6

   8. Where neighbors sit when they visit ....Living room 22, front porch 10, no answer 2

   9. What they do when they visit..Talk, play cards, drink coffee, beer . . .

  10. Description of typical day........Up about 6 AM, go to work or do housework, eat dinner around 6 PM, watch TV, play cards, etc., in bed by 11 PM

  11. What respondent likes least about neighborhood ....Beer joint across street, too noisy because children can only play in streets, trashy and poorly kept yards and streets

  12. What respondent likes best about neighborhood ....Convenience of location and nothing

  13. Commercial services needed in neighborhood ....Most say nothing is needed, but a few say larger chain grocery stores, and washaterias

  14. Community programs needed in neighborhood ....Carpentry, sewing classes, cooking classes, reading and writing classes, and nursing courses

D. Work and school

   1. How long does it take respondent to get to work............45 minutes (average)

   2. Transportation to work ....Walk, bus, automobile

   3. Possibility of carpool ....None

   4. How long does it take children to get to school ....18 minutes (average)

5. Transportation to school ....Walk, 1 bus
6. Services needed in
    neighborhood ....Health centers, day care, sur-
    plus food stores, legal aid

II. Summary of Questionnaire Given to 24 Third Ward Residents in Houston
  A. Facts and figures on people and their conditions
    1. Total weekly income ....$89.50 (average)
    2. Number in house ....Six (average)
    3. Ages of neighborhood
        residents ....Two to sixty-nine
    4. Own/rent ....4 own, 20 rent
    5. Weekly payments ....$14.60 (average)
    6. Number of rooms ....5 (average)
    7. Own a car ....11 no, 13 yes
    8. Who does not drive in
        household ....Wife and children (on the
        average)
    9. How long has family
        lived here ....4 years (average)
  B. What people say about moving
    1. What respondent likes best
        about house or apartment........Ownership 2, convenient location
        7, general condition 10, nothing
        5
    2. What respondent likes least
        about house or apartment........Condition 10, roaches 2, neigh-
        borhood 3, nothing 4, no answer
        5
    3. Desire to move ....13 yes, 11 no
    4. Willing to move to better
        housing ....17 yes, 4 no, 3 don't know
    5. If not why ....Ownership 1, likes neighborhood
        2, hates to move 1, no answer 20
    6. Improvement or repairs
        needed ....Extermination 3, general repair
        19, need more space 1, none 1
    7. Would house be satisfactory
        if improvements were made....18 yes, 3 no, 3 don't know
    8. If looking for house, what
        are first things respondent
        would look for ....More room 5, better neighbor-
        hood 5, convenient location 6,
        condition 8
    9. Prefer to rent or own................Own 20, rent 3, don't know 1
    10. Could make a down payment....Yes 4, no 17, don't know 3
    11. Possibility of someone in
        household helping with
        payment ....Yes 10, no 7, don't know 6, buy-
        ing 1
    12. Building skills ....Painting, carpentry, sheetrock-
        ing, plumbing, roofing

C. What people do at home and in neighborhood

1. Spend time outdoors ....Seldom 6, often 18
2. Thing respondent does outdoors ....Barbecue, work in yard, play with children, sit and talk
3. Like to have porch ....Yes 20, no 4
4. Ways respondent would use porch ....Sit, play with children, flowers, relaxation
5. Choice of small porch or yard..Porch 7, yard 13, don't know 4
6. What respondent does for fun, relaxation and entertainment..Church, movies, TV, bowling, picnics, sports, guests
7. Do neighbors visit ....Seldom 16, often 8
8. Where neighbors sit when they visit ....Inside 15, outside 3, porch 6
9. What they do when they visit..Play cards, talk, coffee, beer, watch TV . . .
10. Description of a typical day....Up about 6 AM, eat breakfast, at work from 7:30 until about 7 PM, eat dinner, watch TV until 10 PM or 10:30, in bed by 11 PM
11. What respondent likes least about neighborhood ....Roaches, too crowded, need to be cleaned up, drifters and drunks . . .
12. What respondent likes best about neighborhood ....Neighbors, convenient location . . .
13. Commercial services needed in neighborhood ....Shopping centers (large), washaterias, barber shops, hardware
14. Community programs needed in neighborhood ....Carpentry, s e w i n g, cooking, electrical, reading and writing classes for adults

D. Work and school

1. How long does it take respondent to get to work............40 minutes (average)
2. Transportation to work ....Car, bus, employer
3. Possibility of carpool ....None
4. How long does it take children to get to school................13 minutes (average)
5. Transportation to school ....Bus or walk
6. Services needed in neighborhood ....Free day care, clinics, parks and recreation, legal aid, library . . .

APPENDIX D

Method Used in Designing the Index of Dissatisfaction For Minority Areas in Houston

This analysis was based on 2,086 "natural dialogue" interviews conducted in seventeen areas of Houston where minority group people reside. The dissatisfaction index was drawn from five questions related to attitudes about the speed of civil rights, about police, schools, job finding, and attitudes toward present job. The index of unrest was computed in the following way: The percentage of the negative response (e.g., "Civil rights going too slowly" or "Bad" for schools) was taken from each geographical area. These then were ranked across the 17 areas, the lower number indicating the higher degree of dissatisfaction or activism. Ranks for each question were averaged: the final ranking indicating the relative amount of dissatisfaction.

APPENDIX E

Evaluation of the Police-Community Relations Program
Sidney E. Cleveland, Ph.D.
Veterans Administration Hospital, Houston, Texas

Analysis of the questionnaires completed by the police and community participants at the conclusion of the fifth seminar reveals attitudes and feelings about the program consistent with the first four seminars. In fact the sentiments expressed by the officers and community regarding this program and its impact on them are congruent for all five sessions thus far completed.

On the basis of about 600 questionnaires obtained from citizens participating in the program to date, and approximately 800 questionnaires from officers, we can arrive at the following general conclusions:

1. The program is viewed enthusiastically by the participating community when polled at the conclusion of a six-week session. Ninety-three percent of the participating community rate the program somewhere between Good and Excellent, 18 percent rate it Excellent and only 7 percent rate it Poor.

2. Participating officers are less enthusiastic but at least moderately accepting of the program. Eighty-five percent rate it between Good and Excellent. However, only 4 percent of the police rate it Excellent and 15 percent rate it as Poor.

3. As a result of the program 65 percent of the participating citizens say their feelings about the police are more positive; only 4 percent say their feelings are more negative. Thirty-one percent say their feelings are unchanged.

APPENDIX F

Evaluation of Second Annual Job Fair in Houston*

Two-thirds of the employers in the 1968 Job Fair considered the program "very good, worthwhile" and intend to support the next one.

Better than four out of five Job Fair employees (students) found their employers friendly and helpful and felt their experience would help them in their next jobs.

This was the highlight of a special evaluation carried out after exhaustive study by the Community Welfare Planning Association's Research Bureau. The report has been submitted to the mayor's office.

Fifteen hundred summer Job Fair applicants and 175 Job Fair employers responded through a 20-item questionnaire for students and a 12-item questionnaire for employers.

The CWPA researchers learned that approximately 84 percent of all applicants were in ages 16-18 and 88 percent were in grades 9-12; non-white applicants outnumbered Anglos and Mexican-Americans each by a ratio of more than 10 to 1.

Of all age groups, 18- and 19-year-olds had the greatest proportions obtaining Job Fair employment. The major items in order of importance to which Job Fair employees devoted their earnings were clothes, school expenses, savings and family expenses.

The 175 employers who responded to the questionnaire provided 1,149 Job Fair youths with summer work. Most hired five youths or less. The largest employer in the sample hired 103. Only one in 12 employers found the youths "unsatisfactory" in work performance.

The most common problems reported were the lack of dependability and the need for closer supervision. More than a third of the employers reported no problems. Two-thirds of the employers said they would hire again either all or most of the youths. Thirteen and one-half percent said they would not re-hire any of the same youths. Employers in the

*From Community Welfare Planning Association Newsletter, March 1969.

sample registered said they intend to support the next Summer Job Fair by a ratio of about nine to one.

The Job Fair committee, which is responsible for the annual event to hire disadvantaged young people, is an example of coalition efforts that have brought community resources together to work on community problems. In cooperation with the mayor's office, a wide spectrum of organizations and agencies volunteer their time and energy to the Job Fair. These groups include the Houston Chamber of Commerce, the Junior League, the Junior Chamber of Commerce, the Harris County Community Action Association, the Texas Employment Commission, the Vocational Guidance Service, the Community Welfare Planning Association, the Assistance League, the Employers' Voluntary Council for Merit Employment, the National Alliance of Businessmen, the Houston Independent School District, the National Association for the Advancement of Colored People, the Concentrated Employment Program, the Harris County AFL-CIO, the Citizens Chamber of Commerce, the League of United Latin American Citizens, the Political Association of Spanish-Speaking Organizations, Casa del Amigos Community Center, SER (Service, Education and Redevelopment), the Houston Personnel Association, various federal agencies and a number of individual companies that donate personnel and supplies. The Job Fair committee has no budget or paid staff and operates on a voluntary basis.

NOTES TO CHAPTER 1

1. Trans Century Corporation, *From the Street*, an evaluation for the Department of Health, Education and Welfare, Washington, December 15, 1967, p. 2.
2. James Q. Wilson, as quoted in the *Wall Street Journal*, September 27, 1968, p. 12.
3. Mayor J. H. Reading, talk given at meeting sponsored by Plans for Progress, Washington, January 23, 1967.
4. *Report of the National Advisory Committee on Civil Disorders*, U. S. Government Printing Office, Washington, 1968, p. 203.
5. George Fuermann, *Houston, The Feast Years*, Press of Premier, Houston, 1962, p. 1.
6. *Ibid.*
7. *Ibid.*, p. 12.
8. *Ibid.*, p. 13.
9. *Newsweek*, March 31, 1969, p. 58.
10. Cited in Fuermann, *op. cit.*, p. 34.
11. Henry A. Bullock, *Pathways To The Houston Negro Market*, distributed by J. W. Edwards, Ann Arbor, Michigan, 1957, p. 31.
12. Research Committee, *Population and Houston Analysis of Metropolitan Houston*, September 1961, Section C., p. 4.
13. *Saturday Evening Post*, August 10, 1968, p. 36.
14. Bullock, *op. cit.*
15. H. Edward Ransford, "Isolation, Powerlessness, & Violence: A Study of Attitudes and Participation in the Watts Riot," *American Journal of Sociology*, 73 (March 1968), pp. 584-585.
16. William Brink and Louis Harris, *The Negro Revolution*, Simon and Schuster, New York, 1964, p. 127.
17. Paul B. Gillen, *The Distributions of Occupations as a City Yardstick*, King's Crown Press, Columbia University, New York, 1951, p. 91.
18. Alvin L. Schorr, *Slums and Social Insecurity*, U.S. Department of Health, Education and Welfare, Social Security Administration, Washington, 1962, p. 91.
19. U.S. Bureau of Census, *U.S. Census of Population: 1960*, Vol. 1, *Characteristics of the Population*, Part 45, Texas, U.S. Government Printing Office, Washington, 1963.
20. U.S. Bureau of Census, *General Social and Economic Characteristics, U.S. Summary*, *ibid.*, Table 152.
21. U.S. Bureau of Census, *ibid.*, *Standard Metropolitan Statistical Areas*, Table B.
22. Houston-Harris County Economic Opportunity Organization, *Dimensions of Poverty*, Houston, 1965, p. 13.
23. Episcopal Society for Cultural and Racial Unity, *Nowhere to Go*, Houston, 1963, p. 3.
24. U.S. Bureau of Census, *op. cit.*, *Standard Metropolitan Statistical Areas*, Table 6A.
25. John Kraft, Inc., *The Report of a Survey of Attitudes of Harlem Residents Toward Housing, Rehabilitation and Urban Renewal*, New York, August 1966.

26. See Blair Justice, "Effects of Racial Violence on Attitudes in the Negro Community," *Law Enforcement Science and Technology II,* Port City Press, Baltimore, 1968, pp. 99-103.
27. William Serrin, "God Help Our City," *The Atlantic Monthly,* March 1969, p. 115.
28. Interview with Rev. William Lawson, Houston, November 9, 1965.
29. Kenneth Myers, "Effects of Density and Space on Sociality and Health in Mammals," paper given before American Association for Advancement of Science, Dallas, December 30, 1968.

NOTES TO CHAPTER 2

1. John Dollard, et al, *Frustration and Aggression,* Yale University Press, New Haven, Conn., p. 1.
2. E. Franklin Frazier, *The Negro in the United States,* MacMillan Company, New York, 1957, p. 647.
3. Gunnar Myrdal, *An American Dilemma,* Harper and Row, New York, 1962, p. 975.
4. Erik Erikson, "The Concept of Identity in Race Relations: Notes and Queries," *Daedalus,* 95 (Winter 1966), pp. 145-146.
5. Lee Rainwater, "Crucible of Identity: The Negro Lower-Class Family," *Daedalus,* 95 (Winter 1966), p. 204.
6. *Ibid.,* p. 205.
7. Lewis Yablonsky, paper presented at the American Association for the Advancement of Science meeting, Philadelphia, December 1962.
8. *Ibid.*
9. Alex Pokorny, "A Comparison of Homicides in Two Cities," *Journal of Criminal Law, Criminology, and Police Science,* 56 (December 1965), p. 481.
10. The President's Commission on Law Enforcement and Administration of Justice, *The Challenge of Crime in a Free Society,* U.S. Government Printing Office, Washington, D.C., February 1967, p. 44.
11. Marvin E. Wolfgang, *Patterns in Criminal Homicide,* University of Pennsylvania, Philadelphia, 1958.
12. Henry Bullock, "The Houston Murder Problem: Its Nature, Apparent Causes and Probable Cures," *Report to Mayor Lewis Cutrer,* Houston, June, 1961, p. 55.
13. *Ibid.,* p. 51.
14. City of Houston Police Department, *Annual Report,* 1963, p. 7.
15. Federal Bureau of Investigation, *Crime in the United States,* Washington, 1963, p. 117.
16. Gunnar Myrdal, *op. cit.,* p. 967.
17. Arnold Rose, (ed.), *Race Prejudice and Discrimination,* Alfred A. Knopf, New York, 1953, p. 412.
18. *Ibid.,* p. 413.
19. Seith M. Scheimer, *Negro Mecca,* New York University Press, New York 1965, p. 119.
20. Frazier, *op. cit.,* p. 652.
21. *Newsweek,* August 16, 1965.
22. Federal Bureau of Investigation, *Uniform Crime Reports,* Washington, 1965.

23. Father August Thompson as quoted in Bradford Daniel's *Black, White and Gray*, Sheed and Ward, Inc., New York, 1964, p. 149.
24. Roy Wilkens as quoted in *ibid.*, p. 34.
25. Austin L. Porterfield and Robert H. Talbert, *Crime, Suicide and Social Well-Being*, Leo Potishman Foundation, Fort Worth, Texas, 1948, p. 69.
26. *U.S. News and World Report*, August 9, 1965.
27. *The Challenge of Crime in A Free Society, op. cit.*, p. 17.
28. *Ibid.*
29. Dollard, et al., *op. cit.*, pp. 112-141.
30. The President's Commission on Law Enforcement and Administration of Justice, *op. cit.*, p. 63.
31. *Ibid.*, pp. 63-64.
32. Sheldon and Eleanor Glueck, *Unraveling Juvenile Delinquency*, The Commonwealth Fund, Harvard University Press, Cambridge, Mass., 1950.
33. Daniel P. Moynihan, *The Negro Family: The Case for National Action*, United States Department of Labor, March 1965, p. 5.
34. *Ibid.*, p. 18.
35. *Ibid.*, p. 30.
36. See *Saturday Evening Post*, August 10, 1968, p. 27.
37. City of Houston Police Department, "Cumulative Report of Offenses for 'The Bottom'," 1966.
38. Robert Lindner, *Rebel Without a Cause*, Grune & Stratton, New York, 1944.
39. *Ibid.*, p. 2.
40. Thomas F. Pettigrew, *A Profile of the Negro American*, D. Van Nostrand Company, 1964, p. 16.
41. F. R. Scarpitti, et al., "The 'Good' Boy in a High Delinquency Area: Four Years Later," *American Sociological Review*, 25 (August 1960), pp. 555-558.
42. W. Mischel, "Father-Absence and Delay Gratification: Cross-Cultural Comparisons," *Journal of Abnormal and Social Psychology*, 63 (July 1961), pp. 116-124.
43. O. H. Mowrer and A. D. Ullman, "Time as a Determinant in Integrative Learning," *Psychological Review*, 52 (January 1945), pp. 61-90.
44. Thomas F. Pettigrew, *op. cit.*, p. 22.
45. See Hyman Rodman and Paul Grams, "Juvenile Delinquency and the Family: A Review and Discussion," in The President's Commission on Law Enforcement and Administration of Justice, *Juvenile Delinquency and Youth Crime*, U.S. Government Printing Office, Washington, D.C., 1967, p. 199.
46. *Time*, July 28, 1967, p. 11.
47. E. Palmore, "Factors Associated with School Dropouts on Juvenile Delinquency Among Lower-Class Children," *Social Security Bulletin*, October 1963, p. 6.
48. See Rodman and Grams, *op. cit.*, p. 196.
49. Thomas P. Monahan, "Family Status and the Delinquent Child," *Social Forces*, 35 (March 1957), p. 254.
50. *Time, op. cit.*, p. 11.

51. Edwin H. Sutherland and Donald Cressey, *Principles of Criminology*, Lippincott, New York, 1960, p. 65.
52. Seymour L. Halleck, *Psychiatry and the Dilemmas of Crime*, Harper and Row, New York, 1967, p. 27.
53. Daniel P. Moynihan, *op. cit.*, p. 44.
54. Harlem Youth Opportunities Unlimited, Inc., *Youth in the Ghetto*, New York, p. 144.
55. Department of Health, New York City, report on "Health Areas," 1964.
56. *Time, op. cit.*, p. 11.
57. Muriel Sterne, "Drinking Patterns and Alcoholism Among American Negroes," Occasional Paper No. 7, Social Science Institute, Washington University, St. Louis, October, 1966.
58. Claude Brown, *Manchild in the Promised Land*, New American Library, New York, 1965, pp. 271-272.
59. Robert Lindner, "Psychopathic Personality and the Concept of Homeostasis," *Journal of Clinical Psychopathology*, VI (January 1945), pp. 517-521.
60. Seymour Halleck emphasizes the influence of "helplessness" and "powerlessness" in the "adaptive value of crime," in *Psychiatry and the Dilemmas of Crime*, p. 68 and the model on p. 81.
61. See H. Edward Ransford's finding on powerlessness as related to riots in *The American Journal of Sociology*, 73 (March 1968), pp. 584-585.
62. Abram Kardiner and Lionel Ovesey suggest a similar concept of "Over-compensation" in *The Mark of Oppression*, W. W. Norton, New York, 1951, p. 178.
63. *U. S. News and World Report*, March 6, 1967, p. 61.
64. *Ibid.*, p. 59.
65. *Ibid.*
66. Loren Eisley, "Man: The Lethal Factor," paper presented at joint meeting of Phi Beta Kappa Society and Sigma Xi, Philadelphia, December 1962.
67. As quoted by Rodman and Grams, *op. cit.*, p. 189.
68. E. H. Powell, "Crime As A Function of Anomie: The Rise and Fall of the Arrest Rate of an American City (Buffalo, N. Y.), 1854-1956," *Clearing House for Sociological Literature*, 1965, pp. 1-21.
69. See Jerry Cohen and William S. Murphy, *Burn, Baby, Burn*, Avon Books, New York, 1966.
70. John Kraft, Inc., report on opinion research poll conducted in Watts in January 1966, p. 25.
71. Jerry Cohen and William S. Murphy, *op. cit.*, p. 287.

NOTES TO CHAPTER 3

1. Henry P. Fairchild (ed.), *Dictionary of Sociology and Related Sciences*, Littlefield, Adams & Company, Totowa, N. J., 1965, p. 259.
2. Crane Brinton, *The Anatomy of Revolution*, Vintage Press, New York, 1957.
3. Howard Zinn, *SNCC-The New Abolitionists*, Beacon Press, Boston, 1964, p. 1.

4. Kenneth B. Clark, "The Civil Rights Movement: Momentum and Organization," *Daedalus*, 95 (Winter 1966), p. 259.
5. Oscar Cohen, "Transcript of the American Academy Conference on the Negro American," *op. cit.*, p. 379.
6. Eric Lincoln, *The Black Muslims in America*, Beacon Press, Boston, 1961, p. 46.
7. Philip Mason, "The Revolt Against Western Values, *Daedalus*, 96 (Spring 1967), p. 335.
8. Eldridge Cleaver, "Prisons: The Muslims' Decline," *Ramparts*, February 1967, p. 10.
9. Mason, *op. cit.*, pp. 334-338.
10. Gary Marx, *Protest and Prejudice: A Study of Belief in the Black Community*, Harper and Row, New York, 1967, p. 113.
11. James H. Laue, "The Black Muslims: The Religious-Historical Identity," *Social Forces*, 42 (March 1964), p. 318.
12. Louis Lomax, *The Negro Revolt*, Harper and Brothers, New York, 1962, p. 177.
13. Marx, *op. cit.*, p. 116.
14. Lincoln, *op. cit.*, p. 4.
15. James H. Laue, "The Changing Character of Negro Protest," *The Annals of the American Academy of Political and Social Science*, January 1965, p. 125.
16. Zinn, *op. cit.*, p. 13.
17. *Houston Chronicle*, August 14, 1967, p. 11.
18. *Ibid.*
19. *Time*, August 4, 1967, p. 17.
20. *Ibid.*
21. *Houston Chronicle*, August 7, 1967, p. 6.
22. *Houston Chronicle*, August 3, 1967, p. 2.
23. *Time, op. cit.*, p. 17.
24. *The National Observer*, July 31, 1967, p. 10.
25. *U. S. News & World Report*, August 14, 1967, p. 23.
26. *U. S. News & World Report*, August 7, 1967, p. 8.
27. *Houston Chronicle*, August 4, 1967.
28. *Houston Post*, August 28, 1967, Page 10, Section 1.
29. *U. S. News & World Report*, May 22, 1967, p. 66.
30. Frantz Fanon, *The Wretched of the Earth*, translated from the French by Constance Farrington, Grove Press, New York, 1963, p. 104.
31. Statement to Afro Asian Missions to the United Nations, signed by James Forman, director of international affairs for SNCC, June 13, 1967.
32. "Negro Freedom and Vietnam" circular, signed by Rev. F. D. Kirkpatrick of "SCLC and SNCC," advertising "Rally for Peace and Freedom," Houston, June 25, 1967.
33. St. Clair Drake, talk at Rice University seminar, May 2, 1967.
34. James Forman, transcription of talk given on Black Power at the University of Houston, October 5, 1966.
35. *Encyclopedia of the Social Sciences*, Vol. 13, The MacMillan Co., New York, 1934, p. 144.
36. Mason, *op. cit.*, p. 336.

37. As quoted by Mason, *ibid.*, p. 336.
38. James Forman, talk given on Black Power at Texas Southern University, October 4, 1966.
39. T. F. Pettigrew, "Transcript of the American Academy Conference on the Negro American," *Daedalus*, 95 (Winter 1966), pp. 353-354.
40. Stokely Carmichael, "Black Power: The Widening Dialogue," *New South*, Summer, 1966, p. 66.
41. See Edwin C. Berry, "Transcript of the American Academy Conference on the Negro American," *Daedalus*, 95 (Winter 1966), p. 354.
42. See Talcott Parsons, "Transcript of the American Academy Conference on the Negro American," *op. cit.*, p. 345.
43. See Rashi Fein, "Transcript of the American Academy Conference on the Negro American," *op. cit.*, p. 347.
44. Talk given by Forman in Houston, October 4, 1966.
45. See Thomas F. Pettigrew, *A Profile of the Negro American*, P. D. Van Nostrand, Princeton, 1964, p. 188.
46. Carmichael, *op. cit.*, p. 76.
47. *Ibid.*, p. 68.
48. Clark, *op. cit.*, p 240 and 254.
49. Talk by Forman in Houston, October 4, 1966.
50. Peter H. Rossi, "Transcript of the American Academy Conference on the Negro American," *Daedalus*, 95 (Winter 1966), p. 349.
51. Talk by Forman in Houston, October 4, 1966.
52. Carmichael, *op. cit.*, p. 76.
53. *Ibid.*, p. 80.
54. See Sol Stern, "America's Black Guerillas," *Ramparts*, September 1967, p. 26.
55. *Forward Times*, March 11, 1967.
56. *Newsweek*, August 2, 1965.
57. Elijah Muhammad, *Message to the Blackman in America*, Muhammad Mosque of Islam, No. 2, Chicago, 1965, p. 270.
58. Daniel C. Thompson, "The Nature of the Negro Protest," *The Annals of the American Academy of Political and Social Science*, *op. cit.*, p. 28.
59. *Ibid.*, p. 28.
60. Lincoln, *op. cit.*, p. 88.
61. Laue, "The Black Muslims: The Religious-Historical Identity," *op. cit.*, p. 381.
62. Samuel Lubell, *White and Black: Test of a Nation*, Harper and Row, New York, 1964, p. 38.
63. *Life*, May 31, 1963, p. 24.
64. Carmichael, *op. cit.*, p. 67.
65. *Life, op. cit.*, p. 32.

NOTES TO CHAPTER 4

1. *Houston Chronicle*, August 30, 1967, p. 10.
2. William Brink and Louis Harris, *Black and White: A Study of U.S. Racial Attitudes Today*, Simon and Schuster, New York, 1966, p. 72.
3. Henry A. Bullock, *A History of Negro Education in the South*, Harvard University Press, Cambridge, 1967, p. 279.

4. Blair Justice, An Inquiry Into Negro Identity and a Methodology for Detection of Potential Racial Violence, unpublished Rice University dissertation, 1966, p. 60.
5. *U. S. News & World Report,* March 6, 1967, p. 62.
6. Granville M. Sawyer, talk before the International College and University Conference, New York, January 1969.
7. *Houston Chronicle,* August 6, 1967, p. 14.
8. Gordon B. Blaine, *Youth and the Hazards of Affluence,* Harper & Row, New York, 1966, pp. 81-97.
9. Nathan Hare, "The Legacy of Paternalism," *Saturday Review,* July 20, 1968, p. 57.
10. *Ibid.*
11. *Newsweek,* November 20, 1967, p. 41.
12. *Ibid.*
13. James Farmer, "Is Violence Necessary," *Children,* March-April 1966, p. 76.
14. *Newsweek, op. cit.,* p. 41.
15. See Richard Evans, *Dialogue With Erik Erikson,* Harper & Row, New York, 1967, p. 67.
16. *Newsweek, op. cit.,* p. 40.
17. *Newsweek,* January 27, 1969, pp. 68-69.
18. John Spiegel, "Hostility, Aggression and Violence," paper delivered at the Lowell Institute, Tufts-New England Medical Center, Boston, March 12, 1968.
19. Elias Canetti, *Crowds and Power,* Viking Press, New York, 1962, p. 19.
20. Carl T. Rowan, "Campus Turmoil Manifestation of Self-Hatred," *Houston Post,* January 23, 1969.
21. See Kenneth Keniston, "Youth, Change and Violence," *The American Scholar,* 37 (Spring 1968), pp. 241-245.
22. For an elaboration on student unrest in general, see Blair Justice, "Group Influences on the Contemporary Campus," keynote address given at annual meeting of Southwest Association of Student Personnel Administrators, Austin, Texas, March 9, 1969.
23. See Blair Justice, "Assessing Potentials for Racial Violence," *Law Enforcement Science and Technology,* Academic Press, London, 1967, pp. 709-716.
24. Rowan, *op. cit.*

NOTES TO CHAPTER 5

1. See Blair Justice, *Detection of Potential Community Violence,* Office of Law Enforcement Assistance, U. S. Department of Justice dissemination document, U. S. Government Printing Office, Washington, June 1968, not only for an analysis of unrest by geographical area but also for an "index of activism," which correlates with the "index of dissatisfaction."
2. John F. Kraft, Inc., *A Report of Attitudes of Negroes in Various Cities,* prepared for the Senate Subcommittee on Executive Reorganization, New York, 1966.

3. Gary T. Marx, *Protest and Prejudice*, Harper & Row, New York, 1967.
4. William Brink and Louis Harris, *Black and White: A Study of U. S. Racial Attitudes Today*, Simon and Schuster, New York, 1967.
5. See also Blair Justice, "Effects of Racial Violence on Attitudes in the Negro Community," *Law Enforcement Science and Technology II*, 1968, Port City Press, Baltimore, Maryland.

NOTES TO CHAPTER 6

1. Arthur Niederhoffer, *Behind the Shield*, Doubleday, Garden City, N. Y., 1967, p. 167.
2. *Ibid.*, p. 170.
3. James Baldwin, *Nobody Knows My Name*, Dell Publishing Company, New York, 1962, pp. 65-67.
4. *Fortune*, December 1968, p. 110.
5. See Alvin F. Poussaint, "A Negro Psychiatrist Explains the Negro Psyche," *New York Times Magazine*, August 20, 1967.
6. *Ibid.*
7. Melvin P. Sikes, "Houston Cooperative Crime Prevention Program," paper delivered before Conference on Urban Minorities and Social Justice, Southern Methodist University, Dallas, November 10-11, 1967.
8. *Ibid.*
9. *Report of the National Advisory Commission on Civil Disorders*, U. S. Government Printing Office, Washington, 1968, p. 70.
10. See John Hersey, *The Algiers Motel Incident*, Alfred A. Knopf, New York, 1968, pp. 103-104.
11. *Report of the National Advisory Commission on Civil Disorders*, *op. cit.*, p. 157.
12. Niederhoffer, *op. cit.*, p. 170.
13. For additional questions asked about police, see Blair Justice, *Detection of Potential Community Violence*, U. S. Government Printing Office, Washington, a study made under a grant from the U. S. Department of Justice, Law Enforcement Assistance Administration.
14. The President's Commission on Law Enforcement and Administration of Justice, *The Challenge of Crime in a Free Society*, U. S. Government Printing Office, Washington, 1967, p. 100.
15. *Time*, July 19, 1968, p. 21.
16. *Report of the National Advisory Commission on Civil Disorders*, *op. cit.*, p. 157.
17. *Fortune*, *op. cit.*, p. 113.
18. *Time*, *op. cit.*
19. *Fortune*, *op. cit.*, p. 111.
20. See John Hersey, *op. cit.*, p. 102.
21. The President's Commission on Law Enforcement and Administration of Justice, *The Police*, U. S. Government Printing Office, Washington, 1967, p. 145.
22. See Seymour M. Lipset, "Why Cops Hate Liberals—And Vice Versa," *The Atlantic Monthly*, March 1969, p. 80.
23. Commission on Law Enforcement, *The Police*, p. 145.

24. Victor Riesel, "Angry Policemen May Go the Union Route," *Houston Chronicle*, January 28, 1969.
25. Michael J. Murphy, as quoted in *The Atlantic Monthly*, March 1969, p. 80.
26. James Q. Wilson, as quoted in *Fortune*, December 1968, p. 111.
27. John Hersey, *op. cit.*, p. 155.
28. Morton Bard, as quoted in *The Atlantic Monthly*, March 1969, p. 104.
29. *Fortune, op. cit.* p. 113.
30. Jerome H. Skolnick, *Professional Police in a Free Society*, National Conference of Christians and Jews report, New York, 1967, p. 21.
31. James Q. Wilson, "What Makes A Better Policeman," *The Atlantic Monthly*, March 1969, p. 135.

NOTES TO CHAPTER 7

1. Seymour M. Lipset, "Political Sociology," in Robert Merton, Leonard Broom, L. S. Cottrell Jr. (eds.), *Sociology Today*, Vol. 1, Basic Books, New York, 1959, p. 84.
2. See Karl Marx, *The German Ideology*, International Publishers, New York, 1939.
3. Max Weber, in H. H. Gerth and C. Wright Mills (eds.), *From Max Weber: Essays in Sociology*, Oxford University Press, New York, 1946, pp. 180-195.
4. Max Weber, *Basic Concepts in Sociology*, translated and with an introduction by H. P. Secher, Citadel Press, New York, 1964, p. 117.
5. Robert S. Lynd, "Power in American Society as Resource and Problem," in Arthur Kornhauser (ed.), *Problems of Power in American Society*, Wayne State University Press, Detroit, 1957.
6. See Robert S. Lynd and Helen Merrell Lynd, *Middletown*, Harcourt, Brace, New York, 1929, and *Middletown in Transition*, Harcourt, Brace, New York, 1937.
7. James Forman, speech at True Light Baptist Church, Houston, June 19, 1967.
8. Lipset, *op. cit.*, p. 107.
9. *Ibid.*, p. 106.
10. *Ibid.*, pp. 106-107.
11. Alexis de Tocqueville, *Democracy in America*, Vol. 1, Vintage Books, New York, 1954, pp. 9-11.
12. Arnold M. Rose, *The Power Structure*, Oxford University Press, New York, 1967, p. 205.
13. Max Weber, as quoted in *Sociology Today, op. cit.*, p. 89.
14. Weber as quoted in J. P. Mayer, *Max Weber and German Politics*, Faber and Faber, London, 1943, p. 128.
15. Rose, *op. cit.*, pp. 247-250.
16. Remarks by W. G. Scheibe, in conference with author, Houston, April 1967.
17. City of Houston mayor's office, *You and Your City Services*, January 1969.
18. Rose, *op. cit.*, p. 43.
19. Floyd Hunter, as quoted by Fred Powledge, *Black Power, White Resistance*, World Publishing Company, Cleveland, 1967, p. 29.

20. Floyd Hunter as quoted by Rose, *op. cit.*, p. 259.
21. See Scott Greer, *The Emerging City: Myth and Reality*, The Free Press, New York, 1962, pp. 151-160.
22. Powledge, *op. cit.*, p. 29.
23. Carol Estes Thometz, *The Decision-Makers: The Power Structure of Dallas*, Southern Methodist University Press, Dallas, 1963, p. 37.
24. Powledge, *op. cit.*, p. 121.
25. Rose, *op. cit.*, pp. 296-297.
26. *Ibid.*, p. 353.
27. VISTA conference, Galveston, Texas, June 2, 1967.
28. Marvin Hurley, *Decisive Years for Houston*, Houston Magazine, Houston Chamber of Commerce, Houston, 1966, p. 298.
29. *Ibid.*, p. 299.
30. *Ibid.*, p. 300.
31. *Ibid.*, p. 300.
32. *Time*, August 11, 1967, p. 14.
33. *Ibid.*
34. See Charles E. Silberman, *Crisis in Black and White*, Random House, New York, 1964, p. 321.
35. *Ibid.*, p. 327.
36. Richard H. Leach, "The Federal Role in the War on Poverty Program," *Law and Contemporary Problems—Anti-poverty Programs*, School of Law, Duke University, XXXI (Winter 1966), p. 12.
37. Silberman, *op. cit.*, p. 356.
38. Houston-Harris County Economic Opportunity Organization, *Community Organization Component Proposal*, 1967.
39. Daniel P. Moynihan, *Maximum Feasible Misunderstanding*, The Free Press, New York, 1969, pp. 77-82.
40. Urban America, Inc., and the Urban Coalition, *One Year Later*, Washington, 1969, p. 116.

NOTES TO CHAPTER 8

1. *Communities in Action*, Office of Economic Opportunity, Washington, August-September 1966, p. 15.
2. *U. S. News & World Report*, September 4, 1967, pp. 68-69.
3. See S. M. Miller in Milton Greenblatt, Paul E. Emery and Bernard C. Glueck Jr. (eds.), *Poverty and Mental Health*, Psychiatric Research Report 21, American Psychiatric Association, Washington, 1967, p. 15.
4. See Blair Justice, "Houston: The 'Sead' Factors of Unrest," The Hogg Foundation for Mental Health, University of Texas, Austin, February 1969, pp. 2-3.
5. Robert Coles, "It's the Same, But It's Different," *Daedalus*, 94 (Fall 1965), p. 1114.
6. Ralph Ellison, "Transcript of the American Academy on the Negro American," *Daedalus*, 95 (Winter 1966), p. 438.
7. Frank Reissman, "The New Approach to the Poor," in *Poverty and Mental Health*, *op. cit.*, p. 37.
8. *Communities in Action*, *op. cit.*

279

9. Cyril G. Sargent and Judith P. Ruchkin, paper on "Education Plan for Parkway, Community Approach Learning," City College of New York, 1967.
10. *Fortune*, April 1965, pp. 130-131.
11. *Business Management*, June 1968, pp. 26-37.
12. *Ibid.*, p. 32.
13. *Ibid.*
14. *Newsweek*, July 1, 1968, p. 21.
15. See *Saturday Evening Post*, August 10, 1968, p. 81.
16. *Ibid.*, p. 27.
17. See *Newsweek, op. cit.*, pp. 23-24.
18. *Communities in Action, op. cit.*
19. National Advisory Council on Economic Opportunity, *Focus on Community Action*, March 1968, pp. 34-35.
20. *Children*, March-April 1968, p. 76.
21. *Ibid.*
22. Daniel P. Moynihan, as quoted in *Report of the National Advisory Commission on Civil Disorders*, U. S. Government Printing Office, Washington, 1968, p. 124.
23. Robert W. Austin, "Who Has the Responsibility for Social Change —Business or Government?" *Harvard Business Review*, July-August 1965, pp. 45-52.
24. *Ibid.*, p. 49.
25. Charles F. Jones, "The Social Marketplace," speech at the National Municipal League, New Orleans, La., December 3, 1968.
26. M. A. Wright, "Business and Human Welfare," speech at the Citizens' Conference on Community Planning, Richmond, Va., February 27, 1969.
27. *Ibid.*
28. H. Ralph Taylor, "Community Development Corporations," speech at Urban America National Conference on Non-Profit Housing and Community Development Corporations, Washington, October 14, 1968.
29. *The Atlantic Monthly*, December 1968, pp. 71-73.
30. See Daniel P. Moynihan, *Maximum Feasible Misunderstanding*, The Free Press, New York, 1969, p. 182.

HOUSTON "NATURAL DIALOGUE" INTERVIEW QUESTIONS

A. Attitude toward present job?
   1. good   2. fair   3. bad
B. Thinks most jobs open to him?
   1. most   2. some   3. very few
C. Thinks salary provides decent living?
   1. always   2. usually   3. never
D. How often do you think you are turned down for a job because you are a Negro?
   1. always   2. usually   3. never
E. How often do you think you are denied promotion because you are a Negro?
   1. always   2. usually   3. never
F. How actively participated in civil rights movement?
   1. not interested   2. no chance yet   3. protested
G. In what situation is violence justified for Negro rights?
   1. always opposed   2. if attacked   3. to gain attention to movement   4. only way to accomplish desired result
H. Opinion of quality of schools?
   1. good   2. all right   3. poor
I. Opinion of integration of schools?
   1. doing it fairly   2. all right   3. not doing it fairly
J. General integration of society?
   1. too fast   2. about right   3. too slow
K. Houston police treatment of Negro?
   1. fair   2. some okay, others not   3. abusive
L. Attitude toward Black Power?
   1. against   2. never heard of   3. in favor of
M. How important is religion to people today?
   1. very   2. not so important   3. not at all
N. Opinion of War on Poverty in Houston?
   1. good   2. fair   3. bad
O. Opinion of Houston housing?
   1. good   2. fair   3. bad
P. How have riots eleswhere affected tension in Houston?
   1. not at all   2. somewhat   3. very
Q. What effects have talks by mayor in Negro areas had?
   1. good   2. bad/very little   3. never heard of
R. Do you think the riots in Watts and other cities helped or hurt the Negro cause?
   1. helped   2. neither   3. hurt
S. What are the causes of racial tensions in Houston today?
   (open ended)
T. What can be done to reduce this tension?
   (open ended)
U. What is the worst problem in own neighborhood?
   (open ended)*

---

*Other pertinent questions were substituted for final three in some of the survey series.

Index